S0-AVJ-345

Praise for *Imagining Head-Smashed-In* by Jack W. Brink

"Brink combines years of archaeological experience with ethnohistorical research, modern biological knowledge and master storytelling abilities into a potent investigation of an ancient Great Plains phenomenon – the mass bison hunt."
Ian Dyck, Curator of Plains Archaeology, Canadian Museum of Civilization

"This is a wonderful book. It is written in a way that captures the character and spirit of the great buffalo kills of the Plains. Brink draws together archaeology, Post-Contact historical information, and First Nations perspectives better than any other author I can think of."
Douglas Bamforth, Professor of Anthropology, University of Colorado at Boulder

"Chock full of First Nations culture, *Imagining Head-Smashed-In* is unlike most history books you are likely to read … (Brink's) knowledge about the area (and) his subject is keen and colourful … Brink has done an outstanding job of bringing the past to the present ... [written in a] down-to-earth, matter-of-fact style that highlights the author's brilliant storytelling ability. An outstanding book with a unique tale to tell."
Alberta Native News

"An important and engaging book … this is an easy-going, almost conversational narrative, but it's easy to detect the author's passion and the solid science … I cannot recommend this volume highly enough to professional archaeologists, to Native Americans, and to anybody interested in a good read about the deep history of North America."
David Hurst Thomas, *Great Plains Research*

"[The author] presents a deeply felt and frequently poetic narrative in which he not only gives us a solid introduction to the issues of Northern Plains archaeology, but also brings his experience with this magical site into play."
Edmonton Journal

"Jack W. Brink, who knows more than anyone else about the hunting of buffalo by natives ... tells us most of it, and makes this reader grateful for his ability to handle rich detail. In his hands [the story] becomes absorbing, dramatic and almost urgent."
Robert Fulford, *National Post*

"The book is scholarly in the scope of its research, but Brink is a rare combination of scientist and storyteller."
Legacy Magazine

"This profusely illustrated work takes readers on a journey through a history of Head-Smashed-In … Brink's great depth of knowledge of the site, its history and context, and its development is evident on every page, as is his intense respect

for the First Nations people … written in a highly engaging and personal style for a broad audience. Brink makes what easily could be a very dry treatise a delight to read."
Canadian Journal of Archaeology

Awards

Society for American Archaeology, Best Book Award, Popular Writing Category, 2009
City of Edmonton Book Prize, Best Non-Fiction, 2009
Calgary Public Library Foundation Literary Awards, Best Adult Non-Fiction, 2009
Alberta Book Publishing Award, Best Trade Non-Fiction, 2009
Canadian Archaeological Association, Public Communications Award, 2009

Imagining Head-Smashed-In

Imagining Head-Smashed-In

Aboriginal Buffalo Hunting on the Northern Plains

Jack W. Brink

AU PRESS

© 2008 Jack W. Brink
Second Printing 2010

Published by Athabasca University Press
1200, 10011 – 109 Street
AU PRESS   Edmonton, AB T5J 3S8

Library and Archives Canada Cataloguing in Publication

Brink, Jack
Imagining Head-Smashed-In : aboriginal buffalo hunting on the
northern plains / Jack W. Brink.
Includes bibliographical references and index.
ISBN 978-1-897425-04-6 (pbk.)–ISBN 978-1-897425-00-8 (bound)
ISBN 978-1-897425-09-1 (electronic)

1. American bison hunting–History. 2. Head-Smashed-In Buffalo
Jump National Historic Site (Alta.). 3. Indians of North America–
Hunting–Great Plains. 4. Buffalo jump–Alberta. I. Title.

E78.G73B682 2008   639'.1164308997   C2008-900089-7

Printed and bound in Canada by AGMV Marquis
Cover design by Rod Michalchuk

This book has been published with the help of a grant from the
Canadian Federation for the Humanities and Social Sciences,
through the Aid to Scholarly Publications Programme, using funds
provided by the Social Sciences and Humanities Research Council
of Canada. Also, this project was funded in part by the Alberta Historical Resources Foundation.

Canadian **Federation** for the
Humanities and Social Sciences
Fédération canadienne
des sciences humaines

This is for my mother, Jenny Lou.

And for my late father, consummate journalist William J. Brink Jr., wishing that I had the benefit of his keen editorial eye to whip this book into shape.

Long ago, in the winter time, the buffalo suddenly disappeared. The snow was so deep that the people could not move in search of them, for in those days they had no horses … the people began to starve. One day, a young married man killed a jack-rabbit. He was so hungry that he ran home as fast as he could, and told one of his wives to hurry and get some water to cook it. While the young woman was going along the path to the river, she heard a beautiful song … The song seemed to come from a cotton-wood tree near the path. Looking closely at this tree she saw a queer rock jammed in a fork, where the tree was split, and with it a few hairs from a buffalo, which had rubbed there. The woman was frightened and dared not pass the tree. Pretty soon the singing stopped, and the I-nis-kim spoke to the woman and said: 'Take me to your lodge, and when it is dark, call in the people and teach them the song you have just heard. Pray, too, that you may not starve, and that the buffalo may come back. Do this, and when day comes, your hearts will be glad.' The woman … took the rock and gave it to her husband, telling him about the song and what the rock had said. As soon as it was dark, the man called the chiefs and old men to his lodge, and his wife taught them this song. They prayed, too, as the rock had said should be done. Before long, they heard a noise far off. It was the tramp of a great herd of buffalo coming. Then they knew that the rock was very powerful, and, ever since that, the people have taken care of it and prayed to it.

George Bird Grinnell, Blackfoot Lodge Tales

Contents

Foreword

Archaeology on the northern plains spans the second half of the twentieth century. Although people had found objects from the old stone age, the dedicated inquiry that goes with the profession only appeared when universities and museums supported researchers. These curators and professors, such as Richard Forbis (1919–1999) and Marie Wormington (1914–1994), made their occupation the full time search for traces of ancient people. That first generation brought with them the methods of an observational science. Their immediate goal was to systematically excavate through the different strata and record their findings. Their long-term objective was to make sense of the artifacts and features in order to understand the cultural history of the northern plains. Their motivation was to establish a chronology or devise a taxonomy from patterns in the material culture they unearthed. More importantly, they trained the students who would pick up the task of interpreting the archaeological record and find the explanations that fit the data.

From then to the present generation, the sites that persistently pique the imagination are the enigmatic buffalo jumps. Interpreting the archaeological record may seem like trying to find answers in the entrails of a badger. However, archaeologists possess many methods that help them understand the life and culture of people who in ancient times called the northern plains their home. The modern era in archaeology benefits from breakthroughs in other disciplines, but in return archaeologists contribute food for thought. Like many in this profession, Jack Brink feels fortunate that he can conduct research that continuously stokes the sense of wonder that makes his job worthwhile. He also recognizes that there exists strong public interest in archaeological work and that we have a duty to report the results of our inquiries in an accessible manner. Thus he can inject his wry sense of humour into the text to illustrate a point he wants to make.

When Jack began his studies in archaeology he was able to concentrate on that topic at university. As a young student he learned his trade from his elder academics, but he was not content to merely absorb data. He has devoted his career to expanding the knowledge base he inherited from them. Of course the challenge for him was not just to look for answers, but also to look for questions. What remains to be done in northern plains archaeology? What questions will preoccupy the current generation of archaeologists? You might well ask. Jack certainly has. He has picked up the task initiated by his intellectual predecessors and continues to look for insights amid the buffalo jumps. The reader will easily find the humanity in both the author and his subject. Nowhere is there a hint of the stereotypical researcher preoccupied with minutiae while ignoring the big picture around him.

Curiosity and wonder drew Jack to the cliffs and crevices that fired his imagination. This memoir of his contemplations about the buffalo jumps, and other artifacts of ancient people, is a synthesis of his life's work. Together with his knowledge he takes on the role of storyteller, relating the personal anecdotes that spiced up his research. He also poses challenges for the next generation. What research questions will they formulate to imagine the northern plains in ancient times? How will they use the knowledge they gain? Well, that is up to them to determine, but at least they will have Jack Brink's narrative to guide their thoughts.

The vantage point from his perspective is similar to the expansive view of the plains from the edge of the precipice. His endeavours have culminated with this inspired volume. From his pen flows a quixotic tour through archaeology; with his own practical guide for imagining northern plains antiquity, including all the blood and guts. More than anything, Jack shows us yet again that buffalo do not jump; they have to be pushed!

Eldon Yellowhorn
Assistant Professor
Department of Archaeology/First Nations Studies
Simon Fraser University
Burnaby, British Columbia

Preface

A great archaeologist once told me not to let facts get in the way of a good story. For the most part I have ignored that advice. In the following pages I have tried to make an ancient, dusty, nearly forgotten story come alive. To do so I have had to expand my assumptions and my thinking well beyond the realm of facts. Over twelve thousand years of residency in North America, the Native inhabitants left us no written records of their dreams and aspirations, or of anything else. To put flesh on the skeletons of these people's lives we have to dream along with them. Capturing people and events that disappeared from our world centuries ago requires a judicious helping of imagination, hence the title of this book.

The book isn't about what are traditionally considered the great historic achievements of our species. There are no magnificent cities built, no colossal monuments erected, no gigantic statues carved, no kingdoms conquered. It was very much this deviation from classical concepts of "civilization" that motivated me to write this book. Modern society seems to equate human achievement with monumental substance and architectural grandeur. Asked to name the greatest accomplishments of ancient cultures you would certainly hear of the Great Wall of China, Stonehenge, the Great Pyramids, and the civilizations that ruled Greece and Rome. Shunted off to the side are many ancient cultures that achieved greatness through their skill, knowledge, and ingenuity – cultures that managed to survive in demanding environments for extraordinary lengths of time without leaving towering monuments to themselves. In the coming pages I hope to show how simple lines of rocks stretching across the prairies are every bit as inspirational as rocks piled up in the shape of a pyramid.

This is a book about one of the truly remarkable accomplishments in human history. It is the story of an unheralded, unassuming, almost anonymous group of people who hunted for a living. They occupied an open, windswept, often featureless tract of land. They lived in conical skin tents that they lugged around with them in their search for food. A life of nearly constant motion negated permanent villages and cumbersome material possessions. They shared this immense landscape with herds of a wild and powerful beast – the largest animal on the continent. In a land virtually without limits, people of seemingly unsophisticated hunting societies managed to direct huge herds of buffalo to pinpoint destinations where ancient knowledge and spiritual guidance taught them massive kills could be achieved. It was an *event* that guaranteed survival of the people for months to come, a *process* that ensured their existence for millennia. Using their skill and their astonishing knowledge of bison biology and behaviour, bands of hunters drove great herds of buffalo over steep cliffs and into wooden corrals. In the blink of an eye they obtained more food in a single moment than any other people in human history. How they accomplished this is a story as breathtaking in scope and complexity as the country in which the events unfolded.

Head-Smashed-In Buffalo Jump in southern Alberta, Canada, is but one of many places where herds of bison were brought to their deaths by the Native inhabitants of the Plains. It forms the nucleus around which my story unfolds. But this is not so much the story of one place, one people, or one time. It is the story of countless people who thrived over an enormous expanse of time and territory by orchestrating mass kills of bison. There were two reasons I wanted to write this book. First, to bring to a wider audience a story that I felt was so compelling and inspirational that it should not be allowed to fade from contemporary memory. And second, to do justice to the people who orchestrated these remarkable events.

For the most part I have built my story around the fascinating accounts of early explorers, fur traders and missionaries who roamed the Great Plains and witnessed the final episodes of traditional hunting. That these important records are flawed is a given; the authors often felt compelled to embellish their stories and to overlay their own social values on the Native people they encountered – seldom in a way that favoured the Aboriginal characters. Yet they provide a richness of detail that the archaeological record alone could never supply. There is nothing quite comparable to the words, reactions, and sentiments of those who were at the scene of the great buffalo kills. When Henry Youle Hind stood beside the rotting carcasses of a Cree buffalo pound in the 1850s and remarked, "it is needless to say that the odour was overpowering, [with] millions of large blue flesh flies, humming and buzzing over the putrefying bodies," nothing that I could imagine, or add, could convey this in the sense of his own words. Notes at the end of the book provide reference for the citations. A much more extensive bibliography, organized by chapter, is available at www.aupress.ca.

While there is an authority and immediacy to historical records, using them comes with a cost. Aside from the obvious issue of bias, reliance on historical records compresses the element of time. Europeans witnessed bison killing on the Plains for little more than a century and a half; a mere fraction of the span of Aboriginal history. By telling the story from a historical perspective, I am essentially telling how the *last* hunting of bison took place. In so doing I mask some important events that transpired on the Great Plains over many millennia. Animal species changed, populations rose and fell, severe droughts came and went. The buffalo hunting that I describe is true to a period and a place. It is not the only story of buffalo hunting on the Plains. It is not likely the one that consumed the bulk of the time people who have occupied this region. What the long view of archaeology teaches us, that historical records cannot, is that nothing ever persists unchanged over great spans of time. Stretching over six hundred generations of Plains life, we should expect nothing less than an ebb and flow of different people and different cultural adaptations across the vast prairies.

Perhaps as well as any bison kill site, Head-Smashed-In Buffalo Jump documents the complex, fluid nature of prehistoric life on the Great Plains. Herds of buffalo were first driven over the cliff at Head-Smashed-In nearly six thousand years ago; a time when no other buffalo jump in North America was being used. How do we explain such an early use of this site? In short order Head-Smashed-In was abandoned, possibly for as long as two thousand years. What's that all about? Why would people walk away from an ingenious trap, the tricks of which they had clearly mastered? Then about two thousand years ago, Head-Smashed-In became a veritable cornucopia of bison killing. So rich in bones and artifacts are these more recent kill events that some (including me) have argued that the great buffalo kills had evolved into "factories," producing bison products beyond the immediate needs of the people, products destined for trade to distant regions of North America.

These are stories that document the unceasing flux of ancient life across the Great Plains and beyond. They are important and incredibly interesting, but I can't address them all. I have directed my efforts to capture just a snapshot of the saga of buffalo hunting in North America. Snapshots have inherent limitations – they freeze a moment in time, failing to illuminate a subject in the moments before and after the captured event. The rest I leave to another author.

Finally, the pages that follow document a personal journey – one of exploration, bewilderment, and exhilaration. In an academic sense the journey is unconventional; it is filled with my own experiences, many of them part of my own process of discovery. And it begs the reader to traverse the vastness of the Great Plains and the cultures of its Aboriginal inhabitants along with me.

Jack Brink
Edmonton, Alberta, 2008

Acknowledgements

It has been a long journey, taken with the help of many people. None more so than Dr. William J. Byrne. Bill first hired me as a staff member of the Archaeological Survey of Alberta and gave me the opportunity to take on the Head-Smashed-In project. Without Bill's years of friendship and support I would never have been in a position to write this book. Dr. Frits Pannekoek, then the Director of the Historic Sites Service, gave me free reign to pursue research and development at Head-Smashed-In. Later, as President of Athabasca University, Frits was instrumental in getting this book to press.

Thorough and thoughtful reviews of the entire manuscript were undertaken by Drs. Douglas Bamforth, Bill Byrne, and Ian Dyck. Colleagues who read and commented on select parts of the book include Susan Berry, Sheila Greer, Bob Hudson, and Wes Olson. All of these folks improved the book and kept me from making a number of mistakes. Thanks to Drs. Brian Reeves and Brian Kooyman for their important work at Head-Smashed-In allowing my use of information I have gleaned from their studies.

I have benefited greatly from the writings of and conversations with Dr. George Frison. His impressive knowledge of bison, bison hunting, and buffalo kill sites has influenced my thinking and my writing in ways I no longer recognize. Norm Cool, Dr. Cormack Gates, Dr. Bob Hudson, Wes Olson, and Hal Reynolds have aided me immeasurably in my understanding of bison behaviour and biology.

Thanks to Wes Olson and Johane Janelle for permission to reproduce drawings and photographs of bison from their personal collection and from their beautiful book, *Portraits of the Bison*. Thanks also to Clarence Tillenius and Shayne Tolman for permission to use their artwork. And to Jeannine Green at the University of Alberta, Bruce Peel Special Collections Library, for permission to use images from their fine collection.

Archaeologist Bob Dawe has worked with me on the Head-Smashed-In project from the moment it began. His contribution to the development, archaeological excavation, and on-going operation of the site is immeasurable. Milt Wright worked with Bob and me through the early years of the project. Milt turned in yeoman's work on the excavation and site development, always with a sense of dedication and humour that has no equal. Dr. Caroline Hudecek-

Cuffe helped me excavate at Head-Smashed-In, and decades later helped even more by shepherding this book towards publication. Initially conscripted to assist with images, Caroline morphed into a researcher, editor, fact checker, indexer, late-night email confidant, and most importantly – after being the very first person to read the manuscript – a believer. I hope that finally seeing this in print is partial compensation for the enormous contribution that Caroline made in getting it there. When the book was still in its infancy, Dr. Claire Allum was the second person to read it. Her comments, encouragement, and kindness are remembered. Karen Giering helped in many ways as I struggled towards the finish. Thank you, Karen.

Staff of Head-Smashed-In Buffalo Jump have been my comrades in arms for more than two decades. It would be impossible to name all that have passed through my life and through the interpretive centre during this time, but I have to single out a few and hope that those not named will know that they have all been a part of this great story: Delorale Brown, Ken Carson, Ian Clarke, Alan Collar, Quinton Crowshoe, Ken Eagle Speaker, Linda Eagle Speaker, Dennis Erich, Blair First Rider, Ronald Four Horns, Trina Healy, Susan Koots, Terry Malone, Jim Martin, Pat Ness, Leo Pard, Louisa Crowshoe, Florence Pilling, Travis Plaited Hair, Trevor Kitokii, Angie Provost, Dean Smith, Jacinta Wells, and Chris Williams. Special thanks to the late Walter Crowshoe, the kindest man and greatest ambassador the site has ever known. And to the late Lorraine Good Striker, the great matriarch of the jump, whose vision and dedication we are committed to honouring. Reg Crowshoe became a friend and instructor in Blackfoot culture. Reg, and the late Sam Good Rider, were instrumental in helping me during interviews with Blackfoot elders, and in telling jokes in Blackfoot at my expense. Thanks to Billy Strikes With A Gun and Nick Smith for sharing so much.

Likewise, I can't name all crew members who worked on my digs over the years but want to single out a few: Harley Bastine, Rita Morning Bull, Hazel Big Smoke, Jody Dersch, Chris Hughes, Caroline Hudecek-Cuffe, Karie Hardie, John Priegert, Maureen Rollans, Tim Schowalter, Craig Shupe, and the volunteer efforts in the field of the late Armin Dyck and his wife, Gerry, and in the lab Maurice and Elsie White.

Cattle ranchers living close to the jump treated my crews with courtesy and friendship that can't be described until you reside in ranching country. The Dersch family, Harvey and the late Collette and their children, opened their home, barbeque, arrowhead collection, and beer fridge to us, and shared their long history of three generations living next to the jump. Jim and Denise Calderwood, and their land managers Paul and Patty Runion, treated us with grace, respect, and made their land our land. John and Donna Viens of Fort Macleod invited my crew to their home for countless pizza dinners and games of bocce. To Connie and Don at the Sunset, I am your guest forever.

The late Joe Crowshoe and his remarkable wife, the late Josephine, welcomed me into their home, their lives and their culture. Joe and Josephine influenced me – and hence this book – in ways that I may never fully appreciate. Their spirit lives on inside and outside the great buffalo jump. I am indebted to Josephine Crowshoe and Lisa Monsees for appropriation of their character and their spirit. I thank the staff of the Royal Alberta Museum for their support.

Sylvia Vance edited this book, but she also championed it, massaged it, coaxed it (and me) along. To you, Sylvia, my heartfelt thanks. Walter Hildebrandt, Director of Athabasca University Press, welcomed this unconventional "academic" book and embraced it as a project for his press. Erna Dominey, Senior Editor at AUP, helped in myriad ways. She tightened up my prose, caught mistakes, defended my rights as author and – most astonishingly – made it fun. Many thanks, Erna. And thanks to Helen Adhikari and Adolpho Ruiz for the design and layout of the book and to Carol Woo at AUP for helping us get to the finish line.

The opinions expressed in this book are strictly my own and do not necessarily reflect those of my employer, the Government of Alberta. I receive no remuneration from the sale of this book. Royalties normally directed to the author have been redirected to the Cross Cancer Institute, Edmonton, Alberta.

To Jonathan Thatcher and Arryn Bronson who stuck with an absentee father.

CHAPTER 1

The Buffalo Jump

[The prairies are a] vast and worthless area ... a region of savages and wild beasts, of deserts ... cactus and prairie dogs ... to what use could we ever hope to put these great deserts? – Daniel Webster cited in *Lewis Henry Morgan,* 1859–62

These great Plains appear to be given by Providence to the Red Men for ever, as the wilds and sands of Africa are given to the Arabians. – David Thompson, 1784–1812

A couple of dusty pickup trucks ease their way off the gravel road onto the hard, baked prairie. The archaeology crew drops to the ground, dressed in hi-tech hiking boots, white sport socks, shorts made of space-age material with countless pockets and zippers, T-shirts and ball caps emblazoned with a variety of logos, dumb jokes, and names of rock bands. Shovels, pails, and toolboxes in hand, they shuffle over towards the imposing sandstone cliff, setting up for another day of routine work. Within moments their casual stride has them standing on soil where, long ago, people once ran frantically in all directions, their hide clothing covered in blood and guts, shouting instructions, whooping with excitement, sometimes crying in anguish, all trying to kill buffalo and to get out of the way of the wounded ones determined to kill them first. The screens for sifting soil from the dig are hung from tripods made of two-by-four lumber, set up at the same place where tens of thousands of bison came flying over the edge of a high cliff – the thundering of the deadly stampede ending with an eerie moment of silence as the animals became airborne, followed immediately by a series of horrible thuds, bellowing, and groans as the massive bodies slammed onto the earth and into each other. The crew members swing their legs into the excavation pits, dragging their simple digging tools with them, inspecting the dense layers

Archaeologists excavate the same piece of earth where ancient people once butchered buffalo. (left: Courtesy Royal Alberta Museum; right: Courtesy Head-Smashed-In Buffalo Jump)

of smashed bison bones they were working on the day before – the very same bones that once supported the mighty buffalo whose blood flowed into the parched soil and whose subsequent butchering left behind mounds of steaming entrails, wretched stomach contents, and stinking excrement. As you set up a lawn chair and pour the first cup of coffee from your thermos, it can seem a little incongruous. Welcome to Head-Smashed-In Buffalo Jump.

The archaeological crew and the ancient buffalo hunters occupied the exact same place on the earth, just separated by time. When you become attuned to studying the past, it can be a strange and humbling experience to know that you are walking on the very same patch of earth as did people who, not such a long time ago, were of an utterly different culture and walked it under such unimaginably different circumstances.

There may be no other type of archaeological site that can match the drama, can fire the imagination, and has a story as utterly compelling as that of a buffalo jump. Certainly the archaeological richness of the globe – pyramids, temple mounds, ancient cities, and great stone monuments – is one of imposing structures and fantastic stories. But I wonder if any can compare to the sheer excitement of watching a buffalo jump or pound (a wooden corral) being used. Eyewitness accounts of mass bison kills reflect the horrific moment. "A dreadful scene of confusion and slaughter then begins," wrote Henry Youle Hind in 1857, "the oldest and strongest animals crush and toss the weaker; the shouts and screams of the excited Indians rise above the roaring of the bulls, the bellowing of the cows, and the piteous moaning of the

calves. The dying struggles of so many huge and powerful animals crowded together, create a revolting and terrible scene."

It is surely one of the great dramatic stories in the course of human history. If a herd of one hundred bison were run off a cliff at a single event (a number considered average), there is nothing in the four million years of human evolution when a comparable amount of food was procured at one time. Elephants, mammoths, rhinos, giraffes, and other animals larger than bison have been preyed upon for thousands of years. But these were usually killed individually or, at most, a few at a time. Caribou and various members of the deer family have been killed in great numbers by hunters over various regions of the earth, but the resulting biomass of the carcasses would never approach that of a bison kill. Even the killing of a huge bowhead whale by the Inuit of the Arctic, the largest animal ever hunted by indigenous people, would yield less meat and fat than an average buffalo jump. Through millions of years of adaptation, mass killing of bison on the Great Plains

A successful buffalo jump would have been a spectacular event (literally earth-shaking) that provided a staggering amount of food, hide, and bone. (Courtesy Head-Smashed-In Buffalo Jump)

Next page: The beauty of the landscape masks the deadly purpose Head-Smashed-In served. The killing cliff is in the distance. (Courtesy Royal Alberta Museum)

of North America, using jumps and wooden corrals, was the most productive food-getting enterprise ever devised by human beings.

And of all the buffalo jumps known from across western North America, there is perhaps none more imposing, more perfectly designed, more consistently executed, more lethal than Head-Smashed-In. It has been recognized by the Province of Alberta as a Provincial Historical Resource, by the Government of Canada as a National Historic Site, and by the UNESCO World Heritage Organization as the premier example of a bison jump in North America. It is, if I may use the phrase, the Mother of all Buffalo Jumps.

This book is the story of Head-Smashed-In Buffalo Jump. But it is more than that. It is the story of tenacious people in their relentless pursuit of an extraordinary way of life. With few exceptions these people were, and still are, nameless and faceless. They exist in a land of shadows we call the past, a period as vast as it is murky. It is a period that, despite its intrinsic opacity, never fails to stir our curiosity and imagination. The past is the ultimate abyss. We can venture to the moon, to the bottom of the oceans, penetrate the deepest jungles, and explore the far reaches of the universe. We can never go to the past; hence, we can never truly know it. We can only approach it obliquely: poking, prodding, conjecturing, and mostly puzzling, as if peering around corners through the narrow lens of a periscope – seeing only little pieces of the past at any one time. But it is important to peer into this abyss. Because it reflects, mirror-like, what it means to be human. Because we learn about what human beings have been and of what they are capable. And because, if we look back far enough into this shadow land, we are all one.

People who are anonymous need not be unknown. It is the role of archaeology and history to breathe life into those whose voices have been stilled by time. Studying the past comes with many serious obligations, just one of which is to engage in what is admittedly speculation when creating reconstructions of what life might have been like in ancient times. It can be a daunting prospect, knowing that you have to speak for people who are no longer here to speak for themselves. A great weight can descend upon you as you wonder if you have represented these voiceless cultures fairly, accurately, respectfully. But to not speak up would certainly be a disservice. It would condemn great amounts of information about ancient peoples to dusty library shelves and arcane academic publications, and deny most of humanity the knowledge of spectacular triumphs and dismal failings of our fellow humans. More importantly, it would be a disservice to the history of a people who left no written history – people who deserve, as much as any of us, to have their story told. Why else study the past if not to bring it back to life?

For more than twenty-five years I have been linked with Head-Smashed-In Buffalo Jump. Sometimes, just as a visitor, I have walked along the top of the cliff where so many bison plunged to their deaths, and strolled through the interpretive centre where two million people have experienced the story of the jump. But mostly, Head-Smashed-In has been my career. As an archaeologist I directed excavations at the site for ten years, was a member of the team that planned and developed the interpretive centre, and I have stayed involved in the research and operation of the site. It is a place to which I continuously return: helping to train new guides, leading public tours, giving lectures, assisting with renovations to the display galleries. The story of the jump, and all that went into making the great bison kills possible, has captivated me. It's a story that should not be left, like the bones of the mighty beasts, to fade and decay with time.

The saga of hunting and killing buffalo at Head-Smashed-In is a paragon for the many stories from across the reaches of North America and beyond. At its core it is a story of courage and cunning, of violence and bloodshed, of survival and defeat, of a people's mighty struggle, spanning thousands of years, in one of the most challenging environments on earth. Before the development of agriculture and, eventually, industrialization, Aboriginal people all over the world hunted game animals as the staple of their ancient way of life. But none did so in a more spectacular fashion than the Aboriginal people of the Great Plains when hunting bison. The lesson from this story is simple; there is practically no limit to the depth of creativity human beings have brought to bear in order to make their world liveable. The ingenious solutions these hunters devised to stalk and kill mighty herds of bison were little known to archaeologists to begin with – existing in obscure and out-of-print historic literature and in the memories of Native elders – and are in danger of fading completely from modern knowledge. This should not happen. The story is simply too compelling, too inspiring, too important. It needs to be remembered for what it was – an astonishing triumph of intelligent humans over circumstances stacked overwhelmingly against them.

Horses were introduced to the Northern Plains early in the 1700s, giving rise to new methods of communal hunts such as this surround. Painting by George Catlin. (Courtesy Bruce Peel Special Collections Library, University of Alberta)

Communal Buffalo Hunting

Now ye manner of their hunting these Beasts on ye Barren ground is when they seek a great parcel of them together they surround them with men which done they gather themselves into a smaller Compass Keeping ye Beasts still in ye middle and so shooting ym till they break out at some place or other and so get away from ym. – Henry Kelsey, 1691, cited in *Ewers*, 1955

Head-Smashed-In is just one type of what are commonly called communal bison kills. These are not the result of a solitary hunter out searching for food for his family, nor of a couple of people working as a team. They are communal in the sense that many people, indeed many groups of people, had to come together and work co-operatively to make these great kills possible. In the more than twelve thousand years in which we can trace Aboriginal history in western North America, people discovered and exploited a bewildering array of ways to kill bison. They trapped buffalo that were mired down at watering holes, ambushed them as they plodded along ageless trails, drove them into deep snow banks where their short legs failed them, cornered them in dead-end canyons, killed them as they swam across rivers and lakes, drove them onto frozen lakes and rivers, herded them into wooden corrals, and drove them over every imaginable kind of precipice. Certainly, solitary hunting, of a wide range of game animals, was a regular and continuous part of life for all Plains Indian groups since time immemorial. But communal hunting of bison was the mainstay of their existence.

Communal hunting brought people together, people who normally would not have lived together as one group. This book is about how these massive hunts took place and the aftermath of butchering and processing the spoils. Yet it bears mention that communal hunting, aside from providing critical supplies of food, also served a great number of social purposes in Plains culture. Any large-scale gatherings of dispersed groups of related people would have been precious moments in ancient times. Friends and relatives were reunited. Enemies eyed each other warily. Stories and experiences of times apart were shared. Marriages were arranged, trade goods exchanged, business conducted. Great ceremonies were held, songs sung, prayers offered. David Mandelbaum, the noted scholar of the Plains Cree, said that the meeting of Plains Cree at a mass buffalo kill was "the nucleus for a large gathering of families." When you consider that nearly all the Plains groups spent thousands of years traversing an immense landscape, of necessity split into small groups of probably fifty to seventy people, coming together perhaps once or twice a year in numbers in the hundreds or a few thousand, you can appreciate the magnitude of the importance of these gatherings. They must have been extraordinary opportunities for meeting many necessary and rewarding social needs – something every bit as central to life as the mass provisioning of food. But that is another story, and another book. Whatever the perspective, communal hunts made life on the Plains not just possible but often quite comfortable.

There are many myths and stereotypes about Native people of North America, perhaps none more than for the tribes of the Plains Indians – the great horse-mounted warriors and hunters who have been the stuff of countless movies, books, TV shows and children's toys. Indeed, to many the Plains Indians are the quintessential Native people, the very definition of "Indianness." All a Seminole, a Hopi, a Dene, or a Haida person has to do is don an eagle feather headdress and, in the eyes of just about the whole world, the person becomes an "Indian." In this book I will challenge some of these stereotypes, at least those that pertain to the buffalo hunters of the Plains. And for

For people around the world, horse-mounted Blackfoot people as depicted in this photograph from the early 1900s became emblematic of Plains Indians. (Courtesy Glenbow Archives/NC 48-14)

my immediate purpose, let's consider the common image of ancient Plains people residing in a land as yet unmarked by the hallmarks of settlement and civilization, as living a hand-to-mouth existence in a state of near constant starvation.

The idea that the early life of Aboriginal inhabitants of the Plains might actually have been quite comfortable will come as a surprise to some readers. How could people possibly be comfortable while scrounging the barren, windswept Plains (on foot), subject directly to wild extremes of weather, possessing none of the modern conveniences we take for granted – all to secure a morsel to eat and a safe, warm place to sleep? Many Europeans painted a bleak picture of the Plains. "We have little apprehension of giving too unfavourable an account of this portion of the country," Edwin James proclaimed in 1820; "The traveller who shall at any time have traversed its desolate sands, will, we think, join us in the wish that this region may for ever remain the unmolested haunt of the native hunter, the bison, and the jackal." Lewis Henry Morgan, in 1859, stated "The prairie is not congenial to the Indian … [as it] neither affords the cover and shelter which the Indian both desires and needs ... there is not a tree, not a shrub, nor a thing of timber with which to kindle his fire, nor a spring perhaps to slake his thirst."

It's hard to imagine people living in such conditions as somehow in a state of peace, plenty, and tranquility. Yet the observations of Daniel Harmon, when exploring western Canada early in the nineteenth century, could hardly apply to a desolate people living on the verge of starvation: "In fact, those Indians, who reside in the large plains or prairies, are the most independent, and appear to be the most contented and happy people upon the face of the earth. They subsist upon the flesh of the buffaloe." The bounty of the Great Plains, and the relative good life provided by hunting buffalo, was not lost on the extraordinary explorer and fur trader David Thompson. Nearly starved to death during his trek through the Rocky Mountains, he emerged onto the Plains and exclaimed, "As we are now in the land of the Bison we hope no more to be in want of Provisions."

Let us think back to people who roamed the Great Plains for the past twelve thousand years. There is no denying that life would have at times been excruciatingly difficult and immensely challenging. No doubt tragedy struck often: people died in battle, in accidents while hunting, of starvation and thirst, torn apart by grizzly bears, lost and frozen in relentless winter snow storms, from illness, and occasionally, if they were lucky, from old age. People in their fifties were old indeed, back then, and were probably revered for the knowledge, skill, luck, and spiritual power that had got them that far.

We can think about all the things that could go wrong in ancient times, because we can easily imagine how helpless we would be if suddenly put in that same environment and deprived of all the conveniences that make life both easy and possible. It is harder to think about things actually going right, about being comfortable in the past, because we could never picture ourselves surviving under the extraordinary conditions that confronted ancient hunters on a daily basis. We could never picture ourselves having the skill, stamina, knowledge, luck, and perhaps spiritual power to pull off a massive kill of a herd of huge beasts that could literally feed, shelter, and clothe a people for many months afterward. The stereotype of ancient Native people living on the verge of starvation and scrounging for existence is prevalent because nowhere in the popular media has the opposite ever been portrayed, and the reason it hasn't stems not so much from an attempt to denigrate the ancient way of life of Native people but, rather, from simple ignorance of the incredible story that lies behind the hunting of huge herds of buffalo.

If hunters of the Plains were engaged in the most rewarding procurement of food ever devised by human beings, maybe life wasn't so bad after all. After nearly perishing in the mountains, Lewis and Clark came back out on to the Plains and proclaimed, "Here we halted and dined, and now felt, by the luxury of our food, that we were

† Grinnell was also
a devoted naturalist
who played a key role
in establishing Glacier
National Park. He, not
the namesake, founded
the first John J. Audubon
Society and published the
first *Audubon Magazine*.
A lifelong defender of
Indian culture and rights,
he was, ironically, the
naturalist on George
Armstrong Custer's 1874
and 1875 expeditions
to the Black Hills and
to the Yellowstone.
Grinnell declined
Custer's invitation for the
following season, citing
commitments at Yale's
Peabody Museum. In the
summer of 1876, without
Grinnell, Custer marched
on to infamy at the Little
Bighorn.

approaching once more the plains of the Missouri, so rich in game." If hunting buffalo yielded a life of considerable comfort, you would expect that it would be remembered fondly. George Bird Grinnell, a great chronicler of Plains culture, interviewed Blackfoot elders decades after the end of the buffalo hunting days.† He reported that eyewitnesses to the final communal hunts "even now speak with enthusiasm of the plenty that successful drives brought to the camp."

Not Just Any Cliff

In some part of its course, [the] valley is bounded by precipitous cliffs ... Our guide informed us that the Indians, a few years since, destroyed every individual of a large herd of bisons, by driving them over the brink of one of these precipices. – Edwin James, 1820

I have driven countless times through the country of the northern Plains with friends or guests beside me. And one of the most commonly made statements as we pass yet another bedrock outcrop, steep river bank, sheer cliff – all of which are common to this broken, desiccated country – is, "Do you suppose that's another buffalo jump?" It's easy to be forgiving. After all, they are riding next to someone who studies these features, and it's not always easy to make conversation on arcane topics such as buffalo jumps. More to the point, the casual passenger simply doesn't know of the great range of aspects of the landscape that must be just right for a steep drop to have functioned as a buffalo jump.

As much as anything, this book is an answer to the question my passengers pose. The prairies are littered with cliffs, drops, inclines, and precipices that were never used by anybody for anything. Why a very few cliffs were selected to be something very much more is the story behind how a buffalo jump works (or in the negative sense, why so many seemingly suitable places were ignored by Native people). It all has to do with the application of ingenious trickery and astounding knowledge to an exceedingly complex set of landscape requirements that made most steep drops entirely unsuitable for driving bison to their deaths.

Many early European visitors to the Great Plains were privy to the inner workings of the great communal hunts and wrote of their amazement at the skill and cunning of the Native inhabitants in the art

of rounding up, driving, and killing huge herds of bison. But occasionally the true genius of the trickery escaped them. Alexander Henry,† an otherwise astute observer of Native culture, attributed efforts to drive bison over a cliff to sheer laziness: "So much do these people abhor work that, to avoid the trouble of making proper pounds [wooden corrals], they seek some precipice along the bank of the river, to which they extend their ranks and drive the buffalo headlong over it." This book aims to dispel such misconceptions. Not only were buffalo jumps an extraordinary amount of work; they were the culmination of thousands of years of shared and passed-on tribal knowledge of the environment, the lay of the land, and the behaviour and biology of the buffalo.

Most people who have ever heard of a buffalo jump by name have only heard of one: Head-Smashed-In. For over twenty years it has featured an award-winning interpretive centre, which has attracted over two million visitors. But the Plains of North America are littered with the remnants of buffalo jumps as well as other mass bison kill sites. The great majority of these are known only to a few archaeologists and local residents. We will never know how many buffalo jumps were constructed and used over the past thousands of years; many have yet to be discovered, many have disappeared due to natural erosion and to the destructive encroachment of modern settlement.

Select locations, such as this rocky edge of Pine Coulee in southern Alberta, fit the stringent criteria for use as a buffalo jump. (Courtesy Royal Alberta Museum)

† Confusingly, two Alexander Henrys figure prominently in the early fur-trade history of western North America, the older one being the uncle of the younger. Henry the elder travelled the west between 1760 and 1776. His nephew travelled the same territory between 1799 and 1814. All my references to "Alexander Henry" are to the younger; I have designated his uncle as "the elder."

It would be wrong to think these kinds of sites are rare. There are about a hundred sites in Alberta alone that are considered to be buffalo jumps or other mass kill places. There must be thousands of known jumps on the Great Plains and thousands more yet to be discovered. Of all the known jumps, Head-Smashed-In was chosen by UNESCO as the very best example of an extant site that typifies all the attributes of a classic Plains buffalo jump. If you only ever get to know the story of one site, Head-Smashed-In is it.

The Site

Twice I have seen buffalo corralled. The first time I was a small boy about four years old. We were camped near the North Piegan in the Porcupine Hills west of the present town of Macleod (Alberta). I don't remember anything about it except that I saw the dead buffalo in the corral. – Weasel Tail, as told to John Ewers, 1947

Head-Smashed-In Buffalo Jump is located in southwestern Alberta, Canada, about a hundred and seventy kilometres south of Calgary and twenty kilometres west of the town of Fort Macleod. It lies at the very southern terminus of a group of beautiful rolling hills known as the Porcupine Hills. They are not true hills, in the sense that they were never uplifted by massive forces within the earth, as mountains were. Rather, they are the remains of a landscape that was once all at the same level as the tops of the hills. That is, they are an erosional remnant (called a *peneplain*). The land all around was once all of this same height, and erosional forces over millions of years wore most of it down to the current level of the surrounding plains. But the sandstone bedrock that lies within the area now known as the Porcupine Hills was just slightly harder than elsewhere and so resisted the erosion and remained higher than other areas. The Porcupines, since they lie just to the east of the towering peaks of the Rocky Mountains, are often thought to be part of the mountain foothills. They are not. The Rockies and foothills were uplifted from within the earth, and the Porcupines are unrelated to this event. But the erosion of the Porcupine Hills sandstone left be-hind many jagged escarpments of bedrock along the flanks of the hills, so that every now and then, although not often, these bedrock walls just happened to lie in precisely the right place for Native hunters to make use of them.

Head-Smashed-In Buffalo Jump is located in south-western Alberta, about one hundred kilometres north of the Montana border. (Courtesy Head-Smashed-In Buffalo Jump)

The Porcupine Hills stretch for about a hundred kilometres, rising from the Plains south of Calgary and ending to the west of Fort Macleod. They lie like a giant cigar on the land, but a convoluted one, full of wrinkles. The rolling nature of the hills makes for perfect country for bison to live and perfect country in which to hunt them. The wrinkles on the landscape afforded places for bison to graze in a diverse set of environments. The high, exposed hillsides offered sparse grass cover but had the advantages of strong winds for relief from insects and a commanding view for monitoring predators. The deeply carved valleys provided water, thick grass, and trees and brush for shelter from storms. The very same convoluted topography offered many opportunities for ancient hunters to manage the herds, to locate and spy on them, to follow the animals but still remain hidden, and to show themselves when appropriate to do so. One of the key reasons why Head-Smashed-In is one of the premier bison kill sites is because of the deeply complex nature of the topography of the Porcupine Hills. Many other buffalo jumps are simply steep drops at the edge of a broad prairie. They offer no cover for the hunters to use in manipulating the herds. Accordingly, many of these sites were used only a few times, some only once, and some were constructed but never saw a single bison fall to its death. Head-Smashed-In was certainly used hundreds of times, possibly more. It is estimated that the blood of more than one hundred thousand buffalo has soaked into the earth at Head-Smashed-In.

Head-Smashed-In, in the centre of the picture, is situated on an east-facing cliff of sandstone in the Porcupine Hills. (Courtesy Head-Smashed-In Buffalo Jump)

The Cliff

On the north we passed a precipice about one hundred and twenty feet high, under which lay scattered the fragments of at least one hundred carcases of buffaloes, although the water which had washed away the lower part of the hill must have carried off many of the dead. These buffaloes had been chased down the precipice in a way very common on the Missouri, and by which vast herds are destroyed in a moment. – Lewis and Clark, 1804–06

Unlike the Rockies, where the beds of rock are thrust up and tilted, the sandstone that forms the jump-off at Head-Smashed-In lies in straight, horizontal layers. This is to be expected when the sand that composes the hills was deposited at the bottom of a great inland ocean. The fine layers of slightly different sediment within the massive sandstone of the hills form bedding planes, which cause the exposed edges of the rock to break off in large angular blocks and topple from the cliffs. This process has been going on for millions of years, and as rocks keep toppling, the face of the cliff slowly retreats toward the centre of the hill. The fallen blocks land at the base of the cliff, where they roll, shatter, and are slowly covered with fine wind-blown sand and silt. The result is an apron that forms all along the exposed edges of the cliff. This apron is naturally highest up against the bedrock, where most of the toppling occurs, and it tapers as it slants down to meet the

16

lower level of the surrounding prairie. The killing took place at the high end of the apron, near the rock face, where a small bench lies in the shelter of the cliff.

The top of the cliff at the main kill site of Head-Smashed-In is now about ten metres higher than the bench of the apron, but it would have been even higher during the millennia when bison were being slaughtered. While the cliff has not got any higher (in fact, continuing erosion has made it slightly lower) the apron has. Over the years that the site was used, bedrock continued to topple, vegetation grew and died, soil drifted in, and the bones of countless buffalo were added. From the main kill site, the edge of the cliff trends roughly north to south, and as it moves in both directions, it gets gradually lower until it is just a few metres high.

The deepest and oldest buffalo bones and stone tools recovered at Head-Smashed-In are found nearly ten metres below the current surface of the apron. The math is easy: the cliff is currently ten metres

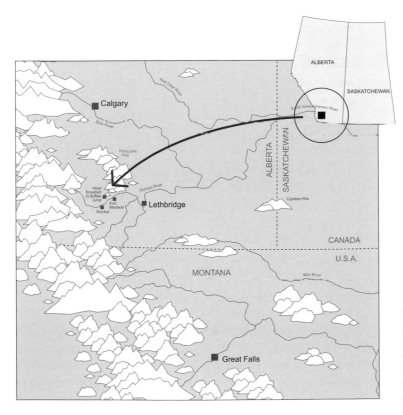

The buffalo jump is located at the very southern end of the Porcupine Hills, north of the Oldman River, and west of the town of Fort Macleod.(Courtesy Royal Alberta Museum)

17

The cliff face at Head-Smashed-In is now a ten-metre vertical drop. It was likely higher in the past. (Courtesy Royal Alberta Museum)

above the apron, and the oldest bones are buried nearly ten metres below the top of the apron. This means that the first animals to plunge over the cliff at Head-Smashed-In were falling nearly twenty metres. Undoubtedly this was a lethal drop, and few of the fallen animals would survive. Many buffalo jumps shared this same deadly trait. Alexander Henry wrote in 1809 that bison "not killed or entirely disabled from the fall ... are generally so much bruised as to be easily dispatched with the bow and arrow." But over time, as the apron at Head-Smashed-In rose against the face of the cliff, the height of the drop continued to diminish, which meant that more animals would only have been wounded and would have to be killed by hunters waiting below.

How Long Have Buffalo Jumped?

The usual manner of hunting buffalo was by making pens at the edge of a precipice and driving the animals over, sometimes killing them by hundreds and even thousands. – Lt. Bradley, cited in *Ewers*, 1968

With the oldest bones and artifacts buried some ten metres below the current ground surface, Head-Smashed-In surely ranks as one of the deepest sites in North America. It also presents enormous challenges to archaeologists. Excavating to that great depth is both tricky and dangerous. The sides of the excavated areas must be shored up with massive beams and plywood to prevent what would surely be a fatal collapse of soil on the crew members. Besides being one of the deepest and thus most hazardous, Head-Smashed-In is also one of the oldest buffalo jumps, maybe the oldest, depending on who you believe.

The oldest layers of buffalo bones and stone tools at Head-Smashed-In date to about fifty-eight hundred years before present (BP). The only known exception is a site in Texas called Bonfire Shelter. Excavation of the small shelter in the rock at the base of a high, steep cliff produced artifacts and bison bones dated to ten thousand years BP. Those excavating Bonfire Shelter argued that bison were driven over the high cliff and butchered at the mouth of the small rock shelter. But others are not so sure. The site lies near the end of a narrow gulley, and some archaeologists think that herds of bison were ambushed as they grazed in the canyon and the butchered parts were then brought into the shelter. The jury is still out on this debate, and so the status of Head-Smashed-In as the oldest buffalo jump remains ambiguous. It does seem odd that Native inhabitants of Texas discovered how to drive bison over a cliff ten thousand years ago but another four thousand years would pass before anyone else would try the trick again.

Whatever the case, Head-Smashed-In is among the oldest of buffalo jumps. Furthermore, there is solid evidence that ancient hunters

The first major dig at Head-Smashed-In was begun in 1949 by Boyd Wettlaufer, a pioneer in the archaeology of western Canada. (Courtesy Royal Alberta Museum)

These are typical styles of spear points found at archaeological sites on the Northern Plains, arranged by age from left to right. (Courtesy Royal Alberta Museum)

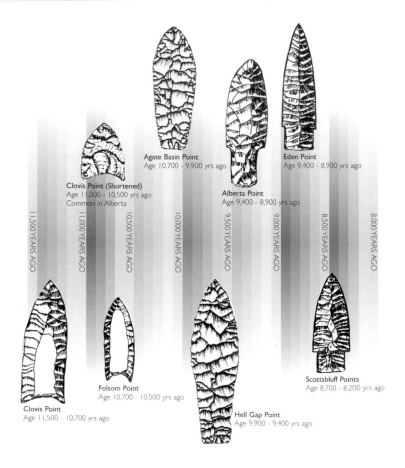

Agate Basin Point
Age 10,700 - 9,900 yrs ago

Eden Point
Age 9,400 - 8,900 yrs ago

Clovis Point (Shortened)
Age 11,000 - 10,500 yrs ago
Common in Alberta

Alberta Point
Age 9,400 - 8,900 yrs ago

11,500 YEARS AGO

11,000 YEARS AGO

10,500 YEARS AGO

10,000 YEARS AGO

9,500 YEARS AGO

9,000 YEARS AGO

8,500 YEARS AGO

8,000 YEARS AGO

Scottsbluff Points
Age 8,700 - 8,200 yrs ago

Folsom Point
Age 10,700 - 10,500 yrs ago

Clovis Point
Age 11,500 - 10,700 yrs ago

Hell Gap Point
Age 9,900 - 9,400 yrs ago

inhabited the site more than nine thousand years ago. One of the earliest archaeologists to excavate Head-Smashed-In, Boyd Wettlaufer, was working at the site in 1949. The farmer working the land at the time had made good use of the natural spring that flows out from under the sandstone bedrock. The spring, probably over thousands of years, has carved a narrow V-shaped channel that cuts through the slope beneath the cliff and then flows across the prairie. The farmer bulldozed an earthen dam at the base of the slope, making a pond of a small pool of spring water for his cattle. Bulldozing the earth beneath the cliff exposed a wealth of artifacts, including stone tools and buffalo bones. Among the stone tools Wettlaufer found were two spear points of a style known to be extremely ancient.

If the truth be told, archaeologists can't tell much about the age of many stone tools simply by looking at them. The reason for this

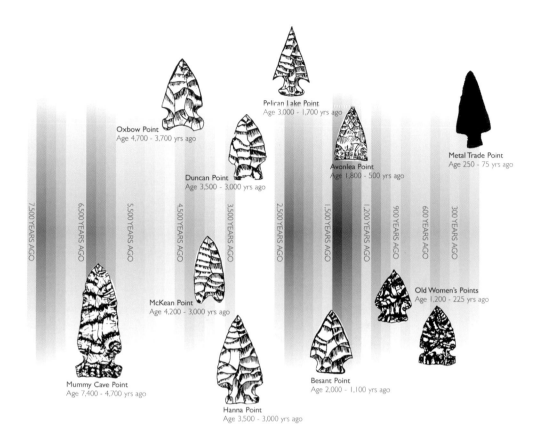

Pelican Lake Point
Age 3,000 - 1,700 yrs ago

Oxbow Point
Age 4,700 - 3,700 yrs ago

Avonlea Point
Age 1,800 - 500 yrs ago

Metal Trade Point
Age 250 - 75 yrs ago

Duncan Point
Age 3,500 - 3,000 yrs ago

7,500 YEARS AGO
6,500 YEARS AGO
5,500 YEARS AGO
4,500 YEARS AGO
3,500 YEARS AGO
2,500 YEARS AGO
1,500 YEARS AGO
1,200 YEARS AGO
900 YEARS AGO
600 YEARS AGO
300 YEARS AGO

Old Women's Points
Age 1,200 - 225 yrs ago

McKean Point
Age 4,200 - 3,000 yrs ago

Mummy Cave Point
Age 7,400 - 4,700 yrs ago

Besant Point
Age 2,000 - 1,100 yrs ago

Hanna Point
Age 3,500 - 3,000 yrs ago

ignorance is simple: the style of many stone tools didn't change for thousands of years. Over much of North America, stone chipped or ground into tools used for cutting, scraping, drilling, and hammering remained pretty much the same over great periods of time. Thus, handed a simple stone knife I can't tell you if it is eight thousand or five hundred years old. To find out the age of generic-looking tools, such as stone knives and scrapers, you need to recover them lying in the ground next to something that can be dated using the radiocarbon technique, such as bone or wood. Stone tools themselves cannot be dated with the radiocarbon technique, but points used to tip killing weapons are a different kettle of fish.

Points changed in style over time, both with different groups of people and with different types of weapons. The oldest type of weapon used in North America is the simple thrusting spear. The stone points that tipped them were large and heavy – much too big to have been used on arrows. (The bow and arrow is relatively recent on the Great

These styles of points were attached to long throwing darts and, beginning with Avonlea, to arrow shafts, by Northern Plains hunters. (Courtesy Royal Alberta Museum)

Plains, dating to just the last two thousand years.) Spear points come in all kinds of shapes and sizes, reflecting the people who made them at different places and in different times. Now that many sites have been excavated and dated across North America, we have a pretty good idea of the changing styles of spear points, and archaeologists have usually named these styles based on the first place they were discovered. Thus, Clovis spear points, first discovered near Clovis, New Mexico, are known to date to about eleven and a half thousand years ago, while Folsom points, also from New Mexico, date to about ten and a half thousand years ago. And so on.

What Boyd Wettlaufer found scraped up on the earthen dam in the spring channel at Head-Smashed-In were two examples of a spear point type known as Scottsbluff. These are large, beautifully made points first recognized as a distinct variety at a site near Scottsbluff, Nebraska. They have been repeatedly dated in the age range of nine to nine and a half thousand years BP. What does this tell us about Head-Smashed-In Buffalo Jump? Does it indicate that people were driving bison over its sandstone escarpment at the same time that Bonfire Shelter was being used?

Boyd Wettlaufer found this Scottsbluff-style spear point on the prairie beneath the cliff at Head-Smashed-In. The find indicates the site was occupied some nine thousand years ago. (Courtesy Royal Alberta Museum)

22

Nine thousand years ago the people who made Scottsbluff spear points may have driven herds of bison into the spring channel at Head-Smashed-In. (Courtesy Head-Smashed-In Buffalo Jump)

The simple answer is no. The two Scottsbluff spear points that Wet-tlaufer found came from within the spring channel at the base of the slope where the prairie begins. They did not come from the deep excavations conducted at the base of the cliff where the oldest layers of buffalo bones and artifacts had been discovered. In other words, these ancient points were not found in association with the use of Head-Smashed-In as a buffalo jump. Rather, they indicate that some-time around nine thousand years ago people occupied the flats that extend to the east of the sandstone cliff.

Until more excavations at the site are conducted, it is anyone's guess what people were doing at Head-Smashed-In that many years ago. Perhaps they camped on the pleasant flats beneath the cliff, cut up parts of game animals they had killed, cooked a few meals, collected local berries or wood for fires, erected some form of shelter, and then moved on. Intriguingly, makers of the Scottsbluff points may have even driven bison to their deaths at Head-Smashed-In, but they would not have done so by bringing them to the edge of the cliff. It's possible that Wettlaufer's finding of ancient spear points in the bottom of the spring channel is not fortuitous; perhaps as early as nine thousand years ago hunters ran small herds of bison into the spring channel, then killed and butchered them on the spot. Whatever the case, hunters apparently camped in the shadow of the great cliff, not realizing the lethal potential of the sheer face of rock. That would come thousands of years later, about fifty-eight hundred years ago.

Blood on the Rocks: The Story of Head-Smashed-In

There is no doubt that the name of the site is unusual and intriguing. There are a lot of people who can't quite figure what to make of it. It shows up as a question in the game *Trivial Pursuit*, it appeared in the humour magazine *National Lampoon*, it was jokingly discussed by the widely syndicated newspaper columnist Dave Barry (who just simply couldn't believe that there was a place in the world where you could dial a phone number and someone would answer, "Head-Smashed-In Buffalo Jump. May I help you?"). The unusual name of the site has presumably led quite a few tourists to veer off the main highway just to see what the heck a place called Head-Smashed-In could possibly be. There is a great and tragic story behind the name of the jump, but stories in Blackfoot culture aren't just stories; they are also the way history is reckoned and recorded.

During the ten years I directed archaeological excavations at Head-Smashed-In Buffalo Jump we intentionally set up our dig so that we were located in the heart of the tourist area. We wanted people to see us, approach the dig, linger, and ask questions. Our excavation was right out in the middle of what we call the processing area, a broad expanse of prairie stretching away from the cliff, where the carcasses of the slain animals were dragged down from the kill to be fully butchered (processed). The sheer cliff towered behind us, often lit in a warm golden hue from the mighty sun beating against the beige sandstone rock. The Porcupine Hills sandstone is rich in iron content, and when the iron particles are exposed to the elements they oxidize, turning a rusty orange colour. Portions of the cliff face are swathed with patches of reddish rock. In a decade of greeting tourists at the site of our excavations, I can't count how many people pointed to the red splotches on the cliff face and deduced how clever the Native hunters were to drive the bison over the prairie, up the slope, and smash them face first into the sandstone cliff.

The real story is just as good. Only the iron stains aren't blood, and the blood isn't that of the buffalo. There is a traditional story handed down through generations of Piikani (also known as Peigan, one of the three divisions of the Blackfoot people) elders. One of the times when the jump was being prepared for use, a young man, too young to be involved in the immediate chase and kill, wanted to be part of the great event. He had seen previous jumps take place and, like everyone, was enthralled with the sight of the huge beasts pouring over the cliff. He asked if he could witness this first hand by hiding under a ledge of the cliff, just below where the plunge would take place. And so he scampered along the cliff until he found a protective overhang and plastered himself against the rock face. The drive of animals began.

The spiritual power was strong that day. A great herd was brought forth and buffalo poured from the cliff like a waterfall. The brown, shaggy bodies slammed into the earth and piled one upon each other. Higher the mass of bodies grew until finally it reached the hiding place of the young man. He disappeared from view. When the waterfall of bison finally came to an end, the hunters waiting below scrambled up the slope of dead and dying buffalo, pulling them away from the rock face. They found the young man crushed against the cliff, his head smashed in.

The story has been a source of consternation among the Blackfoot elders who for years helped with the development and interpretation of Head-Smashed-In. It most decidedly is a well-remembered story in their culture, and there is ample historic evidence for a place on the east side of the Porcupine Hills that is called something like Head-Smashed-In. The great fur trader and explorer Peter Fidler trekked through southern Alberta in the late 1700s and early 1800s. Along with fascinating journals (he was the first white person to contact certain Native groups in southern Alberta), he consulted a map of the western Plains drawn for him by an Aboriginal informant. Many of the place names are in Blackfoot, but in one place there is a dot on the map and the notation, "Steep rocks where buffalo fall before and break their skulls all to pieces." Of course, the map is not precise enough to determine the exact location of the site. About a hundred years later, George Dawson, one of Canada's pioneer and legendary geologists, also traversed the country of southern Alberta. He left detailed maps and journals of his journey, recording many place names and significant features including a number of buffalo jumps. Among the names of jumps he recorded is "Where we smashed their heads in the mud." Again, the map he prepared is insufficient to compare with the modern location of the site. There is no doubt that these two travellers recorded a buffalo jump with a name much like the one we now know as Head-Smashed-In. But was this site the jump now known around the world as a UNESCO World Heritage Site? Or was this some other site, presumably nearby but (for the moment at least) a place lost to history?

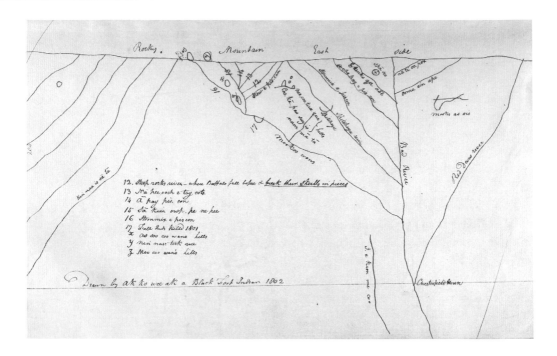

A map drawn by a Blackfoot man, Ackomokki, for Peter Fidler in 1802 plots a place (#12) with the caption: "steep rocks where buffalo fall before and break their skulls all to pieces." This is certainly a buffalo jump but it is impossible to conclude that it is Head-Smashed-In. (Courtesy Hudson Bay Company Archives/N4797)

Many Blackfoot believe the latter. They assert that the story of how Head-Smashed-In got its name is quite correct but that the location is wrong. They maintain that the buffalo jump where the young man met his unfortunate end is actually located elsewhere, often said to be somewhere on Willow Creek, a tributary to the Oldman River to the north of Head-Smashed-In. I sat in many meetings where I was lectured on how we got the wrong name for this place. Patiently I tried to explain that perhaps this was the case, but the name was now enshrined on numerous road signs, plaques, brochures, in travel information, the World Heritage list, and throughout the displays inside the interpretive centre. I hinted at how difficult it would be to change it now. Inevitably I was met with knowing smiles and nods of heads. The elders understood the economics and the politics of the situation. They knew the name was likely fixed for good. They just wanted to make sure I knew that we got it wrong. Of course I had to ask, so what did you call this place? I only ever got one answer: "We always just called it the buffalo jump." Which seemed to make sense: if there was one jump that stood out against all others, if there were a Mother of all Buffalo Jumps, I think that's what it might be called.

CHAPTER 2

The Buffalo

The American bison, or ... buffalo ... seems to have been spread over the plains of this vast country, by the Great Spirit, for the use and subsistence of the redmen, who live almost exclusively on their flesh, and clothe themselves with their skins. – George Catlin, 1832–39

If you had to pick an animal that was going to be the soul of your existence, the one thing that made life possible, you would be hard pressed to choose better than the North American Plains bison *(Bison bison bison)*. From the earliest evidence that people inhabited the Great Plains, about twelve thousand years ago, the bison has been the pivot around which all else revolved. In an old and somewhat overworked cliché, the bison has been called a walking supermarket for the people of the Plains. Like most clichés, this one contains an element of truth. Seldom in prehistory, if ever, have a people relied so heavily on one resource to provide such an overwhelming part of life's necessities (the reliance of some Arctic people on caribou is a fitting rival). Bison provided the bulk of food year-round, durable hides for making lodge covers and blankets, and strong bones for making a wide variety of tools. The great scholar of the Blackfoot, John Ewers, counted eighty-seven different tools and implements made of bison parts, adding that a more exhaustive search would probably bring the list to over one hundred items. To be sure, other resources were needed: wild plant foods to supplement the diet, other animal meat and fat when bison were not available (and to provide a little variety in life), hides from smaller game to make soft, pliable clothing (something for which the tough hides of bison were unsuited). But bison was the kingpin, the backbone of life, and in a very real sense it was the centre of the universe.

There has been a great deal written about bison. After all, they are the largest land mammal in North America. Bison have a fascinating

The supreme importance of the buffalo is reflected in these images of the animal carved and chipped out of stone. (Courtesy Royal Alberta Museum)

and complex evolutionary history spanning millions of years and several continents. Most of this is not relevant to our story. Bison have been in North America for hundreds of thousands of years, long before there were people here to hunt them. They have changed considerably in this time; most notably, they have gotten smaller. Bison have especially diminished in size since the last Ice Age, and continue to do so today, although the change is imperceptible in our lifetime. At the end of the last great Ice Age, about twelve thousand years ago, bison were about 25 per cent larger than their modern counterparts. These were formidable beasts indeed, made all the more so by the fact that their horns were huge. The distance from tip to tip on the horns of a modern adult male bison averages about a three-quarters of a metre. You can drop into museums in Idaho, Nevada, and Utah and see horns with a spread of more than *two metres.* While these monsters had died out by the time humans appeared on the scene, it is certainly true that Aboriginal hunters stalked and ran up next to wild, enraged beasts of nearly their size, and killed them with simple wooden spears tipped with stone points.

If you ever get a chance to see a live bison, please do so. It's not that hard these days, because bison have enjoyed an explosion in popularity in recent years, thanks in part to the superior nutrition they offer compared with beef and the ease of managing a herd. There are ever-increasing numbers of public and private herds throughout North America, thousands in all, containing more than half a million head. I haven't met a private bison rancher yet who doesn't love owning these animals and who will proudly take a few minutes to show them off. Take a long and studied look, but from a safe distance.

One of the giant bison that lived during the Pleistocene Era (the last Ice Age) – was Bison latifrons. *These monsters stood two and a half metres tall but died out in favour of smaller bison before the first hunters appeared on the scene. Painting by Ludo Bogaert. (Courtesy Royal Alberta Museum)*

Next page: With or without horses, bison hunting under any conditions was dangerous business. Painting by Albert Bierstadt (Courtesy Buffalo Bill Historical Center, Cody, Wyoming; Gertrude Vanderbilt Whitney Trust Fund Purchase)

Remember that, unlike cattle, bison have not been domesticated. They are wild animals, and the illusion of domestication is created by the fact that we can lean on a fence and watch them, much like we do cattle and horses. They are magnificent beasts. It is little wonder that their visage has appeared on everything from clothing, beverages, food brands, shipping companies, and the American nickel. The bison is the epitome of power, emblematic of individualism and freedom, an icon of a continent.

The bison was certainly a worthy foe for early hunters, who were armed only with simple weapons such as spears and bows and arrows. The general resemblance of bison to cattle, and our impression of cattle as slow and stupid – an attribute gained from generations of inbreeding for meat production – might lead the casual observer to think bison are plodding and cumbersome beasts. Nothing could be further from the truth. The preeminent naturalist John J. Audubon was astonished by the agility of Plains bison. Though we associate bison with the flat prairies, they possessed remarkable climbing ability. "The activity of Buffaloes is almost beyond belief," Audubon observed; "they can climb the steep defiles of the Mauvaises Terres [Bad Lands] in hundreds of places where men cannot follow them." His companion, Lewis Squires, expressed amazement that bison exhibited "most surprising speed, for an animal apparently so clumsy and awkward … I could hardly imagine that these enormous animals could move so quickly, or realize that their speed was as great as it proved to be."

The Earl of Southesk, like other Europeans, vastly underestimated the speed and agility of the bison, a consequence, he said, of the perceived "lumbering awkwardness of his action, and the grotesque wildness of his appearance."

In every sense but one, bison must be credited with having the upper hand in any encounter. Considering their massive size, they are incredibly fast animals. Over short distances they can run with a race horse, reaching speeds of fifty kilometres per hour. And over the long haul they have amazing endurance, being able to run at somewhat slower speeds for extended periods of time, long after their predators have tired and faded. Their squat, stocky, heavy-bodied appearance belies a remarkable quickness. Ask anyone who works regularly with bison. They can turn on a dime, twirling with their heads down and horns out. Many a coyote, wolf, and human hunter have been gored and flung through the air by a buffalo that just a moment before had been standing still. Audubon again provides witness:

When wounded and mad they turn suddenly round upon the hunter, and rush upon him in such a quick and furious manner that if horse and rider are not both on the alert, the former is overtaken, hooked and overthrown, the hunter pitched off, trampled and gored to death. Although the Buffalo is such a large animal, and to all appearance a clumsy one, it can turn with the quickness of thought, and when once enraged, will rarely give up the chase until avenged for the wound it has received.

Hunters, who were on foot for twelve thousand years before the horse was returned to this continent, standing in the open, often featureless landscape, were at a decided disadvantage. There was only one way humans had the upper hand – their intellect, their cunning, their ability to observe and to learn.

Is it Bison or Buffalo?

There certainly is a great deal of confusion over the two competing names for the same animal. The source of the problem is as follows: there is the name given by the scientists whose job it is to provide order and classification to the animals of the earth, and then there is the popular, colloquial name that is technically wrong but is deeply entrenched in public parlance. How did we end up with two names for the same animal? You can blame that on the early European visitors to this continent. They sailed the Atlantic from places like France, Spain, and England and were familiar with other members of the Bovidae family – the Asian *(Bubalus)* and African *(Syncerus)* buffalo. These look roughly similar to the great beast of the Plains. When they first saw the bison of North America they noted the general similarity and erroneously proclaimed them "buffalo." (In fact, many of the early historic accounts talked about the "cattle" of the prairies.) But since it was European explorers, not Aboriginal people, who wrote books and letters, made sketches of the animal, and communicated these around the world, the name given by the Europeans came into common usage. While their correct name is bison, the word buffalo is in such common use that it is pointless to fight. Just as the animal most people call gophers are really ground squirrels, the name gopher will live on.

What did Native people call bison? Obviously they used their own languages, of which there were many in use in western North America at the time of first European contact. Each group had their own word for bison or, actually, many words. You can imagine that an animal so critical to their existence was not referred to by a single term. Many cultures had distinct words for important aspects of their lives, say, for male and female bison, old and young ones, fat and lean. The Omaha had separate words in their vocabulary for a single family hunt, a hunt by a single man or few men, for men who go out and stay with game, for groups to go out and drive game. In a very real sense, the survival of the Plains hunters depended on knowing and recognizing the differences in bison and how best to hunt them. When your life depends on food from one main source, not all bison are created equal.

In Numbers, Numberless

Mr. Kipp told me that while travelling from Lake Travers to the Mandans ... he rode in a heavily laden cart for six successive days through masses of Buffaloes, which divided for the cart, allowing it to pass without opposition. He has seen the immense prairie ... look black to the tops of the hills, though the ground was covered with snow, so crowded was it with these animals.
– John Audubon, 1843

For many millennia bison roamed the Great Plains in vast numbers. Just how vast no one knows, but there has been much speculation.

As shown in this sketch from 1853, the Great Plains of North America once teemed with buffalo. Sketch by John Mix Stanley. (Courtesy Glenbow Archives/NA 1274-2)

Some have said seventy-five million bison were on the Plains at the time of first European contact. Some put the figure as low as fifteen million. Many think thirty million is a reasonable compromise. It almost doesn't matter. The point is that there were maybe tens of thousands of Native people on the Plains before European arrival, and there were tens of millions of buffalo, which means there was plenty to go around, especially for hunters on foot and armed with simple hunting weapons. There is no evidence that Aboriginal hunting of bison, over at least twelve thousand years, was making any serious dent in the population. On the contrary, evidence from the bones at many different sites of differing ages suggests that bison were certainly holding their own in terms of numbers, if not actually becoming more numerous through time.

There can be no doubt that Native hunters did their best to kill these mighty beasts. They devised an astonishing array of ingenious traps to deprive bison of their natural advantages – speed, mobility, strength, endurance, sense of smell – and to turn the tables so that the hunters at least had a modicum of a chance. But despite the hunters' best efforts, bison flourished. One has only to read some of the statements by early European observers on the Plains, who saw before them a breathtaking virtual sea of brown fur covering the land as far as the eye could reach. On ascending a small hill, Lewis and Clark remarked that bison were so numerous "that from an eminence we discovered more than we had ever seen before ... and if it be not impossible to calculate the moving multitude, which darkened the whole plains, we are convinced that twenty thousand would be no exaggerated number." The great explorer Peter Fidler, in southern Alberta in 1792–93, was convinced that he witnessed a much greater number: "The Buffalo are very numerous on the NE side the Red Deers river & near ... the ground is entirely covered by them & appears quite black. I never saw such amazing numbers together before. I am sure there was some millions in sight as no ground could be seen for them in that complete semicircle & extending at least 10 miles."

Alexander Henry was an experienced fur trader and hunter. He spent fifteen years in the Canadian and U.S. northwest. Few Europeans had more experience than Henry when it came to life on the Great Plains and living off the buffalo. Thus, when he rose on the morning of 14 January 1801 and expressed his astonishment, it must be taken seriously:

At daybreak I was awakened by the bellowing of buffaloes. I got up, and was astonished when I climbed into the S.W. bastion. On my right the plains were black, and appeared as if in motion, S. to N. Opposite the fort the ice was covered [with buffalo]; and on my left, to the utmost extent of the reach below us, the river was covered with buffalo moving northward ... I had seen almost incredible numbers of buffalo in the fall, but nothing in comparison to what I now beheld. The ground was covered at every point of the compass, as far as the eye could reach, and every animal was in motion.

Many found themselves at a loss for words when faced with the teeming herds. Zebulon Pike (the namesake of Pike's Peak) stated, "I will not attempt to describe the droves of animals we now saw on our route; suffice it to say, that the face of the prairie was covered with them ... their numbers exceeded imagination." The emphasis in the following statement by Audubon is his own: "*it is impossible to describe or even conceive* the vast multitudes of these animals that exist even now, and feed on these ocean-like prairies." Others doubted that readers

† How did Native people count bison? For the most part they didn't. Counting systems were rudimentary, often limited to numbers in the tens. Indians assessed the size of bison herds, as David Thompson records, more by "the space they stand on; for numbers is to them an abstract idea, but space of ground to a certain extent they readily comprehend and the animals it may contain."

would believe their accounts of enormous herds. Robert Rundle, near Rocky Mountain House, observed, "The immense quantity we saw would scarce be credited by an inhabitant of old England." Travelling up the Missouri in 1811, H.M. Brackenridge reported this thought:

I am conscious that with many, I run the risk of being thought to indulge in romance, in consequence of this account: but with those who are informed of the astonishing number of the buffaloe, it will not be considered incredible … On the hills in every direction they appeared by thousands. Late in the evening we saw an immense herd in motion along the sides of the hill, at full speed: their appearance had something in it, which, without incurring ridicule, I might call sublime – the sound of their footsteps, even at the distance of two miles, resembled the rumbling of distant thunder.

Even when they were not seen, the presence of the teeming prairie herds had other ways of making their presence known. John Bradbury, on the Missouri in 1811, tells of distant, massive herds that he could not see but whose location was known "by the vapour which arose from their bodies." The Earl of Southesk in 1860 noted the presence of immense herds by the "deep rolling voice of the mighty multitude [that] came grandly on the air like the booming of a distant ocean." Of course there was the ubiquitous buffalo chip; the round patties of dung must have dotted the prairies like an immense checkerboard. John Audubon said that chips were so abundant on the Plains that the traveller could not step more than a few feet without coming across one. In 1820, Edwin James provided the most harrowing account when, struck by a torrential thunderstorm on the Plains, the river rose and "was soon covered with such a quantity of bison's dung, suddenly washed in from the declivities of the mountains and the plains at its base, that the water could scarcely be seen." Dinner that night, made with brown river water, tasted like a "cow-yard" and was thrown away.

Attempts to quantify the size of bison herds in the eighteenth and nineteenth centuries must be seen for what they were – subjective, often intentionally exorbitant, and mostly useless at providing reliable documentation.† It's a matter best left to the imaginative realm of poetry. Robert Rundle, travelling through western Alberta in 1840, perhaps said it best. Remarking on the immense herds that stretched out before him, he stole a line from the poet Milton and wrote: "They were in numbers – numberless."

Tricks of the Trade

Every spring as the river is breaking up ... the buffaloe [are] tempted to cross ... on their way they are often insulated on a large cake or mass of ice, which floats down the river: the Indians now select the most favourable points for attack, and as the buffaloe approaches dart with astonishing agility across the trembling ice, sometimes pressing lightly a cake of not more than two feet square: the animal is of course unsteady, and his footsteps insecure on this new element, so that he can make but little resistance, and the hunter, who has given him his death wound, paddles his icy boat to the shore and secures his prey. – Lewis and Clark, 1805

† Yet they were occasionally caught on thin ice. Maximilian, Prince of Wied, who traversed the Great Plains between 1832 and 1834, reported an event in which eighteen hundred bison drowned at one place on the Missouri, where their bodies temporarily dammed this great river.

Aboriginal bison hunters of the Plains had to somehow take away the natural advantage of the swift and powerful bison and turn the tables in their favour. Clearly they could not do this with speed, strength, endurance, or formidable weapons (like a gun that in the right hands can kill an unsuspecting animal a kilometre away). They had to do it by outsmarting the animals. Almost every type of mass communal bison kill archaeologists have discovered, and those recounted by Native elders, involved some kind of trick, one that was played in a deadly game of survival.

Here's just a sample of many tricks employed. Plains hunters donned the dressed hides of many other animals – deer, wolves, coyotes, pronghorn – and so disguised were able to approach a herd close enough to loose several arrows. Bison are excellent swimmers, crossing major rivers and lakes easily.† But hunters knew bison were slow and vulnerable in the water and so waited at known crossing locations to kill them from the shore, or sometimes even shipped out in small boats to kill them as they swam. Adding insult to injury, these boats were made of the hides of bison from previous kills, stretched over a simple wooden frame. In winter bison crossed frozen lakes and rivers, but their footing on ice was poor. Hunters exploited this limitation by ambushing herds at winter crossing points, sending the beleaguered herds scattering on icy surfaces. In December 1857, the Palliser Expedition witnessed just such an event:

The slipperiness of the ice, which gave us so much trouble in crossing the lake, was turned to good account the other day by the Indians, as they drove a band of buffalo cows so that they had to go out on the ice of the lake, when of course they fell and stumbled, and could make no progress, while their pursuers, approaching them on foot, with ease killed the whole, to the number of 14.

Although winter hunting was difficult, deep snow could become a kind of trap into which hunters on snowshoes could force the animals, then kill them easily. Painting by George Catlin. (Courtesy Bruce Peel Special Collections Library, University of Alberta)

Hunters knew that bison avoided deep snow (it greatly reduced their mobility) and would seek out for their winter trails the crests and side slopes of ridges, which are blown clear of snow. Lying in wait in the lee (downwind) of a ridge (to hide their smell), hunters would storm up one side of the ridge and drive the bison down the other side into deep snow banks where they could be killed easily. They tricked bison into entering the mouths of box canyons leading only to steep-walled dead ends, where they could be picked off by hunters clinging to the canyon walls. Often such tricks were combined, as George Bird Grinnell reports for the Cheyenne, who used snow and gullies to deadly effect: "they followed them [buffalo] in winter on snowshoes and chased them into snowdrifts in ravines. When they had driven buffalo into such drifts, they set the dogs free to worry them, and ran up and killed them with the lance."

The list goes on. Each bison kill site that archaeologists excavate forces us into a protracted scouring of the surrounding landscape, searching for clues as to how the kill was executed. Inevitably there was a trick or trap of some kind; there practically had to be, for the bison in its prairie home was the master of the house. People took them when their intellect had given them the ingredients to strip the bison of its natural advantage and when it was the will of the spirit world.

The skill, planning, and requisite knowledge that went into tricking buffalo to plunge over a cliff may not have been any greater than what went into the other forms of communal killing. But the outcome was certainly more spectacular. In subsequent pages we will examine the details of what made a buffalo jump work. But first we need to know more about the animal itself. Everything about a buffalo jump was rooted in Aboriginal knowledge of the behaviour and biology of bison. It is impossible to understand the operation of a jump without knowing much (though certainly not all) of what Native people knew about the animal they sought. I have studied this topic for some twenty-five years, and I continue to learn new things about bison. Often I learn them first from the scientific literature on wildlife. And as I think about what I have read, I come to realize that these very facts were played out over and over again in the Aboriginal stories and the archaeological traces left behind. It is a humbling experience.

The Fats of Life

To us who had so long desired a healthful portion of bodily exercise in that quarter, it [fat] was the very marrow and life-blood of whatsoever is good and wholesome for famished carniverous animals like ourselves … it loosed our tongues and warmed our hearts towards one another … it made our faces to shine with grease and gladness.– Thomas Farnham, 1839

As far as Aboriginal hunters were concerned, what makes one bison a better catch than another is the amount of fat different animals have. In our modern world, it is difficult to imagine fat being a good thing, let alone being critical for survival. We have been indoctrinated on the evils of fat – causing everything from clogged arteries to obesity. We carefully trim and discard fat from the steaks we grill, and *bacon* has become a dirty word. Most of this carefulness is appropriate, because we get fat from almost every food we eat; every slice of bread, cheese, pie, cake, and donut. We don't need extra fats in our diet, and it is detrimental to our health. But such is not the case for people who don't have the great variety of foods that we have, who live on a diet dominated by meat, and who must survive out on the land, coping with the extremes of the elements. Living such a life burns up body fat much faster than our lifestyle, and it must be replenished. Native hunters of the West craved and sought out fat. They didn't just like it (there's no denying fat tastes good), they perished without it.

If you are not getting fat in your diet from other sources, you must have adequate fat from your main food source – in this case bison.

† John Audubon, during his bison hunting days in the 1800s, observed that wolves also chose the fattest animals to attack.

A lean animal was almost useless to Native hunters, unless they already had some fat stored from a previous kill that they could add to the lean meat. Captain John Palliser, in his famous trek across western Canada from 1857 to 1860, frequently found himself in the position of having to eat lean meat: "we could not get any fat or grease to trade from the Indians, which was a bad look out, as it is nearly as hard to live on the dried meat of a lean animal alone without grease, as it is to starve altogether." It seems improbable, but despite eating kilograms of meat a day, people died because it was lean meat. In such cases, the body craves but does not get the fat it needs to provide energy and maintain normal body function. On another occasion, when he and his men had only a lean moose for food, Palliser vividly conveys the frustration of trying to satisfy one's appetite on a fat-free meal: "Our appetite was tremendous, so that, although the flesh of the animal was so lean that at other times we would not have eaten it, we continued cooking, eating, and sleeping the remainder of that day, and the whole of the next."

There are countless examples in the historic literature of hunters even refusing to kill lean animals, as they knew they were worthless as food. Hunting buffalo in February, Lewis and Clark spied many animals but rejected them as "too poor to be worth hunting" (the term *poor* was used by many Europeans to denote lean animals, as *good* or *fine* were used for fat ones). Or once killed, many lean animals were rejected unless the hunter was in dire straits. Edwin James, on the Plains from 1819 to 1820, killed a bison "so extremely lean ... that nothing but the most urgent necessity could have induced us to taste it."

This is why Native hunters exclaimed with joy when a fat animal was obtained and bemoaned the killing of a lean one. With few exceptions, such as when animals were hunted for needs other than food, finding and killing fat animals was the objective of every hunt. Traversing the southern Plains in the 1830s, Josiah Gregg noted, "In the chase, the experienced hunter singles out the fattest buffalo as his victim." John McDougall, buffalo hunting in Alberta in the 1860s, confessed to the purpose of the quest: "of course every one of us secretly in his own mind wanted to kill the very fattest." Life (and good tasting food) depended on it.

This discernment wasn't just a characteristic of early bison hunters; it is true of any person put in the same environmental situation.† Europeans, originating as they did from heated homes and diverse diets, often arrived on the Plains without an appreciation of the importance

of fat. But it didn't take them long to come to the same understanding as Aboriginal hunters. The literature is full of statements of Europeans craving fat after only a few months living on the Plains. They couldn't help but notice this sudden change in their own diet. Travelling with Native groups through Alberta in 1872, Donald Graham said, "I think that in cold countries where the diet is practically all meat, the human system requires a good deal of fat. Personally, I used to detest it, but on occasions I could take a large chunk of wolf fat and not only eat it, but enjoy it." Edwin James reported that his men got sick from eating currants. Nothing wrong with the currants, he concluded, "but that the stomach, by long disuse, had in a great measure lost the power of digesting vegetable matter."

Some of my friends and I, lucky enough to have the opportunity to do archaeological field work in the Canadian Arctic, likewise found our diet undergo transformation. Camped in the middle of a barren, demanding landscape, living on a restricted diet and with limited source of heat, we found that in a matter of a few weeks we experienced a craving for fat – devouring chocolate bars, peanut butter, oily sardines, and even eating spoonfuls of margarine right out of the tub. Though I shudder at the thought now, at the time there was nothing I wanted more than fat.

Knowing that only fat bison were useful to the hunters, the next step is to know which animals will be fat at any given time of year. It should come as no surprise that Native people were acutely aware of the facts governing different bison conditions. Through experience gained over millennia, they knew precisely which bison could be counted on to supply a nutritious meal: male, female, young, old, spring, summer, fall, and winter. They knew the patterns (though not

By observing subtle differences in body contour and coat characteristics, Native hunters could pick out the fattest animals in a herd. (Courtesy Clarence Tillenius)

the scientific explanations) that governed the gain and loss of fat, and they planned every kill with these patterns in mind. Failure to do so could spell starvation. Not only did the hunters know the natural patterns the bison followed, they also learned how to spot fat animals in a herd. An experienced hunter would pick out the pronounced curves of the body and eye the sheen of the coat that indicated a fat animal. To appreciate the detailed knowledge Aboriginal people had of when bison were fat, witness the statement Buffalo Bird Woman gave to Gilbert Wilson early in the twentieth century:

At this time of the year the fat ones have a patch of black hair over the eyes for the fat under the skin makes the animal shed earlier and the new-grown hair is very black. Also, there is a black stripe on the highest point of the spine over the shoulders and there is a little black hair around the horns.

To understand Aboriginal planning and execution of buffalo jumps, we need to know at least a little of what they knew about patterns of fat in bison and about seasonal changes in buffalo behaviour, habitat, and biology. This information is instrumental in answering how, when, and why the great hunts took place.

CHAPTER 3

A Year in the Life

Our ears were assailed by a murmuring noise. As we drew near it grew to a tremendous roaring, such as to deafen us … several thousand of these furious animals, roaring and rushing upon each other … the earth trembled beneath their feet, the air was deafened, and the grove was shaken with the shock of their tremendous battle. – Henry Brackenridge, 1811

A review of the life cycle and seasonal round of bison may seem academic, but it is crucial to understanding the operation of a buffalo jump. The physical characteristics of the animal change dramatically over the course of a year based on such factors as age, sex, and season. Hunters were acutely aware of these changes; they had to be, for the differing status of bison throughout the year spelled the difference between life and death. It is not hard to imagine that people who lived mainly on a meat diet, and had done so for thousands of years, had long ago worked out which animals were best suited to keeping them alive and which are relatively useless. As will be seen a number of times in this book, modern science is just catching up to what Aboriginal people have long known and used to their advantage. We should expect no less. After all, one group has been researching, observing, and generally paying attention to these facts for a vastly longer period of time. For one group it was a matter of life and death, for the other it's a research project.

The bison family: from left, cow, calf, and bull. (Courtesy Wes Olson)

Calves

The Calves in the Womb are now all well covered with hair. These all Indians are remarkably fond of even when not more than the size of a quart pot they eat them. – Peter Fidler, 1792–93

Although newborn calves can be seen in a herd at almost any time of the year, most bison calves come into this world in April and May. With a gestation period of nine months, this means that the females are getting pregnant in the rutting season in late July and in August and early September. Humans are one of the species that give birth year round. Many species need to time their birth cycle to give the young a chance to grow during times when risks to their survival are minimized. Humans must nurture and protect their young for years after birth, so it really doesn't matter when they are born, especially since we started living in shelters and crowding around fires. Most other animals have to survive on their own relatively quickly after birth and thus need all the advantages they can get to make it into adulthood. Bison on the northern Plains live in a part of the world noted for strong pulses in the seasons – hard, cold winters and warm, lazy summers. Peak calving in the spring gives the newborn an opportunity to graze on the best forage they are going to find. The fast-growing grass of spring, rich in flowers and seeds, is much richer in protein than the drier grasses of mid- and later summer. Calves put on weight, gain strength, and build up body reserves in muscle

Bison calves, which are reddish brown at birth, can walk within hours. (Courtesy William S. Keller, U.S. National Park Service)

and fat that will give them a decent chance of making it through their first winter. Calves born out of the normal season are often doomed to be removed from the gene pool. Thus does the benign indifference of nature construct its tendencies, promoting the regularities and discouraging the deviations that enhance the chances of survival.

Calves weigh a surprisingly light fifteen to twenty kilograms at birth, not much larger than an elk calf and smaller than beef calves. Most of this initial weight is muscle, bone, and hide. They have little fat when young, and their immediate need is to walk with the mother and the herd and to run from predators. These needs are met by the early development of muscle and bone. If you have ever watched a foal drop from a mare, it is an amazing experience. This gangly, slime-encrusted baby falls to the ground, looking like all legs and a head. But within minutes, with nudging and licking from the mother, it is trying and succeeding to stand. A human will take a year or more to reach this same stage of development. Human babies aren't expected to run from trouble; parents carry them. By the end of their first summer bison calves have gained more than one hundred kilograms, are starting to put on fat, and are healthy, substantial animals that would make attractive targets for hungry hunters.

Although neither fetuses nor newborn bison are known for high fat content, they make up for this by being tasty. Unlike tough, older animals, their flesh is soft and succulent. As Samuel Hearne noted in 1772, fetal bison were a highly esteemed treat, and "the young calves, cut out of their mothers' bellies, are reckoned a great delicacy indeed." Lewis and Clark exclaimed that young calves "are equal in flavour to the most delicious veal." And if you were eating a fetus, you were also probably dining on the mother, which offered a more complete array of nutrition than the low-fat fetus.

Mothers

The principal beast of chase is the buffalo, or, rather, the buffalo cow.
– Maximilian, Prince of Wied, 1832–34

In the renewed life of spring on the Plains, many, though not all, healthy adult cows will be carrying young. On average about three-quarters of the adult females will be pregnant in any given year. Cows dropping their calves in spring are embarking on their most perilous journey. Nursing the young over the coming months is a wasting,

Cows typically weigh between 450 and 650 kilograms, and are able to reproduce from about the age of two until they are fourteen. (Courtesy Johane Janelle)

depleting experience for the mothers (as in cattle, single birth is the strong norm and twins are very rare). The continuous production of milk depletes the body resources of the cows. Mothers can routinely lose most of their body fat and even some of their muscle tissue during months of nursing. You can see another critical aspect to timing of birth – the mothers, just like the newborn, need the fine graze of spring and early summer to get them through their own period of greatest stress.

Traditionally, it has been thought that pregnancy was a draining experience, that cows carrying calves are under considerable physiological stress associated with nurturing the fetus. This is only partially correct. Pregnant cows tend to be the biggest, fattest, most muscular of all females, and they stay this way through most of their pregnancy. The simple story is that nature has worked out that big body size is good for reproduction. You may have heard stories of peak female athletes being unable to conceive. Some stop having their menstrual period entirely. They have shed all their body fat, and nature has deemed them, temporarily, unfit to carry a fetus. Fat, despite its current bad rap, is essential to life. Especially lean mothers at the time of conception have little chance of providing essential nutrients to the fetus. The fetus may not make it to full term or, worse, it will, and the mother will be unable to feed the newborn calf.

Over millions of years of evolution, Nature has given her priority to the mother, not the calf. The death of a calf, or failure to conceive, is the loss of one animal. Survival for the mother means the potential birth of many more calves in the future when the cow's condition improves. Lean, scrawny cows that become pregnant risk draining all their own resources to nurture the calf, and neither may survive. Fat, heavy cows have the reserves necessary to ensure the survival of the calf and, more importantly, of the mother to breed again another day.[†]

Cows need to be seen as two distinct groups based on reproduction: those that are pregnant and those that are not (that is, barren). When the cows have just dropped their calves in spring, the production of milk kicks in and the nursing mothers become extremely lean, in fact the leanest they will be all year, as they pour all their resources into nursing the calf. Although nursing continues for many months, the effects on the cows are most severe in the first few months and then quickly taper off.

Through the summer, calves start adding grass and water to their diet. The calves depend less on mothers' milk, and the cows, too, eat fine quality spring and summer graze to help them regain weight. By late summer most cows have recovered from the debilitating effects of lactation, only now they are faced with another rut. Those that have recovered the most, and put on the most fat, will likely breed and become pregnant for a second year in a row. Some that have recovered less well, perhaps having dropped their calves a little later in the spring or faced poor summer graze, may be so lean during the rut that nature blocks their becoming pregnant that year. These cows are now out of the reproductive cycle for that year (barren) and are free to focus on building up their own body resources over late summer and fall.

As the cows enter the fall and winter, the barren cows are leaner. The pregnant ones are by definition fatter, as it was their greater fat stores that allowed them to become pregnant. Both groups generally gain weight (mostly fat) through autumn, since grasses on the northern Plains tend to experience a second pulse of growth and remain highly nutritious. Autumn is the season when cows will have more fat than at any other time of the year. This is true for both pregnant and barren cows, though the former will be the fatter. Cow hides are also in prime condition at this time: the skin is thick and free of the insect holes that come with summer; the hair (much of which is shed

[†] There is, of course, an upper limit to fat being a good thing, as when cows on bison ranches are overfed to fetch a better price at auction. Their fat can close off the birth canal, resulting in a difficult delivery (sometimes death) for both mother and calf. In the wild, this is unlikely to happen.

in summer) has grown back bushy and full. Cows simply don't get any better than they are in autumn.

With the onset of winter, the grass freezes, dries, lays flat on the ground, and loses a great deal of its protein. Snow covers much of the land. Bison, unlike cattle, are extremely efficient winter grazers, using their massive heads to sweep the ground clear of snow. But much more energy must be expended in this effort, with a reduced nutrient return from the dead grass, and all bison lose weight. Fat goes first, as the animals draw on their own stored reserves to compensate for poor feed. In a really severe winter, fat may be severely depleted and muscle, and even bone tissue, may be called on to support life. The weight of adult cows may decline as much as fifty to seventy-five kilograms over winter (about 10–15 per cent of body weight), most of which is fat. As winter deepens, all cows are becoming lean, but the pregnant ones are still the fattest. Remember that they started off in autumn as the fattest of the cows, and for most of the gestation period the fetus draws on little of the mother's reserves, so the pregnant cows remain fatter than the barren ones throughout the winter.

As the next spring approaches, the situation begins to change dramatically. The last months of pregnancy finally start to make a substantial impact on the mother's body resources. Fat, already depleted from winter stress, is now drawn on to nurture the rapidly growing fetus. Barren cows don't experience this late winter-accelerated fat drain. Although all cows are lean in late winter, the barren ones may now start to rival the pregnant cows as being the fatter of the two groups. With the appearance of the first green grass the disparity between the two cow groups intensifies. Barren cows begin to replenish fat and rapidly gain weight. Pregnant cows drop their young, begin lactating, and sink into the depths of fat depletion, ameliorated only by the fact that grass is once again nutritious.

So for those few months of spring and early summer, say from March or April through June, the cows that did not calve become the fatter of the cow groups, while those nursing are in terrible shape, with almost no body fat. The barren cows will gain a great amount of summer weight, mostly fat, and be in prime shape to breed and become pregnant during the coming rut. Nursing cows will start to improve through summer, some enough to breed again, others will be spared by low fat levels and remain barren for the coming year. And so the cycle begins again.

Fathers

Bull meat is not regarded, it is seldom fat, and always tough. – David Thompson,
1784–1812

*Small openings are left [in the buffalo pounds] to admit the dogs to feed upon
the carcasses of the bulls, which are generally left as useless.* – Alexander
Henry, 1808

The situation for males is almost entirely different. Nature has conspired to have cows at peak fat levels as they begin their journey on
the road to bearing young, that is, in the fall. Nature has also conspired
to have males achieve maximum fat levels according to the need to
engage in reproductive activity, but for them this season is late summer. As with females, males are more likely to breed if they are big,
fat, and heavy. These will be the dominant males, those that butt
others out of their way, sometimes engaging in fierce battles, to take
control of cows that are in estrus. Not only are they strong enough
to dominate smaller males, there is also evidence that females find
the bigger males attractive, apparently recognizing that pairing up
with a big male will more likely lead to the production of a strong,
healthy calf that will become a competitive son.

Young males will stay with their mothers through the first two
or three years of life, after which they wander off to join the bull
groups. In fact, young bulls look like cows for the first three years of
life, but by the summer of their third year they grow a hair coat that
defines the males and, after the rut, they leave the cow–calf herd.
They remain very junior in the bull groups for several more years,
as they continue to increase body size, and only start to flirt with the
prospect of sexual activity at about five or six. As you would expect,
adult males reach peak physical size and condition (including body
fat) in mid- to late summer to coincide with the rutting season, as this
will increase their chances of attracting cows. And then an amazing
thing happens. They lose a large proportion of their body fat just as
cold weather is approaching.

Wildlife biologists used to think that the primary purpose of body
fat in large game animals was to serve as a reserve energy source to
help the animal survive the rigors of winter. While there is still some
truth in this belief, the emphasis has shifted to recognizing the profound role fat plays in reproduction. Nowhere is this seen more vividly

This bull is in prime condition and thus fit for breeding. Adult males weigh between 650 and 900 kilograms. (Courtesy Johane Janelle)

than in the fact that males of many North American large mammals experience a drastic crash of their fat stores shortly before the onset of winter. How can the main purpose of fat be that of a winter energy reserve when most of it is lost in the time leading up to the most demanding season of the year? It has become increasingly clear that the primary role of fat is to allow males to participate in reproductive activity. Big, fat, heavy animals have a greater chance to reproduce; skinny, lightweight males are likely to be left out of the game.

In this sense males are more expendable than females. Fat cycles in cows clearly favour survival of the mother, so that a normal cow can breed a dozen times or more during her life. Continuation of the species, then, is better assured by having the cow survive, even at the expense of the calf. For males, however, the emphasis is on doing everything possible to take part in the reproductive effort. If some of them don't make it past this point and perish over winter due to depleted body reserves, there is minimal danger to the overall survival of the species, because relatively few healthy males can (and do) impregnate many cows. Having many cows in a herd is an advantage, as they produce the young that perpetuate the species. It is less critical that a great number of males survive, since a lower number will still be enough to impregnate all the females. No doubt these facts play a role in adult male bison losing most of their fat reserves before heading into winter.

Males come through the long winter on the Plains pretty scrawny, but they soon begin to fatten on the fresh grass of spring. Since they have nothing like the drain of lactation to get in the way, they just keep putting on fat and muscle through the summer and are in peak shape at the start of the rut. But rutting does strange things to male bison (the same could be said of our own species). They become obsessed with finding and guarding cows for mating. They stand by them constantly, ever watchful for other bulls that might have eyes for their cows. This requires vigilance and attention, full time. They will stop eating for days and weeks, as having a head down means taking one's eye off the cows and the other males. They seldom sleep. They pace and chase other males away. They fight. All this extra activity burns calories, lots of them, and yet by fasting they take in almost no new sources of energy to keep up their body tissue. Their fat levels crash. By the end of the rut, adult males lose a great deal of total body fat and even some muscle tissue. But it's all for the cause: the powerful instinct to engage in reproduction. Take a bull completely away from the herd, isolate him in a pen by himself, and he will behave exactly the same and suffer the same physiological changes.

Another thing happens to bulls at this time that affects our story. The rut triggers a rush of hormones pumping through their bodies, and these hormones affect the taste of their meat dramatically. Modern-day hunters of big game are all too familiar with this. They know it is pointless to shoot a bull animal during the rutting season (unless you are only after a trophy), because you won't be able to eat any of the meat. While the musky flavour wouldn't kill you, it sure doesn't taste good. There are plenty of historical accounts of fur traders and explorers who simply had to kill a bull during the rut. They ate it and it kept them alive.† But they didn't like it, and they tossed the meat as soon as there was a chance of something else, preferably a barren cow or a bull too young to be part of breeding activity. You can imagine that for a culture subsisting primarily on the flesh of wild animals, it was a dark day indeed when they were forced to take down a bull during the rut. They did so very reluctantly, and only when survival depended on it.

† Hunting during the rutting season of August 1843, John Audubon and his entourage came across six bull bison. He commented, "Our folks have shot buffaloes, but I have not done so, simply because they are worthless through poverty, and when killed only display a mass of bones and skin, with a very thin portion of flesh; and if you shoot a bull the rankness of its better parts is quite enough to revolt the stomach of all but starving men."

The Big Picture

Which of the two sexes is the fattest at any time of the year is a complex issue, requiring comparison of three groups: cows that are reproducing, cows that aren't, and bulls. It is likewise apparent that if your goal is to hunt the fattest buffalo, different sexes and groups of animals will fill this need at differing times of the year. All adult cows are probably fatter than adult males during the fall and winter. Breeding bulls have lost most of their body fat in the rut, nursing cows have pretty much finished lactating, and non-nursing cows are probably fattest of all and almost certainly have become pregnant. By the end of winter all bison have suffered declining body reserves. Because cows had much more fat than breeding bulls to begin the winter, however, they are still in better shape. By spring the barren cows and bulls rapidly replenish lost fat, but pregnant cows drop their calves and begin nursing. The former two groups will be about equal in fat at this time, while the lactating cows are wholly unacceptable as food. This situation continues into the early summer, at which point the bulls start to gain on the barren cows. Bulls are the fattest animals through mid-summer and at the onset of the rut. But as the rut progresses, bull flesh becomes more strongly infused with musky-tasting hormones. Bulls begin to lose their fat, while at the same time all cows are improving and are soon again the fattest bison.

Adult cows are the fatter of the two sexes for a good part of a typical year. This is true from at least September through April or

Bison are highly sexually dimorphic mammals, which means that males are substantially bigger than females. (Courtesy Wes Olson)

May. Bulls are almost certainly fatter than any cows in mid-summer, from June through August, although by the latter month the effects of the rut are beginning to taint their meat. Recalling that Aboriginal hunters desperately wanted and needed to kill the fattest animals, maximizing fat means killing mostly cows for much of the year. Only in early to mid-summer would bulls be the preferred target. And the difference in fat content isn't just one of relative abundance. Wouldn't it be reasonable to conclude, therefore, that killing a male bison, even if the animal is relatively leaner, would still yield a greater amount of fat simply because male bison are substantially larger than females? It's a good question and the answer is surprising.

Bison are what's termed *sexually dimorphic.* It means that the males are consistently bigger, heavier, and more muscular than the females. The same is true of most large mammals, including humans.[†] And the difference is significant. Male bison are, on average, about 30–40 per cent bigger and heavier than cows. This translates into an advantage of several hundred kilograms of body weight in favour of the males. Accordingly, you might expect that the absolute weight of fat on a bull would exceed that of a cow, even though the cow might have a greater percentage of fat as total body weight. If this were true, then it would make more sense to kill bulls all the time, simply because their much greater size would translate into greater fat weight. Such is not the case; at least not with respect to fat. It is true with respect to muscle tissue (meat). Males are far more muscular than cows, and their muscle mass far outweighs that of the cows, regardless of the season. If your goal was to obtain the most meat you could get from a kill then you would always shoot for the bulls.

However, fat, not meat, was the food source most sought after by all Plains Aboriginal hunting cultures. Despite their smaller size, cows have a greater absolute weight of fat than males do, for most of the year. This is a characteristic of females in many species (again including our own); reproduction requires greater fat reserves for energy, and since the females have to carry and nurse the young, they are genetically disposed to have greater fat reserves. The important lesson here is that different groups of bison differ dramatically in what they offer human consumers by such factors as sex, season, and reproductive status. Aboriginal bison hunters learned this lesson thousands of years ago.

[†] Curiously, and for reasons still debated, some species of birds show the opposite trend.

Science and the Historic Record

The foregoing summary generally accounts for what science teaches us about the differing condition and habits of bison on a seasonal basis. The field of study is called *bioenergetics;* the dynamic processes that operate in the animal body in response to growth, development, and the biological imperatives of reproduction and survival. It is one of the most fascinating areas of literature that I ever delved into, as it helps explain so much of the behaviour we see today in so many species (yes, again including our own). But is it relevant to the real world of everyday hunters and gatherers, those people slogging it out a few thousand years ago just trying to kill some game and provide the next meal? They could not have known of these complex biological processes, but did they appreciate their effects?

Native hunters were keenly aware of these differing conditions and exploited them to ensure procurement of the fattest possible animals at any given kill. European explorers to the Plains soon learned the same biological truths that Native people already knew. Often they learned them from the Aboriginal guides and scouts employed to take them across the Plains. Sometimes they learned these facts on their own, from trial and error, like the famous artist George Catlin in 1832 when he shot his first bison – the biggest, oldest bull he could find. Assuming that bigger was better, he aimed for a massive bull and suffered ridicule and laughter from the rest of his party "for having aimed at an old bull, whose flesh was not suitable for food." Just how much of the intricacies of bison bioenergetics did buffalo hunters really know?

Because no Aboriginal groups of the Great Plains ever developed a system of writing, there always will be some uncertainty regarding what they did and why they did it. True, there are still the memories and voices of the elders. Fortunately, there has been a great upsurge in attempts to document and record the knowledge of the elders before they pass on. But much of this information remains on dusty cassette tapes sequestered in archival storage or in the hands of various Aboriginal cultural centres and museums. Little has been published, and the little that has deals specifically with the finer nuances of buffalo hunting.

Fortunately, there is another source we can turn to: the wealth of literature left behind by the many European explorers, map-makers,

fur traders, missionaries, and adventurers who traversed the Great Plains in the time when bison hunting was still being practised by Native groups. Not only did these people directly observe Native people hunting buffalo, virtually all of them came to depend for their own survival on procuring the great beasts of the prairies.

To be sure, many of these observers were heavily biased against the ways of Aboriginal people; they constantly judged and evaluated these startlingly different cultures by the standards of European civilization. Not unexpectedly, Native culture tended to fare poorly in such comparisons. T.J. Farnham, in 1839, felt compelled to ride around a village of Kansa people asking them if they were humans or beasts. Henry Brackenridge, in 1811, after observing what he assessed to be the filthy, squalid living conditions of the Natives of the Plains said, "The lovers of Indian manners, and mode of living, should contemplate them at a distance ... the world would loose but little, if these people should disappear before civilized communities." Henry Youle Hind's account from western Canada in the 1850s referred to the Native inhabitants as "savage, untutored, and heathen."

In contrast, David Thompson, one of the world's greatest explorers and map-makers, spent three decades with Native people of the

Perhaps reflecting the artist's own encounter with a huge bull, George Catlin painted this scene of an Aboriginal hunter bringing down a great bull, shown out of proportion to the horse and rider. (Courtesy Bruce Peel Special Collections Library, University of Alberta)

West and found much to celebrate in Native culture. He found them to be "brave, steady and deliberate," and praised their sharing of food. Stinginess, Thompson said, "is more detested by them, than by us, from their precarious manner of life, requiring assistance from each other." The sick and aged, he observed, are always well supplied. In contrast to Brackenridge's complaint of Indians as foul smelling, the explorer Edwin James, in 1819–20, reported that Natives were exceedingly pleasant to be around but that the "Indians find the odour of a white man extremely offensive." Further, James reports that bison, too, seemed to find the smell of the white man especially odious and that Natives complained how the smell of Europeans never failed to drive bison from the region. He offered an insightful second reason for the bison's aversion to Europeans: "We are aware that another cause may be found for this than the frightful scent of the white man, which is, the impolitic exterminating war which he wages against all unsubdued animals within his reach."

Travelling among the Métis buffalo hunters of the Red River region of Manitoba in the late eighteenth century, Alexander Ross fully intended to disparage the "barbarians" with the following observation, but he may have, in light of modern values, paid them a backhanded compliment:

These people are all politicians, but of a peculiar creed, favouring a barbarous state of society and self-will; for they cordially detest all the laws and restraints of civilized life, believing all men were born to be free. In their own estimation they are all great men, and wonderfully wise; and so long as they wander about on these wild and lawless expeditions, they will never become a thoroughly civilized people, nor orderly subjects in a civilized community. Feeling their own strength, from being constantly armed, and free from control, they despise all others; but above all, they are marvellously tenacious of their own original habits. They cherish freedom as they cherish life. The writer in vain rebuked them for this state of things, and endeavoured to turn the current of their thoughts into a civilized channel. They are all republicans in principle, and a licentious freedom is their besetting sin.

An alternative view of the value of civilization to the North American Indian is offered by the missionary P.J. De Smet, who traversed the western states and provinces in 1845–46:

Many years have been passed in debates and useless contention, without one single practical effort to secure his real or pretended rights. The poor Indians of Oregon, who alone have a right to the country, are not consulted. Their future destiny will be, undoubtedly, like that of so many other unfortunate tribes, who, after having lived peaceably by hunting and fishing, during several generations, will finally disappear, victims of vice and malady, under the rapacious influence of modern civilization.

As you would expect, there are as many opinions as there were Europeans to provide them. Many of these people were simply trying to sell copies of their books and journals to audiences back home thirsty for vicarious adventure, and so they indulged in bombastic descriptions of buffalo hunts.[†] But in one respect the records of the Europeans left little room for prejudices; when it came to buffalo hunting, virtually all of the Europeans were newcomers to the Plains, rookies in the truest sense. Whatever they thought of Aboriginal people in other respects, they could not but help marvel at the astounding skill and ingenuity of the Plains hunters at bringing down bison. In the 1830s Josiah Gregg proclaimed that Natives were "remarkably expert" with the bow and arrow, "with an accuracy nearly equal to the rifle."

As quickly as they could, Europeans tried to emulate Native tactics and skills at bison hunting, for it now spelled the difference between death and survival for themselves.

Here are the comments from early European visitors arranged by the months of the year to match the bioenergetic processes:

JANUARY
Wounding a bull, which I left for the present ... I pursued after another uncommonly fine fat cow. – Capt. John Palliser, 1847–48

FEBRUARY
Killed three buffalo; they are getting very lean. – Alexander Henry, 1801

[The buffalo are] too poor to be worth hunting. – Lewis and Clark, 1804–06

MARCH
[Natives] had killed two poor Bulls, of which we were glad to get a part. – David Thompson, 1784–1812

[Killed] a fine fat cow. – Josiah Gregg, 1837–38

[†] The Earl of Southesk described the eyes of a bison he had just shot as "emerald furnaces ... that glared with this remarkable expression of intense, everlasting hatred." Edward Harris likewise described a wounded buffalo: "His appearance was now one to inspire terror."

APRIL

[The buffalo are] so weak that if they lie down they cannot rise. – Alexander Henry, 1810

[We intended] if possible, to pick out a barren cow, as they afford the choicest meat at this time of year. – Capt. John Palliser, 1847–48

MAY

Killed a tolerably fat young bull. – Alexander Henry, 1801

I got alongside of the cows; but they were so thin and miserable, being most of them in calf ... At last I spied a barren cow that seemed to promise good meat ... She was in wonderful condition. – Capt. John Palliser, 1847–48

JUNE

In June the bulls are fat and in fine condition while the cows from the ten-dance of their young through the winter are still poor. – Lewis H. Morgan, 1859–62

[Shot a] well-larded body of a noble bull. – James Farnham, 1839

At this time of the year, in the early part of June, the cows are not fit to kill; for they have their young calves, and are very poor. – Charles Larpenteur, 1833–72

JULY

We killed a bull, the flesh of which is more palatable at this season than the cow; bulls are beginning to get in good order ... cows are wretchedly lean and will continue so until the latter end of the month. – Alexander Henry, 1801–09

In the month of July when the Bison Bulls are getting fat. – David Thompson, 1784–1812

AUGUST

Saw ... six bulls ... They are poor at this season, and the meat very rank, but yet are fresh meat; Saw Buffaloes ... on approaching them found only bulls; so returned empty-handed to the boat. – John Audubon, n.d.

A bison ... was killed; but the flesh was found in too ill a condition to be eaten, as is the case with all the bulls at this season. – Edwin James, 1820

The Cows were fat and excellent meat. The younger Bulls kept near the cows,

and were in tolerable order, but the old Bulls fed separate, poor and ferocious.
– David Thompson, 1784–1812

SEPTEMBER

I killed a Bull Buffalo, nothing but skin and bone; took out his tongue, and left his remains to the Wolves ... – Anthony Henday, 1754

I found them only a band of six bulls, which are not good for much at this season. I shot one, but the meat was not worth embarking; Each of us soon killed a good fat cow. – Alexander Henry, 1808

I returned at sunset, having shot a fat cow, the choice pieces of which I brought in. I also killed four bulls, only the tongues of which I took. – Alexander Henry, 1800

OCTOBER

Two old out-straggling bulls [seen] ... We allowed them to go unmolested, as ... we were in hopes that, by waiting a little, we might come across some cows, which would prove a much greater prize to us. – Capt. John Palliser, 1847–48

NOVEMBER

Saw a few Bull Buffalo ... but did not kill any of them. – Peter Fidler 1792–94

DECEMBER

Men running buffalo & killed upwards of 20 fatt Cows. – Peter Fidler, 1792–93

My people killed three bulls ... which served for our dogs. – Alexander Henry, 1800

Bull flesh is not desirable at this season of the year, when the female can be procured. – Paul Kane, 1845

Killed four Bulls, no Cows in sight. We have now plenty to eat, but very tough meat, so much so, we get fairly tired eating before we can get a belly full. – David Thompson, 1784–1812

Month by month there is remarkable correspondence between the preference for, and avoidance of, specific bison and of the known processes of bioenergetics that dictate the different conditions of bison throughout the year. One insurmountable fact tells us that Aboriginal bison hunters knew and manipulated these facets of buffalo biology – for twelve thousand years Native people survived and, even, flourished living off the buffalo of the Great Plains.

The Seasonal Round

Anthropologists use the term *seasonal round* to describe the cyclic and repetitive patterns of movement over a landscape according to the different seasons. It can be used for people or for animals, such as bison. As it happens, the seasonal round for the Aboriginal groups that lived for thousands of years on the Plains and for the herds of bison on which they subsisted share some striking similarities. Since the people depended so heavily on bison, it is not surprising that the seasonal movements of the former roughly paralleled the latter. One of the most common questions I have been asked over the years is, what season of the year did people plan and orchestrate the great communal buffalo hunts? I think a lot of people expect the answer to be that it was used whenever people were lucky enough to find a herd of bison just in the right place behind the cliff. The implication is that the human hunters were not in control of this situation but, rather, were passive observers waiting for nature to smile on them with a fortunate alignment of all the necessary ingredients of a jump. Nothing could be further from the truth. Native groups *orchestrated* every aspect of a communal bison kill, including choosing the seasons in which they were held. To answer the question of what time of year the great jumps were conducted requires consideration of bison behaviour and movement over the course of the year.

Everyone knows bison are synonymous with the Great Plains. And those who aren't familiar with the true character of the Plains think of them as one massive expanse of flatland stretching from the middle of the continent to the Rocky Mountains. But the Plains are in fact much more complex and convoluted. They include great sets of hills, like the Sweet Grass, Cypress, and Black Hills. They include the valleys of deeply incised rivers, creeks, and coulees – broad valleys carved by the water from melting glaciers, many of them dry today. They include patches of evergreen and deciduous forests, which have taken root in local sheltered areas protected from the winds and blessed with a little extra water. And they include an abundance of shrubs and bush growing in the lee of slopes, at the site of groundwater seeps, and in the valleys. The Plains habitat on a gross scale seems monotonous, but on a micro scale it is packed full of diversity. Bison are indeed a creature of the Plains, in all its varied components.

Summer: Summer is perhaps the stereotypical season of the buffalo. As shown in books and movies, teeming herds of them covered the prairie as far as the eye could see. While you couldn't count on this sight every day from every location, it is quite true that summer was the season of the great aggregation of herds on the Plains. Summer is the season when calves are dependent on their mothers and when safety from predators rests in large numbers. Likewise, nursing cows, who are weak and tied to their calves, need the protection of a large herd. Summer is the season when bulls want the company of the cows, to begin courting those they hope to include in their harem. Most importantly, summer is the season when grass is abundant and relatively nutritious, capable of supporting large herds in relatively small spaces. Many of the groups of bison dispersed for much of the year came together in the summer, because the grass growth permitted it, and because preparation for courtship and mating required it. What the movies didn't show was that summer was the only season in which massive herds blackened the Plains.

Huge herds, numbering many thousands of animals, formed on the prairies for summer grazing and for the rut. The aggregation of such large numbers might suggest summer as the ideal time for mass communal hunts by Aboriginal people. For a number of reasons, however, such was not the case. A good percentage of the cows, probably more than half, are nursing calves and are thus badly depleted in fat stores and thus unsuitable as food. Furthermore, nursing cows will not run hard for any length of time because their young calves can't keep up with them. A good, strong run is required for a jump to work. Cows without calves are indeed fine food in summer, and would run without the hindrance of a calf, but they are mixed in with other cows, calves, and bulls and (unless you have horses) would be difficult to single out for selective killing. Bulls are good eating in early and mid-summer, but as we know, their meat becomes unacceptable during the rut and, more significantly, their behaviour becomes unpredictable. Bulls become obsessed with mating, not survival, and will stand and fight rather than run. A summer attempt at running a mixed bison herd towards a cliff would likely be a mess. Nursing cows would only run short distances and stop because their calves were not running with them; non-nursing cows would run like the wind, and adult bulls could stand and defy you, or scatter.

Summer is a unique time in the seasonal round of the bison, when herds of cows and bulls amass in great concentrations. For the remaining three seasons of the year these huge herds disperse, and two basic social groups develop. First, there are the cow–calf groups, which consist of cows (both pregnant and not), calves, and one- and two-year-olds of both sexes. By about the age of three, males begin to drift off, preferring the company of other bulls. Because cows are the more social of the two sexes, they choose to stay in larger groups, typically numbering between one and two hundred. Then there are the bull groups. Bison bulls are relatively solitary animals, increasingly so with age. Following the rut, bulls will wander off, often in groups of one, two, five, or ten. They will stay like this for the remainder of the year, occasionally joined by a few juvenile males and sometimes meeting up with other bull groups. This basic division of the sexes persists until the following summer when the herds once again seek each other's company.

Fall and winter: The huge herds of summer didn't simply disperse and stay out on the great, expansive Plains for the entire year. Bison move a considerable distance over an average year. Some anthropologists have said that, in the past, bison were truly migratory, with great numbers heading south in winter and back north in summer. Others have claimed that migrations were more local in nature and not necessarily directed north–south. We do know this: great numbers of bison overwintered on the northern Plains – just not on the flat and exposed windswept prairies. We know this from Native elders, from numerous historical accounts made by early explorers, and from the many bison kill sites used in the winter season.

Following the rut, the great herds dispersed into smaller bull and cow–calf groups. As long as the forage on the Plains remained fine, and the weather fair, bison stayed out on the open Plains for another month or two. As the air turned crisp and ice began to form on the edges of ponds and streams, their instinct told them that it was time to head for sheltered areas. Seeking shelter during winter on the Plains is a common theme to almost every form of life living there, whether it amounts to burrowing underground, hiding amongst groves of trees, or vacating the Plains entirely.

Bison are incredibly hardy animals and extremely well adapted to cold. They have extraordinarily thick coats of hair for insulation and hides that can be several centimetres thick at certain times of the year. Even so, winter is a brutal time in open northern country. It's not just the temperature, which often dips below -30° C (-22° F) and occasionally much lower; it's the wind. A moderately cool day becomes bitterly cold when whipped by a strong wind. For anything alive that is in the open and exposed, a cold, windy day is utterly unbearable. The only relief is to get out of it.

This is just what bison, and the hunters who depended on them, did. John Palliser, near Morley in 1847–48, made the observation, "the buffalo in winter approach the edge of the woods, and so also do the Indians, seeking fuel and thickwood animals, in case of the buffalo failing them during the winter." As winter set in, both the cow–calf groups and the small bull clusters struck out for places they knew would offer protective shelter. These areas weren't necessarily any warmer or less snow-covered, but they all had one thing in common – they provided refuge from the wind. Typical winter sheltering spots for bison included deep valleys of rivers, creeks, and coulees, thick groves of trees and brush, and hilly or broken country where there are options to move out of the wind. Since these are all local features on the landscape, not huge single areas, it meant that herds had to

As winter approaches, bison herds begin to vacate the open plains and head for sheltered valleys where tree cover offers protection. (Courtesy Mary Meagher, U.S. National Parks Service)

Although winter could be a brutal time on the Plains, bison are exceptionally hardy animals and smart enough to use vegetation cover to ease the fury of winter storms. (Courtesy Johane Janelle)

break up into small groups. The need to scatter was also dictated by the poor quality and reduced quantity of forage at this time of year, which could not sustain large groups of animals. These shelter factors often combine; where you are out of the wind you also tend to find trees and shrubs, for they too require protection from the wind to grow, as well as the greater moisture provided by valleys and the lee sides of hills. In the dead of winter, the open, flat prairies were often barren of large animal life, except for the occasional movement to a new sheltered area or during warm spells when animals emerged to forage.

Spring: Sheltering from winter persisted through the toughest months, December through February. By March the grip of winter loosened and the Plains once again became a tolerant friend. Herds moved out of sheltered valleys and hilly country but stayed close enough to move back in case of all-too-common late winter storms. Sudden snowstorms frequently descended in April and May, but they lacked the bitter cold of winter and could usually be endured. Cows preferred to drop their calves in or near sheltered areas, and so they might linger longer into the spring in areas that afforded protection. But the bulls were on the move, heading for the new grass of the open Plains, and the cows were not far behind. Early summer again finds the herds beginning to coalesce, enjoying the greening-up of the prairie and the pleasure and safety of each other's company.

The Season of Buffalo Jumping

The Savages observe the Time, the Seasons, and the Moons of the Year very punctually, for the better ordering of their Hunting. – Father Lewis Hennepin, 1680s

Head-Smashed-In Buffalo Jump was ideally suited to exploit the patterns of bison physiology and the seasonal round. It is situated in hilly, broken country – the Porcupine Hills. It is only a few kilometres from the major watercourse of the Oldman River and several local streams. Yet it is on the very edge of the expansive Plains. Looking east from the cliff there is nothing but Saskatchewan in your way (which is kind of like having North Dakota in your way). Trees and brush grow in the river and creek valleys and on sheltered sides of the hills. The grass cover of the massive basin area behind the jump is dominated by blue grama and rough fescue; both grasses provide excellent graze for fall and winter, as they are especially high in protein and they stay standing longer into the season (grasses that fall over rot more quickly and lose their nutrients).

Thus, Head-Smashed-In has abundant local water sources, broken, hilly country, intermittent tree cover for shelter, high-quality forage for grazing, and lies next to an immense expanse of prairie. Summer herds would be expected on the Plains east of the jump; fall, winter, and spring herds would find ideal topography and environment in the Porcupine Hills to the west. Quite simply, the jump sits at the confluence of several distinct landscapes and, as such, has the advantages of all of them. If you ask an ecologist what the best place for a species to reside would be, the usual answer is at the junction of several different environments to maximize opportunities for success and survival.

Bison could be expected to frequent the area around Head-Smashed-In in almost any season of the year. But the mere presence of bison in the proper place is insufficient reason to believe that jumps could take place at any time. The overview I have given of seasonal changes in body composition, and the formation and dissolution of social groups, discourages the idea that bison could be rounded up any time and brought to the brink of the cliff. By season, these are some of the issues that would have been considered by Aboriginal hunters:

Spring: Many cows would be calving and nursing and would be difficult to drive; they are also a poor food source. Cows without

The prime buffalo country of the Porcupine Hills greens up dramatically in the spring to provide nutritious grass for the herds. (Courtesy Royal Alberta Museum)

calves would be fine food but could not be driven easily when mixed with other cows. Bulls still live in groups too small for a mass drive. Bison are enjoying the rich green grass of the Plains.

Summer: The situation remains the same for cows with and without calves. Bulls are amassing in larger groups, but are more obstinate than cows and so will seldom run in a large, tight pack as is required for a communal kill. Attempting to round up and move bison during the late summer rut would be difficult because of behavioural patterns characteristic of that time. Most bison are living on the open Plains.

Fall: Cows with calves have largely recovered their body stores, and those without are in prime condition. Cows are separating from the bulls but remain in relatively large groups of a hundred or more. Bulls have depleted their body fat during the rut, are poor food, and are again drifting into smaller groups. Bison roam the Plains but begin to head for sheltered areas.

Winter: Early in winter cows remain in excellent condition and are still in sizable groups. By late winter they are becoming depleted of fat stores. Bulls in early winter are recovering from the rut, but later in winter they are suffering, like the cows, from the effects of poor forage. Regardless of condition, bulls are in small groups unsuitable for deliberate driving. All bison reside primarily in sheltered regions.

From this summary, it is apparent that there was no good season for attempting a communal drive of bull bison. Their social groupings aren't really suitable for rounding up and moving large numbers, and their stubborn disposition would make this a difficult task. Furthermore, bull meat was regarded as tough, and as we have seen they are generally leaner than cows most of the year. Bulls were, of course, hunted occasionally for a variety of reasons including food, but most of this was solitary, not communal, hunting. When horses made winter hunting easier, the selection of bulls probably paralleled the observations of Josiah Gregg in 1837–38: "These [bulls] are generally selected for consumption in the winter and early spring, when the cows, unless barren, are apt to be poor; but during most of the year, the latter are the fattest and tenderest meat."

Communal driving of bison was pretty much restricted to cow–calf groups. It is these bison that for much of the year are found in groups of about the right size. Their protective instinct is to run rather than defy, they are the fattest of the two sexes most of the year, and the meat from cows was regarded as more delicate and tastier.

Two seasons stand out as most suitable to drive cow–calf groups: fall and winter. Their seasonal wandering would likely put them in and around the Porcupine Hills in these seasons. In both seasons, cow hides are thick and full and make the best robes and blankets for winter warmth. Holes burrowed by summer insects have healed. Fat levels for cows and juveniles are at their prime in both seasons (with the exception of late winter). Calves are now old enough to run with the mothers and so won't disrupt the drive attempts. But of the two seasons, fall stands out as the best of all. Not only are cows in the right place, of the right size groups, and at peak body condition in the fall, the weather is also most conducive. Trying to plan and operate a winter bison kill presents serious challenges to the hunters. As these events take days to prepare, the people have to contend with snow and cold and wind. If conditions turn bad it can be extremely demanding trying to round up, drive, kill, butcher, and process the remains of a major kill event.[†] Autumn still has plenty of pleasant days, and the cool nights help chill down the carcasses and slow down spoilage. Another obvious advantage of fall kills is that they allow you to put

[†] Butchering bison in mid-January 1841, Robert Rundle witnessed the physical agony of the process: "The cold was so severe at this time that the blood froze about the instrument employed in cutting up the animal. The person using it was obliged to soak it 2 or 3 times in the warm blood lodged in the carcass."

The buffalo jump in the fall offered pleasant camping, cool weather, herds in peak condition, and ideal circumstances for a communal kill. (Courtesy Royal Alberta Museum)

away surplus meat and fat for the coming winter, when there will be days and weeks when hunts simply can't be conducted.

Since we know that fat animals were the key target of Aboriginal Plains hunters, there is another interesting slant to the importance of the fall season. While to us fat is just fat, in reality it isn't. Fat is composed of many things other than true chemical fat, such as water, ash, and other non-fat chemicals (especially the fat-soluble vitamins that are lacking in a diet with limited vegetables). We know that for large animals of the northern latitudes the relative amount of true chemical fat contained in fat tissue varies with the season. You guessed it: fat tissue has the greatest amount of true fat content in the fall of the year. The difference can be dramatic. For high Arctic reindeer, fat tissue can comprise as much as 90 per cent chemical fat in the fall and as little as 45 per cent in late winter. Thus, settling yourself down to a fine feast of fat from a late winter kill, only half of what you are eating might actually be fat. We don't know comparable figures for bison of the northern Plains, but we can be certain that they follow this pattern to some degree.

Autumn emerges as the finest season for hunting bison on the northern Plains, including in the vicinity of Head-Smashed-In. This preference is generally confirmed in the writings of early European visitors. Daniel Harmon, early in the nineteenth century, wrote that game animals "are therefore killed, principally when they are the fattest, which most of them are in the fall, and some of them in the winter." In the 1830s George Catlin said, "The Indians generally kill and dry meat enough in the fall, when it is fat and juicy, to last them through the winter." And John Bradbury, on the Plains in 1811, stated, "I am informed by the hunters, that in autumn the quantity of tallow or fat in the buffalo is very great." S.A. Barrett recognized the link between the great fall hunts and the need to store provisions for the coming winter: "the Indians had certain spots where the fixed winter camps were established in the fall of the year. At this season the buffalo were fat and prime and the drives to secure a winter's food supply were usually held immediately after this fixed camp was established."

But it would be a mistake to think that fall was the only season of this activity. Indeed, if we have learned anything about the ancient inhabitants of the Plains, it is that they were eminently and infinitely adaptable. Over the vast time they resided on the Plains, they obviously killed bison of all sexes and ages in all seasons. No doubt at times they simply had to, accepting that meat or hides might not be at their prime, or that social gatherings were not ideal, or that the weather was foreboding. Such is the nature of staying alive in a challenging world. At other times, they needed to kill animals for other reasons. The wonderful portable dwelling that Natives used for thousands of years, the tipi, was made of bison hides, and the spring and summer bison hides, much thinner than those of fall and winter, were preferred for making tipi covers. Over time many spring kills occurred, including some at Head-Smashed-In, no doubt dictated as much by the need to obtain suitable hides for tipi covers as for food.

Mass communal kills were not the only, or even the main, method of killing bison. Ancient hunters of the Plains killed bison singly, with a lone hunter skulking across the Plains, perhaps with a wolf skin draped over him. Groups of a few hunters from the same camp would head out for a day or two to scour the local area, hoping to return with the meat of a couple of animals. Sometimes five or ten animals would be killed, and the camp would move to the location of the slaughter rather than haul all the spoils to the camp. And every now and then the great communal kills were planned. How often these occurred we don't really know. The archaeological record isn't that fine in detail. They may have occurred possibly once a year, some years maybe twice. At other times several years may have passed between mass kills if all the requisite parts didn't come together. When they did happen, they would have been something to behold.

CHAPTER 4

The Killing Field

The Great Father of Life, who made us, and gave us these lands to live upon, made also the buffalo and other game, to afford us the means of life: his meat is our food; with his skin we clothe ourselves and build our houses; he is to us our only means of life – food, fuel, and raiment. – Anonymous Chief to H.R. Schoolcraft, 1851

Head-Smashed-In Buffalo Jump is just one of countless places on the northern Plains where prehistoric Native Americans drove bison to their deaths. After all, the buffalo was the centre of existence for Plains people from the very first moment they arrived on the scene until the bison were nearly exterminated in the late 1800s. It stands to reason that the times and places that ancient people found to kill the largest land mammal in North America would be many and varied. But among the thousands of known buffalo kill sites, and countless others yet undiscovered, there is something special about Head-Smashed-In. Something made this particular place one of the most dependable, and hence most heavily and repeatedly used, of all the kill sites that are known. Many were used just once, some a few times, some were built for killing but never fulfilled their promise. Just a handful were used over and over for hundreds, even thousands, of years. Of these, Head-Smashed-In is arguably the greatest kill site of them all. Why?

It is not the height of the cliff that made it so lethal. Some jumps are higher; many others are much lower. It was not, presumably, that people of the region possessed greater skill or knowledge of coercing animals to plunge from a cliff, as it seems reasonable to assume that these abilities would be widespread among many Plains Aboriginal groups. Were there simply more bison in this area, more often? Probably at times there were; the Porcupine Hills, rich in rough fescue and

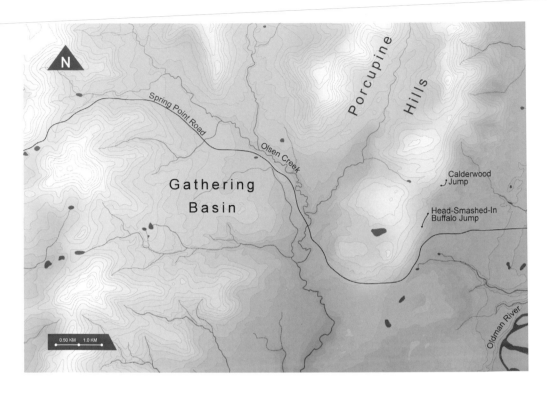

The Olsen Creek valley west of Head-Smashed-In forms the main basin behind the jump, with smaller tributary basins in valleys to the north and south of the creek. (Courtesy Royal Alberta Museum)

blue grama grass, a great attraction. But at other times there would be none anywhere in the region, possibly for extended periods.

Casual visitors who stare up at the imposing bedrock cliff and imagine hundreds of bison plunging to their deaths – the final stanza of an elaborate symphony that played out long before that final drop – see the cliff where the killing took place. It is the focus of all the drama and excitement when conjuring up a buffalo jump. It is the brink of death. It is what most visitors to the site see, and it is all they see. The magic that made Head-Smashed-In perhaps the most long-lived and successful buffalo jump of all time is not found at the cliff, but lies hidden in the grass-covered rolling hills situated behind and to the west of the buffalo jump.

Yet the cliff is just the very end of a story as immense in scope as the vastness of the country in which the story unfolded. Picture yourself at the very end of a horse race, eyes fixed straight ahead at the finish line. Horses thunder past you. You see who wins and who loses. But you don't see any of what got them there. You don't see the blast out of the gate, the jockeying for position, the brilliant moves and the miscues, the strategies leading to success and to failure. Today, silence envelops the sandstone cliff at Head-Smashed-In, broken only by the rushing of the wind, the cries of hawks, and the piercing chirp of yellow-bellied marmots. Gazing at the sheer face of rock, steeped in silence, you are witness to the finish line. But you have missed the race. The story has already unfolded. It must have, otherwise there would be no finish; no ten-metre-deep layer of smashed bison bones lying ghost-like beneath the cliff, no UNESCO World Heritage designation. What only a few lucky visitors to Head-Smashed-In ever see is the incredibly faint evidence of an elaborate network of knowledge, work, and skill that went into making all this come to pass. This evidence lies tucked away, almost imperceptibly, in the rolling shortgrass prairie to the back of the cliff.

Finding Bison

The Indians who reside in the large plains, make no subdivisions of their territory; for the wealth of their country consists of buffaloes and wolves, which exist in plenty, everywhere among them. – Daniel Harmon, 1800–19

The story of Head-Smashed-In begins many kilometres away from the jump, and many thousands of years ago, in a magnificent bowl-shaped depression that lies behind the cliff. It is a place we have come to call the gathering basin. You won't hear that term used for most buffalo jumps, for most don't have one. They have what you might call a collecting area, from which animals were rounded up and moved towards the kill. Typically these areas are flat or gently rolling prairie that happen to lead to a steep drop or sometimes an upland plateau or mesa with sheer edges. But the collecting area at Head-Smashed-In is a natural depression, a huge basin totalling some forty square kilometres in size. There is one main basin located directly behind the jump-off. It extends west toward the mountains some ten kilometres before the land finally rises and you climb out of the bowl. Then there are a number of tributary basins feeding into the main basin. These are mostly to the north side and are formed by a series of ridges and valleys, like fingers of a hand, that meet up with the main basin. These finger basins added yet more territory from which bison could be harvested to bring to the jump, and more complex topography that the hunters could use to their advantage. A small stream, Olsen

Creek, drains the main basin, providing water for hunters and bison alike and, importantly, brush.

There are a few great people in the research and study of buffalo jumps. The Dean of them all is George Frison, now professor emeritus at the University of Wyoming. George not only wrote at length about excavations he conducted at numerous buffalo jumps in the American West, he was also one of the first (and still one of the only) people to give thought to how these elaborate traps worked. Much of his insight into this world came not from academia but from a personal life of hunting large game animals and from hanging around bison herds – hobbies that fostered a deep understanding of animal behaviour, the single most important ingredient to a successful buffalo jump.

I once brought George to Head-Smashed-In. Of course we walked around the cliff and the kill site below where the great slaughters took place. But then we walked up above the cliff, heading west, following the land uphill for the first few hundred metres until we reached the crest where you can see down into the enormous expanse of the basin, where the swell of the land ripples out before you like a churning ocean. I was young, green, and standing next to my idol. Desperate for pearls of wisdom, you can imagine that I haven't forgotten his words. Toothpick in mouth, pocket-protector stuffed full of pens in his snap-buttoned western shirt, with crow's feet–wrinkled eyes that had seen more buffalo jumps than any person on earth, George surveyed the scene unfolded in front of him. Now *that,* he said, is a gathering basin. George was never long on words. In truth, what George probably loved most about Head-Smashed-In was the ten-metre-deep bonebed chock full of artifacts and bones, for this is where archaeologists traditionally get their hands dirty and grub out the evidence they then use to weave their intricate stories of the past. But he had seen enough to know that the rich bonebed only existed because of the pure beauty of the land stretched out before him, a land almost fashioned by the Creator to bring bison to their deaths.

What George Frison and I saw that day was the backbone of what is probably the most successful buffalo jump on the continent. The gathering basin is the substance and structure that held it all together and made everything work. To be sure, there is much more that must fall into place for the drama to unfold, but without the magnificent landscape that lies behind the jump the story would be much more pedestrian in nature. It perhaps would be just a typical kill site where animals met their deaths but a few times. However, the sheer size of the basin at Head-Smashed-In would mean that there was always a good chance of finding bison in this country. The great variety of topography would give the hunters a formidable edge in making sure that at least some of the animals could be led to the brink of the cliff.

Drive Lanes

From this entrance [of the pound] small sticks are laid on each side like a fence, in form of an angle extending from the pound; beyond these to about 1¹/₂ mile distant. Buffalo dung, or old roots are laid in heaps, in the same direction as the fence. – Mathew Cocking, 1772, cited in *Ewers, 1968*

I have often been asked by young students doing an assignment what it's like to be an archaeologist, and especially, what were some of the most important discoveries I have made. The expected answer, I suppose, is to recount the discovery of some spectacular artifact or truly significant site that knocked my socks off, changed our thinking about the past, and perhaps made headlines. I suspect I disappointed the interviewers. I haven't found the Holy Grail, or Atlantis, though I'm not averse to the prospect. Carefully I try to explain what makes a eureka moment for me, and the one I often cite happened one clear, warm summer day at Head-Smashed-In.

When you look southwest into the basin, cattle grazing across the main channel leading toward the kill provide an idea of how bison might have looked when approaching the jump. (Courtesy Royal Alberta Museum)

It was early in my career at Head-Smashed-In, about 1984. I had finished up with some of the required work I had to do in the areas where we were going to build the new interpretive centre (more about this later). You can appreciate that a lot of archaeological testing had to be done in the areas that were going to be disturbed by construction of the building, the parking lot, roads, and so on. How would it look if a UNESCO World Heritage site was partially disturbed by construction of the very facility that was going to interpret it? So with some of this work out of the way, I thought I would take a break and head off for a peaceful walk into the back country behind the jump. This is where I had one of my epiphany moments, the one I relate to inquisitive students researching their first term paper.

I knew there existed an extensive system of drive lanes at Head-Smashed-In, that fabulously complex network of small piles of stone that stretch for many kilometres into the wide basin behind the jump. I had read about them and even briefly seen them from one place in the basin where you can drive a car close. But I had never explored them and, more importantly, never thought about them. On that day, I headed off into the country where the real story of Head-Smashed-In took place, where the race to the finish line was held.

It was a beautiful summer day. The sky was absolutely cloudless, a cobalt blue across the horizon. The wind was strong, as almost always, but not overpowering. You don't sweat on windy days, no matter the temperature, but you do get dirt packed into every corner of your body. And grasshoppers. As you walk into the wind you flush the grasshoppers from the grass in front of you and they are blown back, slamming into your body. It freaks you out at first, but you get used to it. After years of experience, you are only bothered by the ones that drop down your shirt or hit you in the face – especially an open mouth or eye. I've had many of both, and have sat in a doctor's office having body parts of grasshopper picked from a bloodshot eyeball. Then there was the time that a grasshopper, defying all laws of physics, managed to drop into the tiny opening in my can of beer while my crew and I headed for the local swimming hole, but I'll spare you the gruesome details of what happened next.

On that blue-skied day I walked in a gentle zigzag pattern from the top of the cliff, thinking I would soon intersect the small rock piles, called *cairns*, that surely must lead directly to the jumping off point. But I found nothing. The land behind the jump rises gradually for maybe half a kilometre and then crests, on the spot where George Frison and I had stood. From this point you get a spectacular view: west into the rolling Porcupine Hills with the peaks of the front range of the Rockies poking up from behind them, east towards the cliff and the seemingly endless prairie beyond. South lies a ribbon of green where the Oldman River waters this desiccated land, and to the north you follow the crest of the Porcupines like an enormous backbone of the land itself. I reached this crest having seen nothing of the lines of rock and wondered if I was not properly attuned to seeing them. Perhaps I had walked right by them. After all, the few that I had seen had been notable for their nearly inconspicuous nature. These are not true piles of rocks, as sometimes shown in antiquated museum displays or in old encyclopedias. They are more like small circular platforms of rocks, gathered together but not piled up, and now half buried by the dirt that has drifted over them in the centuries of disuse. As I began the descent down the other side into the basin I searched the ground, thinking I must have missed the drive cairns.

Ranchers who run cattle throughout the basin alternate them into different pastures so as to stagger the demand on any one section of prairie. How high the grass is in any one place is pretty much a result of how recently cattle have been in there grazing – that and the annual rainfall. Because grass directly affects the visibility of the ground surface, cairns will show up best in areas recently grazed. My descent into the basin was taking me into parts of the prairie where cattle were grazing. They hurried around in front of me, giving me plenty of walking space and themselves greater social comfort. The grass was cropped very short. I could see almost every rock that poked even a little bit above the sod. Archaeologists train their eyes to look for something out of the ordinary, a pattern where there shouldn't be one. Nature occasionally makes patterns, sorting rocks, sand, and soil according to processes that are understood and predictable. People do the unpredictable, like gathering large, melon-sized stones and putting them in small circular clusters, one after another. Nature doesn't do this.

Walking down the slope into the persistent wind, grasshoppers smacking into me, I began to see small circular arrangements of rocks. Fist-sized rocks, melon-sized, occasionally a little larger, five to ten of them pushed into a tight group. The clusters were not here and there, one to my right, another to my left. They were in a line stretching out

When the grass is heavily grazed, the small rock clusters of the drive lanes show up as a line of faint hummocks on the land, as seen here just to the left of the person standing. (Courtesy Royal Alberta Museum)

in front of me. With the high sun I could just make out slightly raised tufts of grass in the distance, heading west down into the basin, until I lost them in the endless stretch of prairie. The small rock clusters catch and hold a tiny bit more moisture and offer slight protection from the wind, so grass tends to grow a little thicker around them. I walked up to each one in turn, counting the paces between each. I stood over each cluster and looked down at the seemingly insignificant little gathering of rocks. Then I walked to the next, looked ahead to the others in front of me and back to the ones I had just passed, making a line out of them in my mind or, rather, realizing that someone else had made a line out of them long before my leisurely stroll on that warm afternoon.

At first I was just relieved I had found them, that I wasn't somehow deficient to colleagues who had come before me. But as I continued to walk up to each cairn in turn, a powerful feeling came over me. It was a strange blend of exhilaration and yet a creepy tingling. It was not caused by the sudden mind explosion that occurs when you think that you have discovered something. It was just the opposite. I realized that I didn't have a clue what was going on.

My epiphany didn't come from finally intersecting a series of rock piles; any rookie eventually would have stumbled on to them. It came from realizing that I was walking along a line of stone piles laid out thousands of years ago by groups of people who had a plan in mind as to where each pile would go and why. I had no idea what these people were thinking when they did this. Many years later I thought about an often-cited comment on my profession, that investigating the past isn't a search for answers, it's a search for questions. Never was this more true than walking alone on that sun-drenched day in the basin behind Head-Smashed-In.

As I surveyed the land in front of and behind me, watching the line of rock cairns swerve ever so slightly up on a low hillside, then down just a bit into a minor valley, levelling out on a straight plain, I realized that those who manufactured this arrangement were not simple buffalo hunters trying to coax crazed bison to the edge of a cliff. They were ancient architects of the landscape. It was as if, impossibly, they were able to levitate above this immense country and view it from above, detecting every little nuance of change in the roll and sway of the land, figuring out where each rock pile would have to go in order to control the animals. The people who orchestrated this slaughter had laid out maps on the landscape that had at their core some great plan for directing the movement of wild beasts far more massive and powerful than themselves. The evidence of their engineering, a reflection of an enormous knowledge of bison, was lying

As you look west into the gathering basin, you can see the rock cairns spaced about every five metres. (Courtesy Royal Alberta Museum)

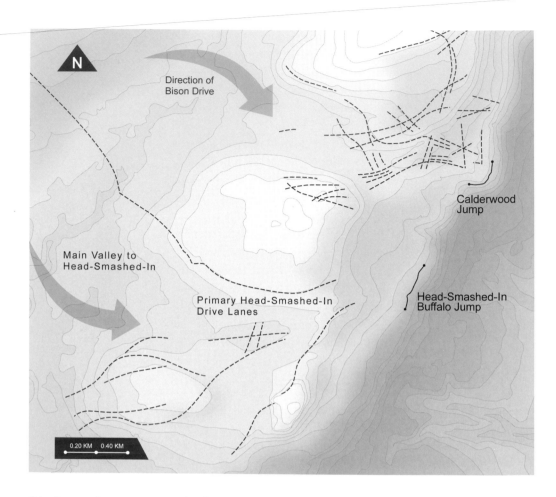

N

Direction of
Bison Drive

Calderwood
Jump

Main Valley to
Head-Smashed-In

Primary Head-Smashed-In
Drive Lanes

Head-Smashed-In
Buffalo Jump

0.20 KM   0.40 KM

Brian Reeves and Maureen Rollans mapped the drive lanes behind Head-Smashed-In and the Calderwood jump. The true magnitude and complexity of the lanes can only be appreciated when seen like this from above. (Courtesy Royal Alberta Museum)

right there at my feet. The humbling thought came to me that this system, for that's truly what it was, is something that was virtually unknown to us.

The reason this day was so memorable for me was precisely because I knew I was looking at evidence for which the archaeological community had no explanation. It was a book written long ago that we couldn't read. I remember smiling broadly as I surveyed the small rounded mounds disappearing into the distance of the Plain. I had walked off in search of answers and instead had found a barrage of questions: Why is this little group of cairns much closer together than others? Why does this line seem to veer uphill, while the one over there angles downhill? Why is there a broad, gentle sweep to the north in this lane? Why do some of the cairns have many more rocks than others? Was all of this built at one time, or over a long period of trial and error? It was truly exhilarating to discover that I didn't have the answers to any of these questions. Why? Ask any scientist and I think you'll get the same answer. It is the thrill of the unknown, a puzzle that has you stumped, a challenge to explain the unexplained. Picture a chemist or physicist in a lab conducting an experiment. Suddenly things don't go as planned. A result appears that was completely unexpected. I'll bet you most of these scientists step back, smile broadly, and whisper in a low voice, "Well, how about that!"[†]

Alone in the basin that day, I knew that I stood among the remains of a huge construction project involving the collection and careful placement of thousands of individual rocks. Each one was selected for certain size and weight and placed in a spot deemed just right by a team of people who must have discussed and debated how the map was to be made. What started off as simple clusters of stone had morphed into a mental blueprint of complex, group-based decision-making on a scale and for a purpose that had mostly eluded consideration by archaeologists, anthropologists, animal ecologists, and pretty much everyone else. I knew that day that there was much to be learned from careful scrutiny of these lines of stone, and I resolved that I would dedicate some of my efforts to trying to tease out the mental maps that ancient people had made and, thankfully, left behind.

Buffalo jumps had been studied by archaeologists for more than fifty years before my first visit to Head-Smashed-In. It was well known that drive lanes of some kind existed to guide the bison toward the impending trap. We knew they were there but knew almost nothing about how or why they worked. Why was precious little known about these ingenious lanes of rocks that made the great kills possible? The answer has much to do with what archaeologists have traditionally considered important evidence of the past.

Points in Time

Our knowledge of virtually every buffalo jump that has been professionally studied comes from excavations at what is known as the bonebed – the thick, tangled, and often deep layers of discarded and broken buffalo bones found at the base of a cliff or steep drop. This is what archaeologists refer to as the rich part of the site, where artifacts are in abundance. In particular, this is where great quantities of the

[†] The great science writer Isaac Asimov once said, "The most exciting phrase to hear in science, the one that heralds new discoveries, is not 'Eureka!' (I found it) but 'That's funny …!'"

points used to tip lethal weapons are typically recovered. Stone points, including those used on arrows, long darts, and spears, are much prized by archaeologists, especially those working on the Great Plains. The reason for this obsession is that, as I mentioned earlier, points are one of the few artifacts that seem to change with time and with different cultural groups. The great majority of artifacts that people made over the past millennia – stone knives, drills, scrapers, hammer stones, bone beads, and awls – often exhibit very little difference over great periods of time. Thus, finding a stone scraper at a site may tell you very little about when the site was occupied and by what people. Points are a more sensitive, or as we say, a more diagnostic artifact.

Finding a certain style of small arrowhead may indicate that a site was occupied about twelve hundred years ago by the probable ancestors of the Blackfoot people. A different shape of arrowhead may suggest it was made by Assiniboine people some five hundred years later. Few other artifacts have this diagnostic ability, so you can imagine archaeologists love finding them, especially in great numbers. Points are made by human beings, not machines, and are thus subject to idiosyncratic characteristics of skill, taste, history, and, of course, the nature of the stone itself. Each point is unique. Therefore if you only find one point, you don't know if you are looking at the normal or typical point produced by a particular culture. What if you find two and each is somewhat different? Is one of them more typical of what most of the people in that group produced, and, if so, how would you know which one? But if you find ten points and six or seven are roughly similar and a couple differ from the majority, then you may have pretty good grounds for saying that the six or seven points are in fact representative of what a certain group produced at a certain time. You then have a style of point, an artifact distinctive of a people who lived and worked together, who shared ideas about how tools should look. Once the style is dated, we know when these people lived. This is how archaeologists build knowledge about the past.

You can see why archaeologists like to recover lots of points. Where better to do this than at a site where the primary activity was killing animals? The fall or drop at most buffalo jumps was probably not in itself fatal for most of the herd. Many would have suffered broken bones, shock, and concussion. For some animals, their wounds would have been debilitating, allowing the hunters to approach safely and dispatch the wounded ones. But many, in a state of panic, would

soon be on their feet and either running or in a mood to fight with their huge heads and dangerous horns. The hunters needed great skill, daring, extreme care, and a lot of weapons to kill off those that came over the drop relatively unscathed. And since points are associated with weapons, lots of them tend to be found at buffalo jumps.[†] Some, like Head-Smashed-In, have yielded literally tens of thousands, so you can appreciate that archaeologists have been attracted to the bonebed portion of jumps, excavating large samples of points which in turn permit a great deal of analysis about when the site was used and who used it. While these excavations have been critical in building up our basic knowledge of the ancient people of the Plains, it has come at a cost.

That cost has been a relative avoidance of other parts of a buffalo jump site. You can pretty well bet that you aren't going to recover many (if any) points spending days following, mapping, and studying the lanes of rocks leading to the jump. In fact, it's quite likely you won't find a single artifact of any kind. People didn't live, work, and leave remains behind in the back country that led to the jumps – to do so would leave the refuse and smell of humans in precisely the area where you don't want the herd to detect them. This detritus could ruin future bison drive attempts.

There is a stereotype that archaeologists are associated with stuff. We dig things up, collect things, analyze things, and cause things to be put in museums. These activities have been a long tradition in our discipline. Not too long ago, to design a research project that didn't involve the recovery of stuff (artifacts), and to seek funding for it, was

Finding a single arrowhead at Head-Smashed-In is exciting but tells us little about the people who used the jump. Finding a number of similar points suggests that a distinct style is represented, possibly indicating a specific group of people. (Courtesy Royal Alberta Museum)

[†] There are suggestions that hunters stationed along the drive lanes may have fired arrows into the stampeding animals, not intending to kill them, but to keep them panicked and running toward the trap. At two buffalo jumps in Idaho, arrowheads were found between the drive-lane cairns, supporting this contention. The practice, however, is not well documented and seems to have been rare.

Sometimes artifacts tell remarkable stories. This front leg bone of a bison has an arrowhead still embedded in the bone; which means that the animal was killed by hunters waiting at the kill site. (Courtesy Royal Alberta Museum)

to risk rejection of your project and funding. Thankfully, this attitude has changed considerably in the past decades. But the history of this tradition helps explain why even as late as the 1980s we still knew very little about how a buffalo jump worked. For decades, the rich bonebeds of buffalo jumps have attracted archaeologists, like metal filings to a magnet, while the pieces of the story that made these bone piles possible lay untouched in the windswept prairie slowly gathering dust. It seemed time to rectify this situation.

My quest to know more about how ancient hunters managed to move bison from their grazing areas to the edge of a deadly cliff cast me into one of the most rewarding and fascinating journeys of my career. It sent me in search of information about bison, their behaviour, biology, and ecology. The more I learned about these amazing animals, the more I realized early hunters had known all this and more long before me. The great respect I now hold for the knowledge and skill that Aboriginal people had in pulling off a buffalo jump didn't come from excavating the bones and tools left at the kill site – these are merely the detritus of people's knowledge. Rather, my respect deepened as I began to comprehend the complete understanding and manipulation of bison that Native people displayed in their laying out of an ingenious trap.

Ancient Knowledge

It may truly be said that they exist on the buffalo, and their knowledge of the habits of this animal is consequently essential to their preservation. – Henry Youle Hind, 1856–57

It is terribly hard for us to even begin to try and imagine what it must have been like to be born into and raised all your life in a society that existed on the Great Plains, say one thousand years ago. We have no experience we can draw upon that would help place us in this world. In the abstract, however, we can consider for a moment a life in a small tribal hunting society. You were born and raised in a small camp made up of perhaps ten related families (roughly eighty people) who travelled and worked together and occasionally met with other related family groups. From the first thing you can remember as a child until now, the world you know revolves around hunting wild animals. The first words you remember are those of your family discussing the hunting events of the day and the plan for tomorrow. As a toddler, a tiny bow and arrow is placed in your hand and you are encouraged to chase after the squirrels that scurry around camp. From the first solid meal you ever taste until the final food brought to your deathbed, the flesh of wild game is the basis of your diet. Imagine times of desperate hardship when your family group has nothing to eat until another animal is killed. Take that one child and repeat the same upbringing about twenty years later, then again in another twenty years, and so on for hundreds of generations.

Although we can't really imagine this world, we can perhaps in the abstract appreciate what thousands of years of continuous reliance on hunting wild animals would produce in the way of accumulated knowledge about the nature and behaviour of the animals upon which these people's lives depended. There are many things that ancient people had to know to survive – where to get stone for tools, how to make fire, how to build shelters – but these pale in comparison to one single absolute: in a land where no plants were ever domesticated, people had to be successful hunters, and to do this they had to have a total understanding of the animals they pursued.

The remarkable thing is not how much Aboriginal hunters understood about the game that they hunted. What else would you expect after thousands of years of having the life of your family and of your people depend on acquiring, remembering, and passing on

The close quarters of Native camp life offered ideal opportunities for young people to learn the traditional ways of the culture. (Courtesy Head-Smashed-In Buffalo Jump)

† Henry Youle Hind reported two hundred and forty bison killed in a pound over several days. Father De Smet is said to have witnessed six hundred brought in. Peter Fidler wrote, "The Pound being quite full laying 5 or 6 deep one upon the other, all thro which in the whole was above 250 Buffalo." But the most astonishing account is Robert Rundle's, in 1841: "Passed near an old buffalo pond, shaped 3 circles, at which my guide 'Friday' was present at the capture of 2450 & left; the Indians still killing them."

this knowledge? The remarkable thing is how long it has taken the rest of us to appreciate the depth of Aboriginal knowledge about game animals. Scientists researching wild animals today are still discovering things about animal behaviour that Native hunters knew and manipulated thousands of years ago. Let me give an example.

The buffalo pound was an Aboriginal method of killing large numbers of bison similar to a jump in nearly every respect except one: the final kill location. Jumps ended at a steep drop, and pounds (an archaic English term for an enclosure) ended in a circular wooden corral. Pounds tended to be located in the lightly wooded areas that surround portions of the Great Plains, where ample wood was available for construction and where the sharply broken country needed for a jump off was absent. The method of rounding up and moving bison along drive lanes was essentially the same for both.

Stop and think for a moment how a wooden corral built one thousand years ago actually served to contain a charging, panic-stricken herd of animals weighing five hundred to nine hundred kilograms each. In days long before posthole augers, pile-drivers, pressure-treated timber posts, how did Native hunters manage to build an enclosure that could contain stampeding herds of bison? And not just a few animals; eyewitness accounts mention hundreds of bison being driven into a corral at a single time.† The answer is simple: by tricking the herds into believing there was no escape. The best they could do was to gather up fallen timber, chop down a few moderate-sized trees, pile and lean logs up against each other, and in the end create a circle of wood that any self-respecting bison could demolish

86

With over thousands of years of observing buffalo, it is little wonder that Native hunters knew everything about that animal that sustained them. Painting by Alfred J. Miller. (Courtesy: Library and Archives Canada/Acc. No. 1946-109-1, Gift of Mrs. J.B. Jardine)

† It is difficult to know just how strong ancient wooden corrals were, but one archaeological site in southern Alberta illustrates how pounds were sometimes strengthened. The Ramillies site, situated in the treeless prairie, used a small natural depression as a pound with the opposite wall as the entrance fortified with piled boulders.

with a single thrust of the head. So how is it that we know (again from wonderfully descriptive historic accounts) that Native people routinely slaughtered countless bison while they milled around inside these rickety pounds, seemingly unable to escape?†

Switch time and place to Elk Island National Park (EINP) in central Alberta. A lovely park more famous for bison than its namesake, EINP has been managing bison for decades. The staff are among the finest authorities on this animal in North America, and the park routinely supplies seed herds of wild bison to reintroduction ventures all over the world. For a number of years I sat on a science advisory committee for EINP and so got to see first hand some of the workings of bison herd management. For the most part, a hands-off approach is taken with respect to the herds, letting nature take its course. An exception is inoculation for disease, and this requires rounding the animals up and containing them. Of course enclosures are built today of massive materials totally unavailable to ancient hunters, but you still have to get up alongside each animal to deliver the shots. For this you need chutes, or squeezes, where the animal can be held almost motionless for a few minutes, constraining them in a very tight, small space. It will come as no big surprise that bison don't much like this. Panicked, they buck and kick and twist their horns into the wooden or wire fence chutes and with their awesome strength can sometimes

† Victims of their own success, buffalo pounds did occasionally collapse under the strain of their bounty. John Audubon reported that "so full does [the pound] become occasionally that the animals touch each other, and as they cannot move, the very weight against the fence of the pen is quite enough to break it through; the smallest aperture is sufficient, for in a few minutes it becomes wide, and all the beasts are seen scampering over the prairies, leaving the poor Indians starving and discomfited."

tear them apart and often injure themselves. Through good old trial and error, EINP herd managers discovered that if you made these spaces solid the bison were far more settled. If you take away the visibility of looking through the slats of the chutes to freedom beyond, the animals did not perceive a means of escape and they were far more manageable. Replacing page wire and rail fences with solid walls of fencing at Elk Island National Park served to create this illusion.

Illusion is the key. Returning to the question of how bison pounds of a thousand years ago managed to restrain an angry herd, a few citations from Euro-Canadians who actually saw these pounds in operation, and those who interviewed traditional Aboriginal people, illuminate the ancient knowledge.

Grinnell reported on the Cheyenne:

In the olden time, before they had horses, the Cheyennes ... also drove them [buffalo] into pens. Such enclosures were usually built under a cutbank or bluff, which formed one or more walls of the pen; the other sides were merely bushes or branches stuck in the ground ... Though the animals might readily break through the walls of bushes, they seldom did so, for they were afraid of them, and merely ran round and round within the enclosure until exhausted.

John Palliser described a buffalo pound as being "on a slope, and the upper part of the fencing was increased in height by skins stretched on poles, for the purpose of frightening the buffalo from jumping out. This is not needed at the lower part of the enclosure, as the animals always endeavour to jump up-hill." From interviews with Blackfoot at the turn of the twentieth century, Grinnell reports that the pound "might be only a fence of brush, but even here the buffalo did not break it down, for they did not push against it, but ran round and round within, looking for a clear space through which they might pass."†

In one of the most detailed descriptions of the workings of a pound, Grinnell again provides compelling testimony of Aboriginal knowledge of the habits of the buffalo:

When it [the pound] was full, or all had entered, Indians, who had lain hidden near by, ran upon the bridge, and placed poles, prepared beforehand, across the opening through which the animals had entered, and over these poles hung robes, so as entirely to close the opening. The buffalo will not dash themselves against a barrier which is entirely closed, even though it be very frail; but if they can see through it to the outside, they will rush against it, and their great weight and strength make it easy for them to break down any but a heavy wall… Sometimes, if the walls of the pis'kun [pound] were not high, the buffalo tried to jump or climb over them, and, in doing this, might break them down, and some or all escape. As soon, however, as the animals were in the corral, the people – women and children included – ran up and showed themselves all about the walls, and by their cries kept the buffalo from pressing against the walls.

Eyewitness to a Cree buffalo pound in the 1850s, Henry Youle Hind likewise recorded the role of women and children in helping to confine the frantic animals in the pen, but this time using hides to block themselves from view: "with the utmost silence women and children on the outside hold their robes before every orifice until the whole herd is brought in." Hind also provides gripping testimony as to the consequences of failing to make the walls of the pound look solid. He recounts an event where some two hundred buffalo were being driven into a pound when a "wary old bull" suddenly spied "a narrow crevice which had not been closed by the robes of those on the outside, whose duty it was to conceal every orifice." The bull made a dash for the tiny opening, smashed through the pound wall, and the entire herd "ran helter skelter through the gap, and [disappeared] among the sand dunes."

You can see the pattern. Ancient wooden corral structures were draped with bison hides, probably with the darker hair side facing in, creating the appearance of a solid surrounding wall. The illusion is complete. Animals thundering into the corral saw only solid darkness surrounding them, no visible escape, and historic records show that they simply circled around in the confines of a structure that they could easily have destroyed.[†] Managers of modern bison herds have rediscovered aspects of the animal's nature that were known and manipulated for thousands of years by Native hunters.

I sometimes wonder how Aboriginal hunters learned such a fact about bison. Since people were without the horse for at least twelve thousand years, stalking and killing animals far larger, much faster, and immensely more powerful than themselves, where do you get an opportunity to work up close to a herd and discover this behavioural quirk? I can only imagine that it came through long periods of observation followed by trial and error. As people first began attempting to drive bison, they must have used certain landscapes as natural traps, cornering them in narrow canyons and valleys. They may have

† Weasel Tail, a Blood Indian, told John Ewers of an additional incentive to keep bison from trying to break through the pound walls: "All around the corral stakes of cottonwood or birch were laid over the lowest crosspoles. Their butt ends were firmly braced in the ground outside the corral. Their other ends projected about 3 feet or more inside the corral at an angle so that the ends were about the height of a buffalo's body. These ends were sharpened to points, so that if the buffalo tried to break through the corral, after they had been driven into it, they would be impaled on the stakes."

This model of a buffalo pound shows hides draped over the edge of the wooden corral to make it look solid. (Courtesy Royal Alberta Museum)

noted that trees or brush in the valleys helped contain the herds and began adding cut brush to the natural vegetation, laying cut branches between existing trees, eventually giving way to the full construction of crescent-shaped wooden enclosures. Presumably it became apparent that herds were tearing their way out through gaps in the walls. Perhaps people piled more wood in places and noticed that where the pound looked more solid the bison tended not to attempt an escape. After using increasingly greater amounts of wood, one day someone, whose name is long lost, had the idea that you could substitute hides for wood to create the same solid appearance. With a few tries, it became clear that hanging hides all the way around the corral had the desired effect.

Back to the Drive Lanes

On each side of [the pound] entrance commences a thick range of fascines [bundles of sticks], the two ranges spreading asunder as they extend, to the distance of 100 yards … but the fascines soon become more thinly planted, and continue to spread apart to the right and left, until each range has been extended about 300 yards from the pound. The labor is then diminished by only placing at intervals three or four cross-sticks … these extend on the plain for about two miles, and double rows of them are planted in several other directions to a still greater distance. – Alexander Henry, 1809

I remember when I was young seeing antiquated museum displays and entries in kids' encyclopedias that showed the final moment of a buffalo jump – animals stampeding toward the edge of the cliff, hunters lined up on both sides of the herd. The hunters were always depicted waving buffalo hides, firing arrows, and standing alongside and behind big piles of rocks. These were towers of rock, often coming up to the chests of the hunters, built with huge boulders. I gave these images no particular thought at the time. But I did when I was out walking in the Head-Smashed-In gathering basin, looking at the small clusters of rocks that didn't rise any higher than the tops of my shoes. Something was wrong. What happened to the towers of rock?

I started bringing my crew back into the drive lanes. We began a search of these rock lines, walking parallel to the small piles, scouring the ground for more rocks. It seemed logical to assume that the piles we see today must have been higher in the past, that the ravages of time, years of neglect, and disturbance by grazing cattle have knocked them down to their current height. If this were true, then we should find a scattering of rocks located near each of the cairns. What we found was just the opposite. The immediate area surrounding most of the rock piles was relatively free of other rocks. We only started seeing the expected amount of surface cobbles as we moved five to ten metres away from each cairn. I should note that surface rocks are common here, as they are over most of Alberta.

The rolling hills of the Porcupines were overrun by mighty glaciers during the Ice Age. These massive sheets of ice brought with them all kinds of debris, including huge amounts of rock picked up by the ice as it ground its way across central and western Canada. The rocks were dropped all over the landscape, often forming a blanket of stone on and just below the topsoil that covers much of Alberta.

As a result, it is perfectly normal to see the tops of rounded cobbles sticking out of the sod everywhere as you walk the hills and plains around Head-Smashed-In. There was no shortage of rocks to choose from when going about building stone cairns. Most of the time, you would only have to scour an area of a few metres to find enough rocks to make a decent pile. Our discovery of an area relatively clear of other rocks surrounding each of the drive-lane cairns started to make sense. Ancient Aboriginal people had scoured the area just as we had, gathering the rocks that lay closest to the place where they wanted to build a cairn. After all, why haul heavy rocks any farther than you have to? They left behind a pattern we can still see today – a zone parallel to the lanes that has been relatively cleared of rocks. But this realization came with a further conclusion: there was no scattering of displaced rocks around the piles that would confirm that they had once been much taller. Where were the rock towers of my youth?

This portrayal of a buffalo jump shows huge rock cairns at the end of the drive, unlike what we find today. (Courtesy American Museum of Natural History)

Crew member Bob Dawe examines excavations along the drive lane where only low platforms of rocks were found. Rocks are concentrated in the cairns and are relatively rare within several metres of each stone pile. (Courtesy Royal Alberta Museum)

If the rock piles hadn't been scattered over time, perhaps they were gradually covered up by drifting soil and we were just seeing the tops of once higher cairns. Investigating this scenario required us to dig, which we did in the mid 1980s. Before this period, I don't think any archaeologist had ever excavated a drive-lane cairn at a buffalo jump. I'm sure the general reaction of my colleagues would be, why waste your time digging around a simple pile of rocks? But I wanted to know what had happened to the other rocks, and I was running out of ideas. So we hauled some excavation gear into the gathering basin and selected a short section of a drive lane, about five cairns in a row, to dig. I didn't want to disturb the existing rock piles if I didn't have to (archaeologists are always conscious of the fact that they can never undo their work, putting things back exactly as they were; nor can we imagine the kinds of analyses that might appear in the decades to come). We left all the existing rocks in place but stripped the soil away from between them and from the sides of the cairns. In a sense we isolated each cairn on a little pedestal of sod as we dug away the surrounding earth. If the small clusters of rock visible today were merely the tops of larger piles, we should have found layers of more rock underneath the surface stones. We didn't.

Under the surface layer of rocks was nothing but dirt. Now I had to wrestle with the looming reality that the small platforms of rock, thousands of them spread across the Head-Smashed-In gathering basin, were never any bigger than what we could see sitting on the surface. It just didn't seem to make any sense. From even a short distance away we had enough trouble seeing them ourselves. How could these innocuous little rock clusters have played any role in directing the movement of such a massive and powerful force as a stampeding herd of bison? I didn't know a lot about buffalo at the time, but I thought I knew enough to realize that these rock piles were insufficient to accomplish the task with which they have been credited. Clearly, I was missing something. Finally I did what I should have done long before. I started reading a great deal from the one source that might hold crucial clues – the literature written by those lucky few who actually saw the last of the bison drives in operation.

It's no wonder that Stephen Ambrose's book and the subsequent television series about the Lewis and Clark expedition were hugely popular. It is quite simply a great story. But read the original; it's even better. There is nothing quite like the day-by-day accounts of people forging a new country, especially an already inhabited one. There is no long-term plot in these early journals, no central storyline, only a matter-of-fact retelling of the day's events. Many days are mundane, others are incredible, and neither you nor the author has any idea what the next day will bring. The journals of the earliest explorers to cross the Great Plains make for compelling reading, and they are especially pertinent here because some of these travellers encountered buffalo-hunting cultures still practising traditional methods of rounding up and moving bison. When it comes to opening windows into the past, it is hard to beat these sources.

Of course contemporary Native people can be an invaluable source of information about traditional bison hunting. But knowledgeable elders freely admit that much has been forgotten, as can be expected given that it has been a century and a half since most of this knowledge was last put to use. Vivid memories persist of the uses of the buffalo, of the importance of the great hunts to the people, and especially of the ceremonies associated with these dramatic events.† In contrast, technical matters tend to be most quickly forgotten: how stone tools were made, or how and why drive-lane cairns were constructed.

Although bison were hunted by whites and Natives alike until there were virtually none left, about 1880, the final decades of Aboriginal hunting were almost exclusively with horses and guns. These two supremely important imports from Europeans put a rapid end to the old labour-intensive and time-consuming ways of hunting buffalo. Not until very recent times have Aboriginal authors put stories of their traditional cultural ways in writing. For first-hand eyewitness accounts of traditional bison drives, then, we turn to the journals and accounts of European explorers, fur traders, missionaries, and others who probed the western frontier.

In a sense, those of us interested in Aboriginal cultures of the western Plains are very fortunate. Europeans generally worked their way from east to west, with Native people being settled in the wake of this push. This means that cultures in the West continued many traditional cultural practices for much longer than those in the east. I can still sit down for coffee with a Blackfoot elder raised by grandparents who hunted buffalo. This is an extraordinarily close connection to the past, one that other anthropologists can only envy. It is a direct result of the very recent settlement of the West, and it is the reason why we have a number of wonderfully colourful and descriptive written accounts that we can draw on for help in interpreting the past.

A number of early European visitors to the western Plains were fortunate enough to witness the Native inhabitants attempting to drive bison to a mass kill, most often into the wooden corral of a pound. There are precious few eyewitness accounts to drives leading to a jump, but the process of rounding up the animals and moving them toward a kill is the same. Only the final kill location differed. It was during

† I have attended a number of Blackfoot ceremonies where the prayers and songs used to call the buffalo to the great traps, or to thank the spirits for the gifts of the buffalo, are perfectly remembered and recited.

† I know of only one
account from an actual
eyewitness to communal
bison kills who mentions
rocks being part of the
drive lanes. Maximilian,
Prince of Wied, wrote,
"A tract is surrounded
with scarecrows, made of
stones, branches of trees,
&c., and the terrified
animals are driven into a
narrow gorge, in which
the hunters lie concealed
... On such occasions the
Indians sometimes kill
700 or 800 buffaloes."

my search of early historic eyewitness accounts of bison driving that I discovered the clues that held the secret to the operation of drive lanes. Once I had this information, the small rock cairns at Head-Smashed-In started to make a whole lot more sense. But there was a curious twist to this secret, one that took me a while to figure out.

Some of the great names in the European exploration of the West are David Thompson, Peter Fidler, Anthony Henday, Lewis and Clark, Alexander Henry (the older and the younger), Henry Youle Hind, John Audubon, John Palliser, The Earl of Southesk, Edwin James, and George Catlin. I read the accounts of these men, and others, and I started to see a pattern in how bison kills were orchestrated. Drive lanes figure in almost every description of luring bison towards a kill. But here's the twist – the accounts of those who were on the Plains during the last years of buffalo hunting almost never mention drive lanes made of rocks.† Rather, individual cairns are said to be made of branches from trees, twigs of brush, clumps of sod piled up, stacks of buffalo chips, and various combinations of these.

In 1772 Mathew Cocking noted that the wings of the drive lane were made of small sticks and that buffalo dung or old roots were laid in heaps in the same direction as the piles of sticks. John Palliser, traversing the Plains between 1857 and 1860, recorded, "To this entrance converge lines of little heaps of buffalo dung or brush from several miles into the prairies which surround the clump of wood in which the pound is concealed. These lines serve to lead the buffalo in the required direction when they have been driven into the neighbourhood." Daniel Harmon likewise observed, "From each side of this opening, they fix two ranges of stakes, at about an angle of ninety degrees from each other, extending about two miles into the plains. These stakes rise about four feet above the ground, and are about forty feet apart."

So where are the rock piles that exist in the thousands at Head-Smashed-In and at most other buffalo jumps that I had seen or read about? Why are these so conspicuously absent from historical accounts of driving bison towards a kill? The literature (an abundance of it, so that it could hardly be dismissed as anomalous) all pointed to cairns made of organic materials, yet a dedicated search of the gathering basin yielded only cairns made of rocks. Something was seriously amiss.

This discrepancy led me to consider the difference between what early European explorers saw and what I could see on the ground today. I could understand why there was no longer any brush, sod, dung, or twigs to be seen along the drive lanes at Head-Smashed-In. In the more than one hundred years since Europeans observed these organic materials, they had decayed long ago. But why didn't the early explorers mention the piles of rocks present at most communal buffalo drives?

Deadmen

[The kill] was formed in a pretty dell between sand hills, about half a mile from the first, and leading from it in two diverging rows, the bushes they designate "dead men," and which serve to guide the buffalo when at full speed, were arranged. The "dead men" extended a distance of four miles into the prairie, west of and beyond the Sand Hills. – Henry Youle Hind, 1857–58

The cairns at Head-Smashed-In are low platforms of stone. Our digging had confirmed that they were never tall piles. In and of themselves, I could not imagine that the cairns would help direct the course of stampeding herds of buffalo, but they could have served as the base on which to construct the organic structures noted by European eyewitnesses. If covered with sod, dung, twigs, and brush, the small basal rock clusters may have been completely invisible during the time the drives were in operation. Early eyewitnesses saw the taller organic cairns and missed the bottom layer of rocks.[†] Clearly this begs the question of why anyone would bother with the small rock piles at all. Why not just stack up chunks of sod and bison chips and brush on the ground and forego all the work that went into gathering thousands of small cobbles?

First, the rock piles would serve as a permanent marker of the correct route for the drive. If the jump was not returned to for several years, the organic materials might be all gone and there would be no trace on the land of where the previous cairns were located. We can be certain that a great deal of thought, planning, and trial and error went into discovering the only suitable places that drive lanes would successfully control the movement of bison. Mistakes were no doubt made, lanes placed in wrong locations, and herds escaped from the trap. Reassessment would have been made, cairns shifted to create slightly different lane direction (or perhaps more cairns added to strengthen a particularly vulnerable spot), and the whole

[†] In contrast, many interviews with Native elders in the years after the end of buffalo hunting make specific mention of the rocks used in building drive lanes, lending support to the likelihood that European eyewitnesses to the hunts simply didn't see the rocks under organic materials.

effort repeated. With such a great amount of effort going into each attempted drive, and considering the importance of success, it is not surprising people designed a method to mark the proper route of the drive in a way that would last for generations to come. Small rock piles accomplished this goal.

Second, rock piles almost certainly played an active role in the actual function of the cairns when they were in use. While sod and dung could be stacked anywhere, brush, if it is to stand up straight, needs to be anchored. Poking the ends of slender sticks into the hard baked earth would be nearly impossible. Furthermore, they would simply blow over in the first strong wind. The low platforms of rock that we see today at Head-Smashed-In are perfectly suited to serve as a base for wedging in the ends of sticks and brush. In almost every instance the rocks are gathered together into a tight group that offers space between individual rocks where the shaft of a branch could be inserted. I am reminded of the little wire mesh grids that are found in the bottoms of some flower vases: the openings in the grid offer places to stick the stalk of the flower so that it stands in just the manner you wish. The purpose of the rocks, in addition to marking the permanent drive lane, is to support the brush so that it can stand

Small rock piles may have served as permanent markers of where successful drives took place. (Courtesy: Royal Alberta Museum)

Preparing the drive lanes at buffalo kills might have looked something like this: fixing branches with rocks and stacking bison dung. (Courtesy Head-Smashed-In Buffalo Jump)

† Grinnell wrote, "Finally, when the buffalo were fairly within the chute, the people began to rise up from behind the rock piles which the herd had passed, and to shout and wave their robes. This frightened the hinder-most buffalo, which pushed forward on the others, and before long the whole herd was running at headlong speed toward the precipice."

up in the wind, and, by doing so, these seemingly innocuous little stands of brush provide a key element that made the buffalo drive work, that is, motion.

European explorers commonly used one word to describe the drive lane markers that they observed: "deadmen." I think this may be a very insightful use of a term. When buffalo chips, chunks of sod, brush, and twigs were piled on top of rock piles, they may have looked, from a distance, very much like human beings – hence the term deadmen. Perhaps the European observers were recognizing the fact that once these cairns were made in the proper form, they served as, and took the place of, Native hunters. Witnessing traditional buffalo drives in the early 1800s, Daniel Harmon seemed to appreciate that cairns were intended to extend the range and numbers of people. He described long lines of stakes extending into the prairies, topped with some dried grass to give a sense of motion, and perceptively noted the human-like quality of the cairns: "Indians are stationed by the side of some of these stakes, to keep them in motion, so that the buffaloes suppose them *all* to be human beings" (my emphasis).

We know that hunters, sometimes including women and children, staged themselves along the path of the drive lanes to help control the bison, ensuring that they did not escape the trap. This was especially true at the end of the drive where the lanes converged (funnel-like) to their narrowest point, where the herd was compressed into a tight mass and where the danger of escape was greatest. There are graphic accounts of Native people standing alongside the cairns, shouting, waving their arms, and flapping bison hides, as a means of keeping the animals contained within the funnel.† Yet clearly there were never enough people to spread themselves along the kilometres of lanes that extend back from the edge of Head-Smashed-In.

To extend the ranks of human figures way beyond the limits of the small population, cairns were built in the likeness of the people. And what better way to imitate a human being (as opposed to having the cairns simply resemble small trees or bushes) than to have the cairns move as if they too were alive.

Fresh-cut brush would accomplish this movement. Branches stripped from trees and sections of small bushes would wave in the wind, especially if they still had leaves on them. When the season was such that the leaves had fallen, small strips of bison hide and hair were tied to the twigs so as to catch the wind. What is the big advantage of having the cairns impart a sense of motion? Once again we look to Aboriginal knowledge of bison behaviour for the answer. Perhaps because they are not very keen of sight, bison are remarkably sensitive to any unusual movement in their environment. People who work with buffalo will tell you that as long as you are positioned downwind you can get quite close to a grazing herd by simply not moving whenever the animals are looking at you. As long as you stand perfectly still, they will gaze at you for a long time, trying to identify the object. Finally, they will turn away or return to grazing and you can continue to approach, freezing once again when they look up. If you want to be noticed by a bison herd, and cause a sense of consternation, simply move around. This is what stone cairns embellished with brush did.

What a great ruse the Plains people had pulled off. They managed to gather together small piles of rocks, wedge some branches between the stones, and maybe pile up a few bison chips or some sod around the base of the brush. In so doing they created a deflective shield, a barrier that existed only in the mind's eye of the buffalo. It was a barrier that could easily be crossed or trashed at a moment's notice by any self-respecting bison herd, but it was one that on most days was not. The people who built it understood that bison would shy away from an unusual object waving in the wind. As the herds stood in the bottom of the basin looking along a lane of cairns, they would experience the famous telephone pole effect, the visual illusion that the fluttering stacks of brush appeared to be closely spaced, especially when viewed from one end ... just like telephone poles parallel to the road we are travelling seem to merge closer together as we view them in the distance. Recall how wooden pounds worked to contain panicked bison because they looked solid. So too, drive lanes worked extraordinarily well to keep the bison contained in a specified area because, by their movement, the stacks of brush gave the appearance of something to be feared – a strange object moving in the distance.

In Small Things Forgotten

I didn't really learn anything new on the first day I walked into the gathering basin. On the contrary, I realized how much I didn't know about how and why ancient hunters constructed this bewildering labyrinth of stone lines. But I knew that these simple, inconspicuous lines must have played a central role in the bison drive. Why else move tens of thousands of stones into carefully crafted positions? My ignorance set me on a course of discovery, determined to understand the same truths that the ancient map-makers understood. My ignorance opened up wonderful doors to new worlds in the gripping accounts of the first explorers and the beauty of the natural world as revealed in the literature on bison behaviour.

A thin but beautifully written introduction to archaeology by James Deetz is titled *In Small Things Forgotten*. How appropriate.

The final configuration of drive lanes at a buffalo jump might have looked like this: V-shaped lines of rocks, brush, and other material leading to the cliff. (Courtesy Shayne Tolman)

For, indeed, the small, innocuous stone cairns of the long-abandoned buffalo jumps of the northern Plains have been very much forgotten. They have been left to gather dust and slowly disappear into the prairie sod. There is an important lesson here. Sometimes the small, forgotten things of the past tell a powerful story. But the stones won't speak to us. The archaeological record is as static and silent as are the voices of the vanished people who produced it. Only when secrets from the past are pondered, probed, wrestled with, debated, is it occasionally the case, and only occasionally, that we stumble through a window into another world.

CHAPTER 5

Rounding Up

When buffalo were needed, the shaman invited several young men into his tipi. He gave them berries to eat, had each one blow on an eagle bone whistle, and then made a pipe offering. At night these young men went out to find buffalo. When they located a herd they surrounded it and drove it steadily toward the opening of the chute by slapping their folded robes on the ground or on the snow. – David Mandelbaum on the Plains Cree

---

T he simple lines of stone cairns are enormously long at Head-Smashed-In, with some single lanes extending for many kilometres into the gathering basin. Yet despite their imposing length, it would have been impossible to have these lanes crisscross the entire area from which bison were to be harvested. There had to be a great expanse of land beyond the reach of the stone cairns where people were on their own in rounding up herds of bison and moving them into the lane complex. Drive lanes can be beautifully constructed, but if you can't coerce bison to file within their ranks, then an enormous amount of work has been in vain. How did ancient hunters manage to slink through the gathering basin behind Head-Smashed-In, coaxing great herds of buffalo to move towards the cliff and into the drive-lane system?

Of the many stereotypes that visitors bring with them to Head-Smashed-In, a prevailing one is that Native hunters simply ran out onto the prairie, waving and shouting, hoping against hope that the animals would just happen to run toward the cliff. Your chances of success with such a strategy are somewhere close to zero. Bison are simply not going to respond in a dependable manner to this kind of hazing, and predictability is the essential ingredient of a successful bison drive. The truth of what happened in the hills and valleys of the basin is much the opposite of the stereotypical pandemonium. Instead, it was a calculated, carefully orchestrated application of

Panicked, uncontrolled efforts to move bison on the open Plains probably met with little success. (Courtesy Shayne Tolman)

human ingenuity that once again shows a deep understanding of bison behaviour and biology.

Imagine for a moment you were charged with the task of getting a herd of buffalo to move in a particular direction. First, we take away your pickup truck or horse, and your rifle, give you a pair of moccasins, and tell you to head out toward the herd and get busy. How would you go about it? Carefully, I suspect. Would you have any desire to get up close and personal with a herd of powerful, wild beasts that weigh ten times what you do, can run much faster, and have sharp curved horns that they routinely use for fighting? Not likely. Yet for thousands of years Aboriginal people did just this, often not even armed, because the purpose was to move the animals, not to hunt them. Over millennia of stalking and observing bison, Native hunters became aware of the animal's natural tendencies. Gradually, no doubt with much trial and error, they converted these observations into an array of ingenious ruses that allowed them to direct the path of bison movement. Few tricks are more inspiring than the hunters' use of disguises.

The Spirit Sings

There is nothing relating to the Indians so difficult to understand as their religion. – John Bradbury, 1809–11

It is a daunting task to try to briefly summarize the rich, complex ceremonial life of ancient buffalo hunters, as it would be for any ethnic group. Entire books have been written on this subject, and I will touch only lightly on a few selected aspects of the Native spiritual world. It will be a fleeting look, as determined by my own limitations and by the need to focus on relevant topics. But some consideration of ceremonialism in the buffalo hunt is essential. To neglect the topic would be a huge disservice to Aboriginal culture, as it might imply that the great kills were a triumph of technique and knowledge, when to the people who orchestrated them they were accomplishments granted by the spirit beings. They were gifts from the Creator.

Aboriginal people of the Great Plains lived in a world full of uncertainty and danger. As is true of many hunting and gathering peoples, this precarious style of life is prone to elaboration of the spiritual world, often to the point that nearly every aspect of daily life has a spiritual or ceremonial reference. There was literally nothing in life (and thereafter) not touched in some way by the powers of the spirits. Living and inanimate objects, to which western culture would ascribe no special abilities, had and still have power to Aboriginal people.

BUGS: Fireflies were the spirits of the ancestors and were revered.

ROCKS: Small round rocks were collected and respected, because they had neither beginning nor end. Large rocks on the prairies were the work of the spirits and were given offerings of food.

BIRDS: Eagles possessed astonishing hunting powers and their feathers were coveted, and stuffed eagles were hung in lodges as good luck. Swallows and bluebirds pecked out rock art images with their beaks. Magpies were not hunted because they helped people win their dominance over buffalo.

REPTILES: Turtle hearts were fed to young children so that they would grow up, like turtles, with strong bodies. Rattles from snakes were symbols of power and were hung on war shields.

Powerful ceremonies, such as the Buffalo Dance of the Mandan, were designed to invoke the help of the spirit world in calling the buffalo to a kill event. Painting by Karl Bodmer. (Courtesy Edward E. Ayer Collection, The Newberry Library, Chicago)

† Archaeologists working in the high country of Wyoming have discovered skulls of game animals completely incorporated by trees. The skulls must have been placed in the notches by respectful hunters.

TREES: Trees were life-giving to the prairie people and were honoured with gifts of food and bones placed in the notches of branches.†

LAKES AND RIVERS: These waters were the source of both people and buffalo.

SMALL ANIMALS: Weasels were revered as magnificent hunters, and their tails adorned shirts and shields.

LARGE ANIMALS: Bears were regarded as ferocious predators. Out of respect, their flesh was seldom eaten, but their claws, worn as ornaments, transferred the power of the bear to the owner.

As can be imagined, societies so intensely focused on hunting a single game animal for their survival had numerous special rites, ceremonies, and taboos associated with buffalo and the hunting of this animal. It is absolutely correct to state that everything about a buffalo hunt, from beginning to end, was steeped in spiritual beliefs and appropriate ceremony. As Fletcher and La Flesche recorded for the Omaha in 1911,

The life of the people depended on this animal, as it afforded the principal supply of meat and pelts; therefore the buffalo hunt was inaugurated and conducted with religious rites, which not only recognized a dependence on Wakon'da [spirit of mysterious life force], but enforced the observance by the people of certain formalities which secured to each member of the tribe an opportunity to obtain a share in the game.

While the days leading up to the great communal kills were filled with numerous preparatory tasks and chores, they were also filled with critical ceremonial events, the successful execution of which would determine the outcome of the effort. Responsibility for orchestrating both jumps and pounds (corrals) usually fell to one or occasionally to a few key individuals. These were shamans, or medicine men and women, credited by their people for possessing extraordinary spiritual powers.† Most importantly, their power enabled them to see where the herds of buffalo were located and also to charm or call the animals toward the lethal trap, ensuring the proper location for the kill. Remember the Plains is a vast area, the distribution of herds was always patchy, and small camps of people would frequently not know the location of the closest herd at any one time. The ability to predict the location was a critical part of being a successful shaman.

† The term "medicine" was widely used by Plains Indians to describe objects and places of power. The first Europeans brought with them certain western remedies, which were used on occasion to heal Native people. This, of course, was magical to the Natives, and when they asked what it was, were told it was medicine. They in turn told Europeans of magical parts of their world, and the closest English word for such phenomena was medicine. Thus we have medicine men and women, medicine wheels, and so on.

Since orchestrating the great communal hunts was relatively rare compared with daily and weekly small-scale hunts, it stands to reason that medicine people had to ply their trade much more often for the smaller hunts, especially when the people were dangerously low on food, or even starving. When the Mandan were desperate for buffalo, George Catlin recorded that "every man ... brings out of his lodge his mask (the skin of a buffalo's head with the horns on), which he is obliged to keep in readiness for this occasion; and then commences the buffalo dance ... which is held for the purpose of making 'buffalo come.' " A typical account of how a medicine person might be pressed into service in desperate times comes from Robert Lowie, one of the prominent anthropologists of the Plains Indians. Interviewing the Crow people at the beginning of the twentieth century, Lowie tells of a remarkable shaman:

Once the people could not find any game. Big-ox bade them get a buffalo skull and put its nose toward the camp. In the night they began to sing. In the morning they saw six head of buffalo and killed them. The following morning they again found several head. When they had had enough, Big-ox bade them turn the skull around, then they did not see any more buffalo.

Frequently, the ability to see the location of the bison came to the shaman in the form of a dream or vision. Having such a vision, Mandelbaum recorded among the Plains Cree, "carried with it considerable prestige," including "the privilege of constructing a buffalo

A small stone structure built on a high hill near Head-Smashed-In was used by Native people to receive visions from the spirit world. Similar structures are still made and used today. (Courtesy Robert van Schaik)

† By "tied" Lowie actually means attached to the back by sharp bone skewers stuck through the skin. Long rawhide cords connected the bone skewers to the skulls, which were then dragged around, often for hours at a time, to induce a hallucinogenic state. Skewering of the chest was done at the Sundance ceremony. Both practices continue today.

pound. A man had to have supernatural guarantees that he would be able to entice buffalo into a pound before he could build one, for its success depended on the aid of the shaman's supernaturals." People who had visions that led to success were revered and consulted again for subsequent hunts. Those whose visions failed would lose respect and might be ignored during future endeavours. Sometimes visions came to people in the form of dreams, but if people were desperate and a vision was needed, it was common for the medicine people to try to induce them by engaging in various forms of self-torture. Subjecting yourself to pain and deprivation certainly had the power to bring on extraordinary hallucinations. These were then interpreted to tease out the deep meaning of how and when a successful hunt might be held. Lowie again informs us that "Some shamans called buffalo by dragging buffalo skins tied to their backs and singing buffalo-bull songs on the way."†

Perhaps the most complete and inspiring account of the incredible amount of ceremonial ritual that went into the duties and events leading up to a major buffalo hunt comes from Fletcher and La Flesche's description of the Omaha. It provides insight into the overwhelming strength of the spiritual world among buffalo hunting people, beginning with a respected man appointed to be the director of the hunt. This was a "grave responsibility and high honor," and was only accorded to men who "possess courage and ability to lead men and command their respect and obedience." The entire tribe was placed under his control: "He directed the march of the tribe, selected its camping places, chose and dispatched the runners in search of buffalo herds, and directed the hunt when the game had been found." A council of respected elders was convened and consulted as to which direction the people were to head in search of the buffalo. It was a decision "considered one of the most important acts in the welfare of the people; on it depended the food supply and also safety from enemies while securing it."

After much speech making, feasting, and pipe smoking by the council, a day was set for departure. The man appointed director of the hunt fasted for four days and waited until all others had left camp. Then he removed his moccasins and walked alone to meet up with the group at the first camp. When he arrived he was left alone in his tipi. During this time he would have no sexual relations, eat little, live apart from his family, and pray continuously, "for on him all the people are depending." He was responsible for all the actions of his people, good and bad. In a sense he became the embodiment of his people as, an Omaha explained, "a man's hand belongs to his body." The purpose of all the deprivation he endured was to disassociate himself as much as possible from the everyday natural world and have him in communication only with the spiritual world from which he received his power.

Days continued in this manner until signs of a buffalo herd were seen. Then the director sent out the runners, scouts whose name translated as "those who look," to find the herds. "Come!," the director implored the runners, "that you may go and secure knowledge of the land for me." Runners scoured the land, and when a sizeable herd was spotted they returned to camp. Amidst elaborate ceremony, they reported their findings, careful not to exaggerate the numbers of animals. If the report was promising, a herald was sent around camp proclaiming, "It is reported that smoke (dust) is rising from the earth as far as the eye can reach!" The director, having remained alone in his tent throughout, now emerged and assumed control of the hunt. Young men were selected to carry sacred objects, such as pipestems and ceremonial staffs. A strict silence was enforced so as not to startle the herd. Barking dogs were muzzled or killed.

Led by the young men, the director took his people toward the herd. The walk was done with great pomp and ceremony and, considering the excitement of the hunters, at an excruciatingly slow pace. Four times the march was halted. Each time, pipes were unwrapped and smoked and prayers were offered for the success and the safety of the people. When the herd was close by, the young men who carried the ceremonial staffs ran first toward the buffalo while, under pain of severe reprimand, the others endured an agonizing wait. The boys circled the herd and planted their staffs in the ground, the signal for the hunt to begin. As the killing commenced, two other young men were charged with securing the first tongues from the slain buffalo. Into the frenzy they rushed, "dodging in and out among the animals and hunters, for they must take the tongue from a buffalo before it had been touched with a knife." A great feast followed the kill, at which there was observance of many restrictions and taboos on eating certain parts of the buffalo. The feast was "a sacred one, the consecrated food was prized, as it was believed to bring health and long life."

Perhaps the most astonishing thing about the historical account of Omaha buffalo hunting is the wealth of ceremonial detail beyond what I have related above. Every nuance of people's actions and thoughts, for weeks and days on end, was guided by their spiritual beliefs. The clothes people wore, the food they ate and abstained from, the direction they faced as they exited a tipi, rules governing whom you could and could not speak to: everything in daily life was drenched in deeply held beliefs that dictated the proper course of action – ritual that time and experience had proven would lead to the successful killing of their staff of life.

The depth of reporting on the Omaha is perhaps unusual, but the rituals cited are not. For the Blackfoot, Grinnell reported that a medicine man, one who possessed the iniskim (sacred buffalo stone), "unrolled his pipe, and prayed to the Sun for success." Another man charged with "calling" the buffalo arose early from sleep and "told his wives that they must not leave the lodge, nor even look out, until he returned; that they should keep burning sweet grass, and should pray to the Sun for his success and safety." This man then abstained from food and water and led his people to find the buffalo.

The actual hunts were accompanied by no less devotion to strict spiritual beliefs. Corrals made by the Plains Cree had various offerings – feathers, bones, cloth – placed under the wooden ramp forming the

The vital importance of ceremony in bison drives is depicted in this detail from a Paul Kane painting showing a medicine man perched on a tree in the centre of the buffalo pound. He is holding offerings and calling the herd into the corral. (Courtesy Royal Ontario Museum)

† Supporting the antiquity of this practice, archaeologists have excavated bison kill sites showing evidence of a wooden pole in the middle of the corral and have found unusual artifacts, presumably offerings, clustered around the spot where the pole would have stood.

entrance to the pound. The intent, clearly, was to place objects that would encourage bison to come to the trap. Palliser states, "I saw a collection of Indian valuables, among which were bridles, powder horns, tobacco, beads, and the like, placed there by the believing Indians." He also noted the placement of a tall central pole in the middle of the pound, "on which they hang offerings. To which piece of idolatry I was in a manner accessory by giving them my pocket handkerchief to convert into a flag."† The Earl of Southesk wrote of a fantastic young man "who had a wonderful power – magical, some thought it – of guiding buffalo in any direction that he pleased." Edwin James tells how hunters approached the herd and paused to allow "the pipe-bearer an opportunity to perform the ceremony of smoking, which is considered necessary to their success."

We know from historic records that medicine people often kept up their prayers and rituals during the entire progression of the hunt, even if it took days to complete. And at the end of a successful venture,

The practice of making offerings at great buffalo kills continues. This small, little-known buffalo jump on the Kainai (Blood) reserve in Alberta is honoured with offerings of coloured cloth, food, and tobacco. (Courtesy Royal Alberta Museum)

the ceremonialists continued to play a key role in how the slaughter and butchering should be done. Describing the final stages of a Plains Cree pound, Mandelbaum gives compelling testimony of the degree to which ceremony permeated every aspect of the kill:

Before the carcasses were butchered, the shaman ascended the wall of the pound and sang his power song, accompanying himself with a rattle. Then small boys undressed and climbed into the enclosure. They threw buffalo intestines over the branches of the central tree, imitating the call of crows as they did so. At the same time, little girls brought wood to the tipi of the shaman. For these functions, each girl received a piece of heart fat and each boy a buffalo tongue. The fatty tissue around the buffalo heart was peculiarly sacred. The person who cut it out of the carcass wailed as he did so.

As hard as it is to believe, documentary records indicate that the actual killing of contained bison was sometimes postponed so that the necessary ceremonies could be observed. In the mid-1800s Audubon stated, "the warriors are all assembled by the pen [pound], calumets are lighted, and the chief smokes to the Great Spirit, the four points of the compass, and lastly to the Buffaloes. The pipe is passed from mouth to mouth in succession, and as soon as this ceremony is ended, the destruction [killing] commences."

When the slaughter was over, the first order of business was to give thanks to those exceptional people who, through their ability to commune with the spirit world, had made success possible. Often this entailed giving choice pieces of the buffalo to key players in the hunt. The Cheyenne allowed the few men who had called the buffalo to make the first selection of the finest cuts from the carcasses. In many cases, the highly esteemed tongues were brought to the medicine people and hunt directors as signs of respect and thanks. As the butchering commenced, a series of formal rituals had to be observed, the specifics of which differed from group to group. Often these displayed a clear belief in the ability of the spirits to transfer specific powers to people. Mandelbaum records that the Plains Cree men drank the warm blood of the buffalo "so that they might not be perturbed at the sight of blood in battle." The Omaha were known to save the fat from around the heart of the buffalo for young children so that they would grow up with strong hearts.

Bones were the subject of much ceremony, as they clearly came to represent the animals themselves. Many groups believed that bones could return to become bison again. Edwin James recorded in 1800, "Many of the Minnetarees [Gros Ventre] believe that the bones of those bisons, which they have slain and divested of flesh, rise again clothed with renewed flesh, and quickened with life, and become fat, and fit for slaughtering the succeeding June." Maximilian also documents the power of bones to control living herds of bison: "In one of their villages they preserve the neck bones of a buffalo, as the Crows also are said to do; and this is done with a view to prevent the buffalo herds from removing to too great a distance from them." It was also common to find great piles of bones, usually horns, near the sites of the great kills. For the Cheyenne, Grinnell reports that "there were formerly to be seen piles of buffalo-horns heaped up, which, as described to me, were similar to the piles of horns made under like conditions by the Blackfeet that I have seen near their killing places." None of the bones were more sacred or used in more ceremonies than the skull.

The attention Native people paid to honouring and respecting the spirit world and the role of bison in this endeavour did not end when the hunts were over. Rather, it permeated every other aspect of daily life, as a simple story recounted by David Thompson conveys: "We had been hunting the Bison, and every horse was loaded with meat, even those we rode on; returning we came to a few Aspins [aspen trees], where everyone made a halt, and from the load of every horse a small bit was cut and thrown on the decayed root of a tree, to appease the spirit of a Man who had died there of hunger many years past."

All the actions laced with symbolism and deep meaning would be impossible to explore fully here. My central point is that to present only the western science-based explanation of how great buffalo kills worked would be to equate them to extraordinary technical achievements (which in fact they were). What is important is that they were so much more; they were interactions between deeply spiritual people and the world in which they lived.

The Nose of the Buffalo

During our stay here a very large herd of buffaloe continued to feed within a quarter of a mile of us. Some of them I observed gazing at us; but as they were to the windward, they had not the power of discovering what we were by the sense of smelling. I found, on inquiry from some of our party who were well acquainted with the habits of these animals, that they seem to rely chiefly on that sense for their safety. – John Bradbury, 1809–11

Bison, like most large mammals, have a highly developed sense of smell. This, not sight, is their primary defence mechanism. Given the right wind conditions, bison can smell another animal, including humans, as much as several kilometres away. It is the smell of trouble that usually causes unease in the herd, and if severe and persistent, it will initiate movement, even a stampede, away from the perceived threat. Bison are constantly checking the wind. Hardly any part of their daily activities – grazing, sleeping, drinking, scratching, playing, or fighting – takes place without frequent reference to what is in the wind.

The importance of smell to the story of buffalo hunting is inextricably linked with wind, as wind is the carrier of the smells that reach the noses of the animals. Wind is so important in Aboriginal hunting strategies that it is safe to say that precious few kill events took place in prehistory without reference to what the wind was doing. European hunters quickly learned the same truth; Josiah Gregg hunting in the 1830s noted that a successful hunt depended on the hunters being downwind of the herd. The herd can be approached, Gregg stated, "provided he 'has the wind of them,' as hunters say – that is, if the wind blows from the buffalo; but if the reverse, he will find it impossible to approach them, however securely he may have concealed himself from their sight." Edwin James, travelling through vast herds in 1820, recounts how the wind blew over his troop and reaching the nose of the bison "it informed them of our presence by the scent which it conveyed. As soon as the odour reached even the farthest animal, though at the distance of two miles on our right, and perhaps half a mile in our rear, he betrayed the utmost alarm, [and broke] into a full bounding run." James was traversing the extremely flat country of the Platte River (French for the river being flat as a plate) and was able to watch the physical effects that human scent had on bison herds:

The wind happening to blow fresh from the south, the scent of our party was borne directly across the Platte, and we could distinctly note every step of its progress through a distance of eight or ten miles, by the consternation and terror it excited among the buffaloes. The moment the tainted gale infected their atmosphere, they ran with as much violence as if pursued by a party of mounted hunters.

Aspects of smell and wind were combined to create just one of many instances of hunters using their knowledge to get the upper hand on their intended prey and to move them in the desired direction. When the wind was wrong, hunts failed. In 1809 Alexander Henry was called repeatedly by a group of Blackfoot to witness a bison drive, but despite plenty of buffalo aligned in proper position, "the wind was still unfavorable, and every herd that was brought near the ranks struck off in a wrong direction." Conversely, Henry noted, when the wind comes from behind, "it is most favorable, as they can then direct the buffalo with great ease."

Bison movement is controlled by a number of short- and long-term needs, especially the search for good grass on which to feed, the need for water, and the changing seasons of the year. All these are under the constant influence of smells carried to the herd in the wind. The instinct to survive is stronger than any immediate need for water or food, and if there is a dangerous scent in the air, an area of fine pasture may be abandoned for the sake of safety. There are two sides to this coin. Bison will move away from a potential threat and will move towards a perceived area of safety. If you are a clever hunter, well aware of these tendencies, how do you make this work to your advantage?

First, you would need to know to what smells bison have an adverse reaction. Given the size and strength of bison, there is not

Grizzly bears were known to attack and kill full-grown bison. (Courtesy Clarence Tillenius)

† In 1859, near the fork of the Bow and Red Deer Rivers, Palliser "saw a good deal of buffalo and many antelopes; also five grizzly bears, two old and three young ones, at which there was much firing and only one killed."

much they fear in their natural environment. We know from records of early explorers that the grizzly bear had a much larger range than at present, extending well onto the Great Plains.† Named the Plains Grizzly, this fearsome animal did occasionally run down and kill bison (and unfortunate Native people as well). While little is known of the long-term history of the Plains Grizzly, it can be assumed that this animal was probably always a part of the northern Plains landscape and a persistent threat to solitary bison. But grizzlies probably never existed in large numbers on the Plains and accounted for very few buffalo deaths.

The status of bison's most constant, relentless, and effective enemy would certainly go to the wolf, and these supreme predators were regular companions to bison herds. Henry Brackenridge, in 1811, observed, "Great numbers of wolves were now seen in every direction; we could hardly go forty yards from the buffaloe, before a half a dozen would shew themselves. It was amusing to see them peeping over hillocks, while we pelted them with stones." At about the same time, John Bradbury recalled a buffalo herd where he "counted fifteen wolves, several of which stood for some minutes looking at us, without exhibiting any signs of fear."

Obviously, a lone wolf was little threat to any adult bison, although a young calf, if caught alone, could be in serious trouble. Kills in winter favoured the wolves because of their superior ability to run through snow. But wolves are pack animals, frequently ganging up in groups of ten or more. At this strength, they were capable of bringing down any adult bison, although they tended to prefer young, old, and sick animals, the ones less able to defend themselves, especially if they wandered away from the main herd. Edwin James tells of a lone bull

Wolves were nearly constant companions of bison herds; they were generally tolerated but closely watched. (Courtesy Clarence Tillenius)

† It appears that wolves adapted to letting humans do the hunting for them. Several observers noted wolves congregating during the hunts. Paul Kane wrote, "As is frequently the case on buffalo hunts, a large band of wolves hovered round us in expectation of a feast." John Palliser said that wolves eagerly watched the hunters, "perfectly aware that the events about to come off were to terminate in an abundant meal after the field was left to themselves." Wolves selected the fattest animals to consume first, then hunters selected the fat wolves. Peter Fidler recorded the practice of Indians intentionally letting wolves feed on discarded bison carcasses, knowing that the gorged predators would be slow and easy to kill.

bison, wounded by hunters and pursued by a gang of wolves: "they saw him several times thrown to the ground by the wolves, and afterwards regaining his feet."

Bison were well aware of the presence of wolves in their immediate environment. Packs of coyotes, as well, would have been a constant companion to the bison-wolf mixture. Coyotes are too small to bring down bison (though the occasional stray calf may have been taken by a pack), but they were supremely adapted scavengers. Lurking on the edges of the action, they readily pounced on the dregs of the wolf kills and on the carcasses of natural deaths in the bison herd. The smell of both these predators would have been pretty much a constant factor of life, and they were generally tolerated lurking around on the outside margins of the herd. Since bison also tended to live and move in large groups, they knew that as long as they stayed close to the main herd they were generally safe. George Catlin recognized this when, in the mid-nineteenth century, he noted that "while the herd of buffaloes are together, they seem to have little dread of the wolf, and allow them to come in close company with them." It was an ecological fact often put to use by Native hunters.†

Fire this Time

The grass of these plains is so often on fire, by accident or design … and the whole of the great Plains are subject to these fires during the Summer and Autumn before the Snow lies on the ground. – David Thompson, 1784–1812

Prairie fires, started by lightning strikes as well as by humans, had the power to wreak havoc on bison herds. There are horrific eyewitness

accounts of fires scorching, blinding, and killing large herds of buffalo, as well as other large and small game. An eyewitness to prairie
fires, Daniel Harmon, reported, "When the fire passes over the plains,
which circumstance happens almost yearly … great numbers of horses
and buffaloes are destroyed; for those animals when surrounded by
fire, will stand perfectly still, until they are burned to death." Robert
Rundle, in Alberta in the mid-1800s, gives the sad report of what
"a sight the poor burnt buffalo presented" since, consumed by fire,
"many [had] perished in that way."

Understandably, bison had a healthy respect for fire, and the
scent of smoke in the air would send a herd fleeing in the direction
opposite the perceived source. Fire was a natural and frequent com-
ponent of the northern Plains. While most were caused by lightning,
the human occupants also learned to set fires to create a number of
desirable conditions. They long ago learned that grassland burned
off in one season came back greener, more nutritious, in the next, as
the burned grass provided fertilizer to the soil. The hunters knew
that bison would be attracted to these greener, freshly burned areas.
Again, many Europeans offer repeated witness to these events, perceiving the processes at work. Edwin James said that Indians "set fire
to the plains, in order to attract herbivorous animals, by the growth of
tender and nutritious herbage which springs up soon after the burning." Lewis and Clark in 1805 noted how bison head off in search of
"the fresh grass which immediately succeeds to the burning." David
Thompson, with decades of experience watching Aboriginal burning,
demonstrated amazing insight into the ecological processes of prairie
regeneration:

*Along the Great Plains, there are very many places where large groves of
Aspins have been burnt … and no further production of Trees have taken
place, the grass of the Plains covers them: and from this cause the Great Plains
are constantly increasing in length and breadth, and the Deer give place to the
Bison. But the mercy of Providence has given a productive power to the roots
of the grass of the Plains and of the Meadows, on which the fire has no effect.
The fire passes in flame and smoke, what was a lovely green is now a deep
black; the Rains descend, and this odious colour disappears, and is replaced
by a still brighter green; if these grasses had not this wonderful productive
power on which fire has no effects, these Great Plains would, many centuries
ago, have been without Man, Bird, or Beast.*

Prairie fires, driven by the fierce winds of the Plains, occasionally caused terrible devastation to bison herds. (Courtesy Head-Smashed-In Buffalo Jump)

† Many relative newcomers to the Plains mistook intentional Aboriginal fires for wanton destruction. John Sullivan, a member of the Palliser expedition failed to appreciate the many purposes of Aboriginal burning and attributed intentional burning to the simple purpose of communication: "The most trivial signal of one Indian to another has often lost hundreds of acres of forest trees which might have brought wealth and comfort to the future settler, while it has brought starvation and misery to the Indian tribes themselves by spoiling their hunting grounds. The Indians, however, never taught by experience, still use 'signal fires' to the same extent as in former years, driving the animals from their retreats and marring the fair face of nature for the future colonist."

So fires were intentionally lit, usually in the fall or spring, to attract herds into a certain region the following summer. Hunters then frequented these same areas, secure in the knowledge that bison would come.†

There has been much speculation about the intentional use of fire by Native people to move and drive bison herds. A casual glance at literature on bison hunting will turn up a number of comments that Native people lit fires to drive herds towards an intended kill site, such as a buffalo jump. In the mid-1800s, Schoolcraft stated that Indians used fire to surround herds of buffalo, "setting fire to the grass [to] encompass them on all sides. The buffalo, having a great dread of fire, retire towards the centre of the prairie as they see it approach, and here being pressed together in great numbers, many are trampled under foot, and the Indians rushing in with their arrows and musketry, slaughter immense numbers in a short period."

Fire may have occasionally been used intentionally to drive bison into a surround of some kind, but I suspect the circumstances permitting this were rare. The widespread use of fire to drive bison seems contrary to all we know about the need to precisely control the circumstances of the hunt. A prairie fire, even when lit by the experienced hands of people who managed fire continuously, is a dangerous thing. The critical things people consider when they set fires are the dryness of the grass, the strength and direction of the wind, and the lay of the land (flat versus sloping). Winds might prevail from a certain direction, but this is not to say they don't vary. A fire lit with a prevailing wind can still swirl, gust, surge in other directions. Not only might this be dangerous to people and their camps, fire and smoke, at the wrong time and place, could foil the efforts of Plains hunters to lure bison into a trap. Henry the younger witnessed Blackfoot men "driving whole herds from different directions, until these came within scent of the smoke, when they dispersed." Coaxing a herd to arrive at a highly specific destination leaves no room for error. It's not good enough to have a herd of bison come close to the opening of a pound, the mouth of a box canyon, or the edge of a cliff. Great effort was invested in making sure bison moved to an exact place where hunters lay in wait for the kill. Predictability was essential, and the unpredictability of a prairie fire argues against its being used for this purpose. Also, if indeed most communal kills took place in fall, grass is driest at this time and would burn fast and hot – not the most desirable conditions for control.

I once had my own encounter with a small prairie fire, and it was a scary moment. I had a crew out in the Head-Smashed-In gathering basin surveying some of the drive-lane cairns. It was a gorgeous sunny summer day. As the afternoon wore on, great thunderhead clouds piled up in the sky well to the north of us. We watched with only casual interest as rain and lightning pelted down on the Porcupine Hills in the far distance. It was a common afternoon occurrence and of no special concern when the action was many kilometres away. Then a bizarre thing happened.

Despite clear blue skies above and all around us, a bolt of lightning suddenly arced its way over from the storm to the north and literally landed at our feet. The moment was made all the more frightening by the fact that our surveying employed tall metal instruments, one of the worst elements to have around when lightning decides to pay a visit. I yelled at my crew to run for a nearby bedrock outcrop that had a small overhang where we could hide. Tucked under the rock, we waited out a barrage of many more very close strikes, with thunder rolling over us like cannon booms. Finally, the storm passed and we emerged to find the grass all around our survey gear on fire. It wasn't a raging fire, so using jean jackets, shovels, and our feet, we managed to put it out before it spread. Native elders have since told me that this was a sign; our work that day offended some spirit power. My own feeling was one of relief that no one was hurt, and this was a first-hand lesson in the unpredictable nature of lightning and prairie fires.

The inherent danger of fire on the prairies doesn't necessarily mean that people didn't harness this power to move bison toward an intended kill site. I just don't think they did it by torching the grasslands and hoping for the best. They may have lit contained fires, ones that they could be the master of rather than a slave to, and one way this might have been done is to carry fire with you as you moved into position for a bison drive. How do you carry fire? Using a mix of dry and moist grass, you make a small fire inside a rawhide pouch, one that allows you to open and close the top. Moist grass on the bottom prevents burning the pouch, and the mixed grasses give off more smoke than heat. Hunters could move behind a bison herd, putting themselves upwind, and then open and close the hide bags to let out puffs of smoke. The smoke drifts downwind into the herd, creating the impression of a grass fire moving towards them. The herd's instinct is to move away from the threat, downwind, and thus toward the intended kill location. Tricks such as this might have been used (there are a few historic accounts in support of it) during the early stages of rounding up the animals; that is, to get them into the general region of the kill site.† Beyond this, more precise means of controlling the herd were needed, and that's where the drive lanes and people who lined them took over.

† The artist Paul Kane seems to have witnessed this trick in the 1840s when he observed a hunter who had circled around a herd: He "strikes a light with a flint and steel, and places the lighted spunk in a handful of dried grass, the smoke arising from which the buffaloes soon smell and start away from it at the top of their speed." Alexander Henry probably observed the use of contained fires when he wrote that "the herd must be started by slow degrees. This is done by setting fire to dung or grass."

Luring the Buffalo

They generally drive the herd faster, until it begins to enter the ranges, where a swift-footed person has been stationed with a buffalo robe over his head, to imitate that animal ... When he sees buffaloes approaching, he moves slowly toward the pound until they appear to follow him; then he sets off at full speed, imitating a buffalo as well as he can, with the herd after him.
– Alexander Henry, 1809

Playing on known aspects of buffalo behaviour, Native hunters employed a great number of tricks to move them into the drive-lane complex. Some of them were relatively simple, others exceedingly complicated. An example of a simple trick would be the advantage hunters took of the fact that bison, like some other large game animals, have a decidedly curious streak. It was nothing as pronounced as seen in pronghorn (antelope), an exceedingly curious animal, a fact that, as James noted in 1819–20, occasionally led to its demise:

Considering the great expanse of territory on which bison had to be found, contained, and carefully moved, the task seems overwhelming. Head-Smashed-In at centre; gathering basin in the top half of photograph. (Courtesy Head-Smashed-In Buffalo Jump)

"The antelope possesses an unconquerable inquisitiveness, of which the hunters often take advantage … [He] conceals himself by lying down, then fixing a handkerchief or cap upon the end of his ramrod, continues to wave it, still remaining concealed. The animal, after a long contest between curiosity and fear, at length approaches near enough to become a sacrifice to the former." Although not as developed as that of the antelope, bison do have a certain curious nature, and if you know the tricks this trait can be manipulated.

Historic accounts of bison drives report Natives stealthily moving near the herds, falling to the ground, jumping into the air, twisting around several times, falling again, running a short distance, and doing it all again. Each action was punctuated by periods of calm where the hunters would lay or stand perfectly still. Understandably, European observers were completely perplexed by the antics of the Natives, although the great student of the Blackfoot, George Bird Grinnell, was one of the few to appreciate the nature of the ruse: "A man who was very skilful in arousing the buffalo's curiosity, might go out without disguise, and by wheeling round and round in front of the herd, appearing and disappearing, would induce them to move toward him, when it was easy to entice them into the chute [of the pound]."

What was going on here was a clever play on the curiosity of bison. These short, interrupted actions were just enough to capture the attention of the herd. Any of these actions alone would have been ineffective. Simply lying down or standing still would have drawn no attention, and persistent running would have spooked the animals. But a carefully timed combination of these, performed by experienced actors, was enough to capture the interest of the beasts.

The hunters would carefully position themselves between the grazing herd and the desired destination, in this case the opening of the drive-lane funnel. The hunters were downwind of the herd, since the wind must always be blowing over the herd and towards the kill site, keeping the scent of the waiting hunters and those at the camp from drifting back to the animals. Once in position, the actors commenced their bewildering charade. The less-than-keen eyes of the bison would stare long and hard at the figures. When the action ceased, they returned warily to grazing but maintained a watchful eye. When action started and stopped several times, the bison simply couldn't resist any longer, and they began to approach the figures. This was exactly the plan. Slowly the hunters retreated towards the cliff or pound, continuing their antics, never moving too much at any one time, drawing the curious but unsuspecting herd toward them and to their impending death.

Paul Kane, western artist and traveller, recorded another seemingly bizarre method of approaching bison herds, one that apparently played on the buffalo's tolerance for foreign sights within their field of view. It was the mid-1800s, near Edmonton, and Kane reports that the trick was used often and with great success:

It consisted in crawling on our bellies and dragging ourselves along by our hands, being first fully certain that we were to the leeward of the herd, however light the wind, lest they should scent us until we came within a few yards of them, which they would almost invariably permit us to do. Should there be twenty hunters engaged in the sport, each man follows exactly in the track of his leader, keeping his head close to the heels of his predecessor: the buffaloes seem not to take the slightest notice of the moving line, which the Indians account for by saying that the buffalo supposes it to be a big snake winding through the snow or grass.

George Frison (the reigning authority on buffalo jumps introduced earlier) has spent a lot of time around bison. He recounted

While the focus of this book is on communal hunting, it is important to remember that individual hunting was an almost constant part
of life on the Plains. Large communal hunts involving many groups
of people coming together to kill many animals were special events,
organized perhaps once a year, and sometimes not even that often.
Except for in the dead of winter, solitary hunting was a regular feature
of life for people who depended on the buffalo. Disguises were an
important part of the methods used in all types of bison hunting.

During their amazing trek westward, Lewis and Clark also had
the opportunity to witness buffalo runners using their tricks to bring
a herd to the intended kill:

*The mode of hunting is to select one of the most active and fleet young men,
who is disguised by a buffaloe skin round his body; the skin of the head with
the ears and horns fastened on his own head in such a way as to deceive the
buffaloe; thus dressed, he fixes himself at a convenient distance between a
herd of buffaloe and any of the river precipices, which sometimes extend
for some miles. His companions in the meantime get in the rear and side of
the herd, and at a given signal show themselves, and advance towards the
buffaloe; they instantly take the alarm, and finding the hunters beside them,
they run towards the disguised Indian or decoy, who leads them on at full
speed toward the river.*

The general assumption is that bison will follow these decoys
because they are fooled into thinking that it is one of their own and
that the decoy is leading them toward an escape from danger. Josiah
Gregg figured this out when he wrote, "A gang of buffalo is frightened
towards the pen, while an Indian, covered with one of their woolly
skins, runs at a distance ahead. Being seen by the animals, they mistake him for one of their kind, and follow him into the pen."

Without doubt my favourite account of buffalo runners using
disguises comes from the journals of Alexander Henry (the elder). It's
my favourite because it reveals the enormous depth of understanding
that Plains people had of their principal prey animal. While travelling
through central and western Canada in the 1760s and 1770s, Henry was
eyewitness to a bison hunt. In preparing to round up a nearby herd,
several buffalo runners draped themselves in the skinned-out hides
of bison. The decoys approached the unsuspecting buffalo "bellowing
like themselves. On hearing the noise, the oxen did not fail to give it
attention; and, whether from curiosity or sympathy, advanced to meet

those from whom it proceeded." Henry could not contain his astonishment as he watched the runners work the herd. So perfectly did they imitate the antics and sound of the bison – their gait, pace, sway, body movements – that Henry paid them the ultimate compliment:

At day light, several of the more expert hunters were sent to decoy the animals into the pound. They were dressed in ox-skins, with the hair and horns. Their faces were covered, and their gestures so closely resembled those of the animals themselves, that had I not been in the secret, I should have been as much deceived as the oxen.

Given the talent these runners had for deception, I can't help but wonder if, on a rare occasion, a disguised hunter was hit by an arrow or ball shot by compatriots who had lost track of the hunter and the hunted. I am likewise astonished when I ponder the degree of skill that must have been required to pull off such a flawless impression of another animal. Yet no one should be astonished. These are a people who spent thousands of years studying the habits of the animal that occupied the centre of their universe.

Lost Calves

When all is ready a young man, very swift of foot, starts at daylight covered over with a Buffalo robe and wearing a Buffalo head-dress. The moment he sees the herd to be taken, he bellows like a young calf, and makes his way slowly towards the contracted part of the funnel, imitating the cry of the calf, at frequent intervals. The Buffaloes advance after the decoy. – John Audubon, 1843

There is yet another remarkable take on the bison disguise trick. Not only did the buffalo runners perfectly imitate the movement of bison, they also duplicated the sound of the buffalo calf. It was not just any sound, but the specific call that is made when a calf becomes separated from its mother. Anyone who works with cattle knows that cows have a strong bond with their own calves. They are constantly checking to see where a calf is, ensuring that it doesn't come to any danger. Calves in turn have a mechanism to alert their mothers when they become separated. They make a loud bleating sound. This distress signal is guaranteed to get the attention of the cows, as they scan the herd and sniff the air, checking to see if it is their calf that has issued

† Thomas Woolsey, in
the mid 1800s, noted
a variation when he
observed a Native hunter
on horseback "imitating
the lowing of the cow.
On this being noticed
by the [herd], they are
instantly in motion and
probably hundreds of
them approach nearer to
him supposing that other
buffalos are contiguous."

the call. Bison cows and calves behave in the same manner. Ancient hunters knew this and took lethal advantage.

Picture a bison herd grazing in the Head-Smashed-In gathering basin. The wind is blowing from the west, over the herd and into the wide end of the drive-lane funnel, providing perfect conditions for a drive to the cliff. Buffalo runners drape bison calf skins over their bodies and move into position, placing themselves between the herd and the drive lanes. Their disguises permit them to move in close to the herd, always staying downwind, perfectly imitating the body movement of the calves. When close enough to be heard they begin making the bleating sound of a calf separated from its mother. Since the herd consists mainly of cows and calves – the preferred target group for nearly all Plains hunters – the trick has the desired effect. Cows raise their heads and check for their calves. Even if she knows her own calf is nearby, maternal instinct dictates that every cow will investigate the source of the plaintive bleating. A calf in danger can-not be ignored. In the distance to the east, they see a couple calves off by themselves, wandering away from the main herd, calling for help. The cows respond and start after the "lost calves."

The buffalo runners continue the hoax, wandering slowly away from the herd, into the mouth of the funnel, toward a mighty hunting party laying in wait. Since the cows can't see or smell any immediate threat to the lost calves, it is unlikely that they would run to their aid. After all, a bleating lost calf is a common occurrence, requiring only that the mothers eventually bring them back into the fold.† The runners keep up their calling and movement away from the herd, and the herd continues to follow, walking into the jaws of the trap.

The artist Paul Kane reported yet another ploy using disguises to attract cows, but this trick involved the clever combination of both wolves and bellowing calves. Hunting with his companion François, Kane described how a wolf attack is staged to attract the adults:

This ruse is generally performed by two men, one covering himself with wolf skin, the other with buffalo skin. They then crawl on all fours within sight of the buffaloes, and as soon as they have engaged their attention, the pretended wolf jumps on the pretended calf, which bellows in imitation of a real one. The buffaloes seem to be easily deceived in this way. As the bellow-ing is generally perfect, the herd rush on to the protection of their supposed young with such impetuosity that they do not perceive the cheat until they are quite close enough to be shot; indeed, François' bellowing was so perfect, that we were nearly run down. As soon, however, as we jumped up, they turned and fled, leaving two of their number behind, who paid the penalty of their want of discernment with their lives.

Although this multiple disguise trick was performed by Europeans, I have no doubt that it was learned from the Aboriginal hunters among whom Kane had spent time. Everything about it smacks of a Native understanding of bison behaviour.

Buffalo runners had a wide variety of clever ploys to move bison, but all of them had a single purpose: to bring distant herds into the confines of the drive-lane funnel. Once inside the lanes, hunters had a great deal more control over the movement of the beasts. The runners had the hardest job of all: getting unrestrained, free-roaming herds of wild animals to move to a single predetermined destination. One wrong move, a gust of wind from the wrong direction, a suspicious bleating call, a distant dog bark, a hunter showing himself at the wrong moment – the slightest miscue could send the herd fleeing off in any number of wrong directions. The efforts of many people could be instantly undone and an even greater effort required to correct the mistake and bring the herd back into position. People who work with modern bison will tell you that once a herd has been hazed and scattered, it is much more difficult to manage and may require several days to settle down before it can be approached successfully. We will never know how many attempted buffalo jumps failed because a herd was spooked at the wrong moment, but I suspect disappointment was not infrequent.†

With skill, an element of luck, and the blessing of the spirits, the carefully orchestrated ploys of the buffalo runners worked as designed, and the bison herds were drawn into the wide end of the funnel. How long this whole operation might have taken depended, of course, on a host of factors, such as the original distance of the herd from the cliff, the number and skill of the runners, the co-operation of the wind, and the peculiar behavioural traits of each distinct herd. On a good day, when everything just happened to fall into place, the entire drive may have lasted just a few hours. In the mid-1800s, Thomas Woolsey reported that a man might continue luring a herd by imitating the sound of a cow bison for up to two days. I'm sure that there were many instances where even greater time was spent getting

† In 1841 Robert Rundle wrote: "I had hoped to witness the capture of buffaloes by the method of decoying them but was doomed to be disappointed. Two or three herds were driven near the entrance whilst I remained there but they escaped by rushing off in a contrary direction to that of the mouth of the pond." An aged Peigan, Lazy Boy, told this story to John Ewers: "Their chief announced, 'Now we are going to make a buffalo fall.' They built a corral below a cliff and piled rocks at intervals in a great V-shape on the slope above the fall. Then they chose a man to lead the buffalo to the fall. But each time he lured them between the lines of rocks, they broke away before they reached the cliff edge. After this had occurred three times, Many Tail Feathers, a young man of that band, became angry. That night he made a fire and burned the corral."

Using the skins of bison calves, hunters managed to draw the predominantly cow–calf herds into the wide end of the drive-lane funnel. (Courtesy Shayne Tolman)

† Alexander Henry, a witness to Blackfoot bison drives early in the nineteenth century, stated that sometimes the lead bison broke through the ranks of people "carrying before them everything," and that "lives are sometimes lost" as Natives are trampled or thrown from the cliff.

herds into proper position. Once this was accomplished, many more people pitched in to contain the herd and keep it moving toward the cliff. These were the people stationed along the sides of the drive-lane cairns, carefully positioned so as to monitor the movement of the herd and to troubleshoot if the animals showed an inclination to turn around or make a break through the line of cairns.

While most Plains tribes shared similar habits of directing bison drives, one notable difference is seen in the composition of the people who monitored the lines of cairns. For some groups, only men partook in the activity. For others, women and older children joined in the efforts to contain the bison. The duties were much the same for everyone and generally consisted of waving arms or bison hides, shouting, and making as much of a scene as possible to keep the animals from approaching the sides of the funnel. At all costs the herd must be kept between the drive lanes and must not be allowed to turn back towards the unguarded gathering basin. Sometimes the cost was dear indeed. We know from historic records that herds did occasionally foil the drive attempt and charge through the line of cairns, trampling all those in their path.†

You might think the buffalo runners had done their duty and retired to rest while others concluded the drive, but written descriptions tell us that in many cases the runners continued to lead the herd right through the middle of the drive lanes, often having to run to keep ahead of the rapidly panicking bison. Some lost their

Once the buffalo runners had accomplished their job of getting the herd into the drive-lane funnel, a great number of people pitched in to keep the animals moving in the desired direction. (Courtesy Shayne Tolman)

lives in the process. Others were seriously injured. Lewis and Clark report that the result of the runners' deception was occasionally catastrophic: "Sometimes in this perilous seduction the Indian is himself either trodden under foot by the rapid movements of the buffaloe, or missing his footing in the cliff is urged down the precipice by the falling herd."

Special provisions were made to rescue these revered men. Though it seems incomprehensible, some runners escaped being trampled by ducking into specially dug holes in the ground, the herd thundering overhead, or into a prearranged hiding place. Again, Lewis and Clark provide compelling testimony, reporting that a runner "suddenly securing himself in some crevice of the cliff which he had previously fixed on, the herd is left on the brink of the precipice." Occasionally runners must have been killed or maimed in the process.

Sometimes prearranged places in heavily fortified sections of the drive lanes were prepared for a quick exit by the runner. People guarding the final stretch of the lane, possibly standing shoulder to shoulder and holding up bison hides, would part at the last moment to create a small opening for the runner to slip through. Interviewing a Gros Ventre woman born in 1854, Flannery was told that the buffalo runner "would run forward toward a steep precipice and just at the edge would jump aside while the buffalo following him would go over." The opening was immediately closed behind the runner to keep any bison in hot pursuit from getting the same idea. Instead of

† Mostly I have described young men as runners and a hectic pace to the rounding up and driving of bison herds, but Grinnell describes a more leisurely progression led by old Medicine Men: "When the old men got near the buffalo, they beckoned to them with the [bird] wings, and soon the buffalo began to come toward them. Then the old men turned about and walked toward the chute in front of the buffalo; and on either side of them, but a long way off, walked the two parties of painted young men. The young men did not sing, but if at any time the buffalo tried to turn aside in either direction from following the old men, the young men held their hands up to the sky and waved them in a certain way, and the buffalo turned back. After the old men had led the buffalo in between the wings, the opening between the wings was filled by the two parties of painted men who had followed them out, and all sang."

a wall of dark hides keeping bison contained in wooden pounds, the wall was formed of humans holding bison skins. Sometimes runners, either by chance or design, ended up leading the herd right to the edge of the cliff. Here they either ducked under the ledge of the cliff, dove through a temporary gap at the sides of the drive lanes, or, on a bad day, sailed over the cliff along with the frantic herd.

Other ingenious techniques were used by buffalo runners and other members of Native society to round up and move bison.† All involved some form of trick to either pull the herd towards something (the twisting, whirling humans; the lost calf) or to push the herd away from a perceived threat (a contained fire; hunters disguised as wolves or coyotes). The historic literature is rich in detail of this fascinating aspect of bison drives, but the literature is far from complete. Communal kills were enacted all over the Great Plains by a number of different tribal groups, many of which were never witnessed by any European visitor. No doubt, some methods of directing the movements of bison went unrecorded and are forever lost. Others still remain in the memories of select elders, waiting to be captured before they, too, fall victim to the passage of time and the end of the buffalo days. Such were the memories of Billy Strikes With A Gun.

Billy's Stories

If I ever had any doubts that contemporary Native elders still retained vital knowledge about the past, they were disposed of during the course of interviews I did before the opening of the interpretive centre at Head-Smashed-In. For many weeks I made the thousand-kilometre round-trip trek from my home to the Piikani (Peigan) cultural centre at the reserve town of Brocket to conduct interviews with elders. Though dozens showed up for the event (we provided free lunch), it always fell to just a few elders to carry the conversation. As I came to know more about Native culture, I realized that this was following proper protocol. In a room full of non-Native elders, when asked about particular experiences of our culture, I suspect that most of us would feel that we would have something to contribute. After all, we all have a personal history, and a family history, that provide us with insights into our culture and identity.

Native culture does not operate in the same manner. While everyone present has stories to tell, there is a matter of, for lack of a better

Piikani elder Billy Strikes with a Gun, centre, talks about the traditional days of buffalo hunting with help from Nick Smith, right. (Courtesy Royal Alberta Museum)

term, authority. When it comes to talking about their history, not everyone has the right to tell stories, not everyone has the recognized authority. There is clear recognition that certain individuals know the most traditional stories, the most correct versions of the people's history. A person doesn't acquire this status from education degrees, or by belonging to an important family, or by being successful in one's own life. It comes from recognition from one's peers that a person was raised in such a way that he or she inherited or was schooled in a great deal of traditional knowledge. Everyone knows who these people are.

In times past, all transmission of knowledge from one generation to the next was done by experienced people telling stories to the young. There were no books to consult, no classrooms, no libraries, no Google. There were just people who had lived through the important experiences of life and who passed this information on to the inexperienced. People living on the reserve today know who was raised in the most traditional families by parents, or often grandparents, who themselves were reared in families with a strong traditional background. These were the ones with authority to speak, the ones to whom everyone else deferred. Few had more authority than Billy Strikes With A Gun.

Billy was in his early seventies when I interviewed him in the mid-1980s. He had been raised mainly by his grandparents. They would have lived through the last half of the nineteenth century, the

† Europeans soon noted the same proclivity, and used well-worn bison trails to help them find water.

‡ While non-Natives might see the obvious benefit of the strong smell of sage in masking human scent, Aboriginal people employed the plant for its purifying effects. Sage was and still is used in many ceremonies: sacred medicine pipes are laid on a bed of sage; buffalo skulls, emblematic of the animal itself, have sage stuffed into the nostrils and eye sockets.

final days of the buffalo hunting culture. Billy was raised by people who had lived in tipis, travelled by horse, and hunted buffalo. When I asked questions about the old days, translated into Blackfoot, there might be some general discussion around the room, but soon someone would say, "Let Billy tell it." The room would become quiet, and Billy would speak, often at considerable length, telling stories and passing on information just as it had been passed to him.

There is a great responsibility that comes with being recognized as one of the precious few who carry the history of a people. It is imperative to recount what you have learned exactly as it was conveyed to you, without embellishment or change. That this code was rigidly followed was made clear to me when I compared Billy's words (when translated) to texts of traditional Blackfoot stories written in both Blackfoot and English in the early twentieth century. Astonishingly, I could follow along with the written text noting an almost word-for-word correspondence with Billy's version (the correspondence was so uncanny that there were fleeting moments where I thought that Billy must have read the same decades-old book, though I assumed this was not possible). But Billy also told stories that have never appeared in any book. One of them struck a special chord with me, because it provided insight into rounding up and moving bison towards a kill.

Billy told how sometimes buffalo jumps were held during winter. The conditions for the people were much more difficult, and they had to contend with cold, frozen ground, and drive lanes covered with snow. The people had to resort to other tricks, had to reach deep into their pool of knowledge. The Porcupine Hills were an excellent wintering place for herds of buffalo, so the animals were often gathered in the hills. The task was to move them toward the cliff. Billy told how people knew that bison are attracted to and will follow their own trails, perceiving them as a safe route of travel.† The trick was to create a fake trail, one that bison would perceive as a means of escape but that, in reality, led to death. Billy recounted how the hunters would first rub their bodies and moccasins with sage so as to hide their human smell.‡ Then they would take several tanned buffalo hides and head into the gathering basin, collecting all the frozen buffalo chips they could find. Chips (now freeze-dried and lightweight) were piled on the hides and dragged by the hunters until they reached the place where the drive would begin. Once in position, hunters walked backwards toward the edge of the cliff, dragging the chip-laden hides behind them. Billy explained how dragging the hides over the footprints of the people further served to mask the scent of the humans. As they walked, the hunters tossed out chip after chip, forming a long line of dark circles set against the snow or frozen ground. They continued this until they reached the edge of the cliff.

Hunters knew that bison preferred to follow an existing trail. After all, if the animals had travelled a certain route many times before, it must lead to safety. There are several dead giveaways that a trail is old. One clue is the deep ruts cut by thousands of sharp hoofs. Another is the ubiquitous dark circles of dung that, in earlier times, surely lined all paths the bison travelled. Hunters knew that this would be a chosen path of escape and so used dried buffalo chips to create a false trail leading to the cliff edge. By walking backwards and dragging hides behind them, they covered their own scent with that of the intended prey. A herd of bison, frightened by hunters circling around them, could see and smell a safe path of escape in the form of a beaten trail marked with a line of chips. Billy's story made perfect sense.

I had never seen this trick recorded in any literature, yet armed with a bit of knowledge about the nature of bison, I had no doubts about the authority of the account.† Billy has now passed away, a sad loss for the community and for all who yearn to know the past. Thankfully, some record of his profound knowledge was made before his passing.

The End of the Drive

When the buffalo appear inclined to take a direction leading from the space marked out by the "dead men," [the people] show themselves for a moment and wave their robes ... This serves to turn the buffalo slightly in another direction – Henry Youle Hind, 1857–58

Getting bison herds into the wide end of the drive lanes was far from the end of the drama and suspense. In terms of excitement and danger, it was just the beginning. Now the herd had to be contained and pressed ever forward. The stone cairns outfitted with brush or other flags could keep the animals on track even without hunters stationed nearby, but there is no question that nothing would contain the herd better than people, and the more the better. I envision

† Yet I did eventually find a variation of it, employing the same idea of creating a false trail for a drive during winter. Interviewing Blackfoot elders at the end of the 1800s, Grinnell wrote, "In winter, when the snow was on the ground, and the buffalo were to be led to the pis'kun [buffalo pound or jump], the following method was adopted to keep the herd travelling in the desired direction after they had got between the wings of the chute. A line of buffalo chips, each one supported on three small sticks, so that it stood a few inches above the snow, was carried from the mouth of the pis'kun straight out toward the prairie. The chips were about thirty feet apart, and ran midway between the wings of the chute. This line was, of course, conspicuous against the white snow, and when the buffalo were running down the chute, they always followed it, never turning to the right nor to the left."

The main drive lanes to the west of the Head-Smashed-In cliff show the general route of the drive out of the basin from southwest to northeast. (Courtesy Royal Museum of Alberta)

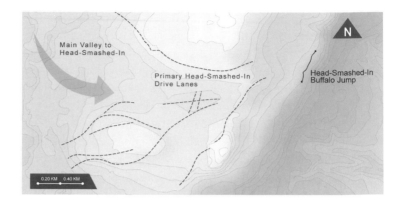

dozens, probably hundreds, of people, often including women and older children, moving back and forth along each side of the funnel, watching the movement of the herd, looking for trouble spots where the animals might test the strength of the lanes. Their job was to augment the cairns.

If the herd made a move toward one of the drive lanes, the waiting sentinels spooked the animals back into the centre of the funnel, then moved on to the next spot that might require attention. Meanwhile, those stationed at the distant end of the funnel waited for the herd to pass and then fell in behind, their job being to eliminate the possibility of the animals turning and heading back out of the funnel. In this way the bison were encouraged to move in one direction only, deeper into the ever-constricting wings of the drive lanes.

Clearly, this was a carefully choreographed event. There must have been frequent and critical communication between widely distant groups of people, presumably using signals of various kinds and shouts. "A man stood at the top of the hill," the aged Blackfoot Weasel Tail told John Ewers, "and gave a signal to the women and children, who were hiding behind the willow piles, when the buffalo were coming. As the buffalo passed them the women and children ran out from their hiding places."

Ewers' mention of women and children working the drive lanes is indeed interesting. Much about bison hunting (and Plains Native society, generally) is heavily male dominated. But the occasion of a great communal drive was an exception for many tribes. Blackfoot, Plains Cree, Assiniboine, Gros Ventre, Crow, and several other tribes are known to have employed women, children, and even old people to help steer bison toward the kill. Their roles were twofold. In some instances they positioned themselves along the drive lanes, shouting, waving their arms and bison robes as the herd thundered past; other times they formed a rear guard, sweeping in behind the herd as it moved past, preventing escape. As Alexander Henry observed in the early 1800s, as the bison enter the drive lanes, "every man, woman, and child runs to the ranges that lead to the pound, to prevent the buffalo from taking a wrong direction."

It might sound as if a full-blown stampede of bison was, at this point, in progress. Far from it. The great majority of movement leading up to and through the drive lanes was almost certainly of a much more gentle, though deliberate, nature. Henry the younger noted just this pattern when he wrote, "Young men are usually sent out to collect and bring in the buffalo – a tedious task which requires great patience, for the herd must be started by slow degrees." Henry, astutely observing the gentle, coercive nature of a drive, remarked that bison are not so much run to their death, but, rather, "they are in a manner *enticed* to their destruction" [my emphasis].

The drive probably consisted of short bursts of movement where the herd scampered ahead, followed by a lull where the hunters purposefully allowed them to rest and remain calm. Patiently, the hunters waited for the herd to regroup, perhaps resume grazing, and then looked for an opportunity to nudge them ahead another short distance. A full stampede any distance from the edge of the

As the herd passed along the sides of the drive lanes, hunters fell in behind to ensure that the buffalo did not turn around to escape out the back of the funnel. (Courtesy Shayne Tolman)

Bison are gregarious animals that travel in large herds. That they run as a group and follow leaders was key to the success of communal kill events. (Courtesy Glenbow Archives/NA 3878-95)

cliff was undesirable and was actively avoided. But why not take full advantage of having the herd trapped inside the drive lanes and run them immediately toward the cliff? Why risk prolonging the event, increasing the chances that something might go wrong and have the animals escape? As with everything connected with a buffalo drive, there were sound reasons behind the human actions, reasons again rooted in an ancient understanding of the nature of the prey.

Bison are herd animals, a gregarious species that prefers to live and travel in large groups. When harassed or in trouble they run as a group, with certain mature cows recognized as the leaders. But imagine a herd of one or two hundred bison running over a long distance, say several kilometres. Every herd will automatically include a wide array of individuals, very old, very young, sick, wounded, and healthy prime animals. A herd of this diversity might well start off running as a tight group, but it won't last long. In short order, the prime animals will sprint into the lead, some of the sick and old will start to lag behind, some of the very young will not have fully developed flight instincts and might run for a bit and then stop, causing the mothers to also halt their progress. Over the course of a moderate distance, a stampeding herd will lose its cohesion, becoming a strung-out line of animals rather than a running pack. Why would this be a bad thing? After all, if the prime cows are in the lead, and these are the most desirable animals, why not just keep driving the leaders toward the cliff and ignore the stragglers?

The answer has everything to do with the difference between a successful massive kill and utter failure. Hunters understood that running a long, strung-out herd of bison toward a cliff might well end with the killing of none, while getting a tight pack of animals to the precipice could end with killing all of them. It led Native hunters to avoid a full blown stampede until the final course of the drive, perhaps the final kilometre, or less. Before that, the drive likely progressed as an admixture of short spurts of movement and periods of rest, both for the bison and the hunters. This continued into the ever-constricting drive lanes. The tapering of the funnel permitted greater numbers of people to congregate along the narrowest parts of the lane, where the need for control, and the danger, was greatest.

Of Illusions, Pickup Trucks, and Curves in the Road

There are a number of important things that happen near the end of the drive to the cliff. Each is seemingly minor, but in combination they are part of the constellation of features that helped transform Head-Smashed-In into a most effective bison killing machine. Many buffalo jumps operated without any number of the special attributes that are present at Head-Smashed-In, but they didn't operate as often or as successfully.

The final stretch of the drive lanes swings through a prominent yet shallow valley that lies behind the jump. This valley perfectly guides the animals toward the cliff and would have been a major help in containing the herd – the buffalo confined to the valley bottom, the

This view across the main channel leading to the jump shows the high points of land on either side of the valley (foreground and background) that may have been used for observing the progress of the drive. (Courtesy Royal Alberta Museum)

† There are a number of theories as to why stone cairns suddenly disappear along the final stretch of the drive at Head-Smashed-In. One informant told me that the rocks were collected to form rip-rap for a weir on the Oldman River. With an abundance of surface rock blanketing the prairie much closer to the river, I find this hard to believe. More likely, given that the final run is both downhill and down wind, silt and sand, blown over the crest of the ridge, may have covered the small rock piles.

hunters and rock cairns commanding the high ground on each side. As you would expect, lines of stone cairns snake their way along both sides of this valley, a silent reminder that this was the path chosen by ancient map-makers thousands of years ago.

From their vantage point above the herds, the hunters had the upper hand in preventing the herd from rising up the sides of the valley and escaping. Other hunters poured into the valley bottom behind the herd to keep them from turning around. But this perfectly formed trap doesn't continue right to the edge of the cliff. Approaching the final five hundred metres of the drive, the valley rises up a gradual slope out of the gathering basin and crests the ridge marking the top of the local hill behind the jump. Here the valley becomes less defined, broader, flatter, and it probably presented a greater challenge to controlling the herd. Unfortunately, stone cairns can no longer be found along this final stretch, so it is difficult to know the exact course of the drive.†

After cresting the ridge, the land drops down a slight slope and begins the final run toward the cliff. A slight valley continues along this downslope run, and in the absence of stone cairns we can assume that the hunters sought to maintain control by keeping the animals in the lowest part of the land. Once, as an experiment, I walked the final distance toward the jump, instructing myself to keep to the lowest point of land. Crossing over this broader, rolling country, I swerved back and forth, always taking the lowest path. I worked my way east toward the cliff, eventually intersecting the sandstone escarpment exactly above the spot where the deep archaeological digs have been conducted, the place we think served as the major kill site. It seems likely that my footsteps that day followed the same path as the thundering herds of buffalo.

The final run to the cliff is all slightly downhill. This fact had two very important consequences that made Head-Smashed-In all that much more deadly. First, a downhill run takes advantage of the weight distribution in bison. They are massive animals, but a great deal of that mass is concentrated in the front end of the beast. The head is huge, with thick skull bones, horns, and massive sheets of neck muscle needed to hold up the mighty head. Also, the thickest part of the hide is found around the neck, which is why Natives used hide from the neck for making their war shields. Poised over the shoulder of the front legs is the great hump of the buffalo, a mass of

The bedrock on each side of the channel leading to the jump has been etched with petroglyphs (rock carvings). The meaning of these grooves, lines, and circles is unclear, but their placement on each side of the final approach to the kill – and nowhere else in the area – suggests a relationship with the bison drive. (Courtesy Royal Alberta Museum)

fat and muscle intertwined around the tall bony spines of the thoracic vertebrae. Below the hump is the deepest part of the chest, and the powerful front legs. Buffalo are like pickup trucks, the engine and weight housed in the front end, the rear end relatively light and poor for traction.

A front-heavy animal running downhill has a much more difficult time stopping or turning. Its weight carries it forward, propelling its motion. To be sure, bison are fantastic runners going downhill. Modern studies have shown bison increase their speed when running downhill, especially during a stampede. A century and a half ago, Edward Harris, ascending the Missouri with Audubon, commented on a chase made over "a long [downhill] slope of a couple of miles, giving greatly the advantage to the Buffalo who run with remarkable speed down hill, while the speed of a horse is sensibly checked." It's not that bison don't run fast downhill; it's that they have much less control than a horse does.

As the animals approached the final metres before the cliff, they would surely try to stop hard to avoid the precipice. Bison have no innate desire to plunge from the edge of a high cliff. Running on level ground, or slightly uphill, they would have a much better chance to take evasive action. But running downhill, the buffalo are at a distinct disadvantage, the momentum of their weight pulls them onward. Last minute turns or stops are just all that much more awkward and difficult. It isn't a requirement that a buffalo jump has a downhill run at the end, but it sure helps. When interviewed in the 1940s by John Ewers, Weasel Tail recounted how "We built a corral near the edge of timber toward the bottom of a downhill slope."

The second advantage of a downhill run at the end of the buffalo drive is more elusive. I had never seen it written about and only noticed it many years after I began working at Head-Smashed-In. Along with several members of my crew, I was exploring the land

As you look down the final run of the drive, the cliff disappears as the lower prairie appears to merge with the uplands. Note the roof of the interpretive centre in the middle of the shot. (Courtesy Royal Alberta Museum)

† A member of the 1960s archaeology crew told me how they made a frightening discovery of the same effect. While moving excavation gear from the back side of the cliff, the driver of the pick-up truck came down the final sloping prairie, failed to notice the precipice, and nearly drove over the edge.

above the cliff. I was further upslope from my crew and turned to look back. As my eyes scanned across the figures and the shortgrass prairie around them, I noticed something amiss, as if I was looking in the wrong direction. Where was the cliff? Had I somehow gotten turned around? I could see my crew, and grasslands extending well beyond them, beyond them forever, as far as my eye could see. The downhill aspect to the final run to the cliff creates an optical illusion. Because you are looking down, the land beyond the cliff simply merges with the foreground, creating the appearance of a continuous stretch of prairie with no interruption, no deadly break in the slope. The cliff virtually disappears.†

Human eyesight is relatively good compared to the weaker eyes of bison. As the animals pounded down the final leg of the drive, they would have been even harder pressed than I to spot the edge of the cliff. They would have perceived a vast prairie in front of them – escape, freedom, relief from the pressing force of the nearby hunters. They may have run even harder over this final stretch, fixated by a belief that safe exit lay just ahead. Again, the illusion created by the downhill run isn't essential to a buffalo drive, but it is one more piece of an enormous complex of factors that contributed to Head-Smashed-In being perhaps the premier of all jumps.

The final important thing that happens at the end of the drive is again subtle, but it is a characteristic that Head-Smashed-In shares with a few other communal buffalo kills. It is a turn in the direction of the stampede. Leading up to the final stretch, the last several kilo-metres of the drive lanes winding their way through the gathering basin have been essentially straight, trending west to east. But as the lanes crest the ridge and begin the downhill run, there is a broad, gentle sweep to the north. The valley of confinement becomes less distinct here, but there still is a definite low point of land – the one I followed that day when I walked to the very edge of the cliff. It is this lowest part of the land that makes a subtle curve to the north. Not due north, parallel to the cliff, but northeast, so that the path of the drive still intersects the cliff edge, just at more of an angle rather than straight on.

This trait seems to have been intentionally selected by ancient hunters, as it shows up at a number of bison jumps and pounds on the Great Plains. Writing about bison pounds built by the Plains Cree, Mandelbaum stated, "The chute took a sharp turn just before the entrance to the enclosure so that the onrushing herd could not see the corral until it was too late to stop. Men were stationed at this bend and at several places along the chute."

The intent of the curve near the end of the drive seems clear. It was to help perpetuate for as long as possible the illusion that no trouble lay ahead, to hide the presence of the cliff until the last possible moment. Bison cresting the ridge and stampeding down the final leg, assuming hunters commanded the high ground and animals were confined to the shallow valley, had to curve their path towards the northeast if they wanted to avoid the people shouting and waving robes who were perched to both sides of them. Running this curve and looking ahead into the distance, even if just for a few moments, takes their eyes off the position of the cliff. Every second the animals didn't see the danger that lay before them was one more fraction of an advantage for the hunters and one more nail in the coffin of the stampeding herd. That this trait shows up at a number of buffalo kill sites suggests that these few seconds were critical to the success of the drive.

The final route of the drive came east through the channel, over the ridge crest, and then turned to the northeast and headed downhill toward the cliff. (Courtesy Royal Museum of Alberta)

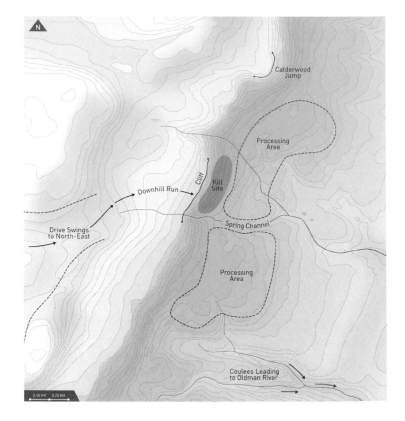

If all went as planned, if the Spirit Beings were appropriately appeased, if the wind was right, if the buffalo runners executed their roles with skill, if the herd was in the right place and of the right composition, and if every other factor fell into place, a thundering herd of perhaps a hundred or more five-hundred- to one-thousand-kilogram animals bore down on the edge of a steep escarpment. The moment of truth had arrived. The most crucial few seconds in the lives of many Plains Aboriginal groups, and for countless buffalo, were about to begin. These few seconds have made buffalo jumps famous and infamous around the world. In a global perspective, they must have been some of the most dramatic moments of any hunting and gathering society on earth.

CHAPTER 6

The Great Kill

The poor affrighted animals were eddying about in a crowded and confused mass, hooking and climbing upon each other; when the work of death commenced. – George Catlin, 1832–39

Probably not many people have spent time wondering what they would do if they had a time machine, but most archaeologists have. It is the ultimate weapon: the invention that will put us all out of work. Before that happened, hopefully we would get a chance to try it out, to act as some kind of quality control specialists, to take it for a test drive. Imagine the range of answers you would get if you were to ask archaeologists where they would go if they had one trip in a time machine. Some would be on hand for the carving and erection of an Easter Island statue. Some would be deep underground in the Valley of the Kings in the burial chamber of King Tutankhamen as his funeral procession arrived. Others would set up their lawn

A stampeding bison herd was a powerful force on the landscape that could be felt, heard, seen, and smelled over great distances. (Courtesy Jim Peaco, U.S. National Parks Service)

The precarious situation of hunters positioned along the end of the drive, where the herd finally appreciated the nature of the trap, is almost impossible to imagine. (Courtesy Shayne Tolman)

† "Still their advance is somewhat frightful," Gregg wrote in the 1830s, "their thundering rumble over the dry plain ... puffing like a locomotive engine at every bound, does at first make the blood settle a little heavy about the heart." In 1811 Henry Brackenridge observed, "Late in the evening we saw an immense herd in motion along the sides of the hill ... The sound of their footsteps, even at the distance of two miles, resembled the rumbling of distant thunder." Despite being two miles from a large herd, Palliser records, "They were in such numbers that their peculiar grunt sounded like the roar of distant rapids in a large river, and causing a vibration also something like a trembling in the ground."

chairs on the Salisbury Plain, soaking up the action as the massive rocks of Stonehenge were raised into place. More than a few would recline on Capitoline Hill to watch the birth of Rome. I'd be standing at the edge of the cliff of Head-Smashed-In Buffalo Jump as a herd of stampeding bison bore down on the precipice. And if I only get to do this once, let it be a big herd.

My favourite scene in *Dances with Wolves* isn't the dramatic buffalo hunt or the panoramas of majestic Great Plains scenery (much as I appreciated these) but a more subtle moment. The character Kevin Costner portrays, John J. Dunbar, is asleep on the ground in his little shack of a home on the prairie. Gradually, a low rumbling sound comes through the theatre speakers. The camera pans past trembling glasses, cups, bottles. As Dunbar stirs, everything in the cabin starts to shake more violently. The rumbling builds to a thunder and the audience begins to shake too. Suddenly aware that his life is in imminent danger, Dunbar rushes outside to find a huge herd of stampeding buffalo bearing down.

This part of the film, at least, isn't your usual Hollywood fabrication. There are numerous testimonials from early fur traders, hide hunters, and pioneers attesting to the sheer physical chaos of a thundering bison herd.† The ground really did shake, apparently for kilometres around. And just like in the movies, an experienced Native scout could put his ear to the ground, listen carefully for a moment, and declare buffalo nearby. Sometimes entire camps and crews of

European hide hunters were obliterated in a tidal wave of brown fur. Such is the power of the pounding of hundreds, if not thousands, of massive hoofs. This is where I'd go if I had a time machine – to the moment and the place of thundering hoofs.

The terminal moments of a great buffalo drive were without parallel in the events of world prehistory. Nowhere else, on any continent at any time, did human beings kill such a staggering amount of food in a single moment. For sheer raw power, unbridled danger, nail-biting suspense, and rampant drama, there may be nothing in the archaeological record that can match the final few seconds of a herd of stampeding buffalo arriving at the edge of a steep cliff. Right there alongside them, standing maybe less than a metre or two away from an out-of-control freight train of biomass, unprotected except for their knowledge of what the animals should do under most circumstances, was a small group of vulnerable, ancient hunters.

Leap of Faith

A dreadful scene of confusion and slaughter then begins, the oldest and strongest animals crush and toss the weaker; the shouts and screams of the excited Indians rise above the roaring of the bulls, the bellowing of the cows, and the piteous moaning of the calves. The dying struggles of so many huge and powerful animals crowded together, create a revolting and terrible scene.
– Henry Youle Hind, 1856–57

It should be obvious that the term *buffalo jump* is a serious misnomer. Bison didn't jump from the cliff into the air. They fell, they stumbled, they sailed, they rolled, they were pushed, but they most certainly did not jump. Still, it's a great name for this type of site and no doubt will be with us for a long time to come. As I noted at the end of the previous chapter, a series of events and circumstance conspired to ensure that the final stretch of the buffalo drive would end in success. The downhill run to the cliff helped hide the existence of the cliff until the last moment and made it especially difficult for the front-heavy animals to turn or stop. A curve in the route of the drive likewise veiled the precipice and kept the animals preoccupied with following the apparent course of escape. But all this trickery and advantage was about to end. The herd was now in full stampede, hunters swarming in from behind, others hazing from the sides.

Perhaps the most preposterous depiction of a buffalo jump has a comic book he-man figure about to club a panicking buffalo over the cliff, while the trusty steed of a mounted hunter prances a mere metre from the precipice. Painting by William R. Leigh. (Courtesy Buffalo Bill Historical Center, Cody, Wyoming; 13.69)

As bison galloped, their heads and shoulder humps rocked up and down, a characteristic of stampeding bison that led early Europeans to compare them, quite appropriately, to the swells of the ocean. A veritable sea of brown hair and ominous black horns rolled toward the cliff like a huge dark wave.

As the final metres flew under hoof, consider this. Bison are wild and intelligent animals. They did not survive millions of years of evolution by being stupid. They emphatically did not willingly or carelessly throw their bodies into the empty abyss that lay waiting one step beyond the shelf of rock. And no matter how many tricks had been played on them, how much they had been deceived, and how well the cliff edge was hidden, eventually they saw it. The leaders of the stampede at some point sensed the imminent danger that lay ahead (and the better designed the jump, the later this happened). If they were so smart, so well adapted to survival, why didn't they stop at the last moment, why didn't they charge into the ranks of frail humans, easily crushing them beneath their hoofs, and run to freedom to live another day?

Ancient hunters had planned and designed everything for this one moment, to ensure there would be no escape. One of the most

The next-most preposterous rendering of a buffalo jump is Alfred Miller's 1837 painting, in which a wave of bison stretching to the horizon pours mindlessly into a gaping chasm in the earth. If these animals were ever to be seen again it would be as hamburger. The mounted hunters are themselves moments away from a deadly plunge. (Courtesy Library and Archives Canada/C-000403)

† In his engagingly written book, *American Bison: A Natural History*, Dale Lott captures the instinct of the bison to run as a group: "Be a bison. A bison cow on the run, adrenaline soaring, heart racing, hooves flying. On the run from what? From whatever the bison all around you are running from. Something scared them, and the voice of your species' experience tells you that when others run, safety lies in running with them. Being left behind is dangerous; so you run, simultaneously spurred and reassured by the pounding hooves beside you, before you, behind you. Predators can't come through another bison, so hold your position and run."

important things they did was to wait until the very last moment to start the full stampede. As described previously, a mixed herd of bison will only run in a tight group formation for a short distance before some members – old, young, weak, sick, or a few obstinate bulls – start to drop out of the race. Even the most fit, run over a considerable distance, will start to stagger into a line of charging animals, rather than a tight pack. And a pack is what is desired, even necessary, when the herd arrives at the edge of the cliff. It is thought that if a *line* of two hundred bison arrives at the edge of a cliff, you end up killing none of them, but if a *pack* of two hundred arrives, you kill them all. Obviously there is little in the way of actual data to back this up, but the theory is compelling.

Bison herds have recognized leaders (usually females). All the animals know who the leaders are and will turn to them in times of trouble to see what the leaders are doing. If the leaders run, then they all run.† European hide hunters quickly recognized this fact and made a point of aiming their long rifles at the leaders first, knowing this would put the rest of the group in disarray, giving the hunters more time to pick off additional animals. Aboriginal hunters wanted the leaders to lead, but they wanted them to guide the entire herd as one unit. Because bison are indeed fast, agile on their feet, and intelligent, hunters knew that when the leaders finally did see the edge of the cliff, they would do everything in their power to avoid it, including crashing through the people stationed along the end of the drive lanes. The only hope of avoiding this stall was to have a great mass of animals arrive at the same time. As the leaders approached the cliff,

There are no living eyewitnesses to describe the sights, sounds, and smells of a herd of bison plunging from a steep cliff. (Courtesy Shayne Tolman)

sensed the danger, and tried to turn, the mass of animals following immediately behind crashed into them, bowled them over, pushed them sideways, forward, rolling, falling. When running as a tight pack, only the leaders saw the danger; the others followed blindly on the tails of those in front. As the leaders tried to stop or turn, it was the crush of those right behind that ensured a wave of bison would go cascading over the edge of the cliff.

Lewis and Clark were among the few European explorers to appreciate this critical aspect of the drive. Describing the final moments of a buffalo jump, as the herd is brought to the brink of the precipice, they noted, "it is then in vain for the foremost to retreat or even to stop; they are pressed on by the hindmost rank, who seeing no danger but from the hunters, goad on those before them till the whole are precipitated and the shore is strewed with their dead bodies."

Everybody should have something that they think about when they turn off the lights at night and stare up at the dim outline of the ceiling. I have often tried to picture the sights, sounds, and smells of a mighty herd of bison plunging from a high rock precipice. The panic of the leaders as they finally realized the terrible fate in front of them; their frantic efforts to dig their hoofs into the earth, shift their weight, move to the side; the chaos of trailing animals slamming into the sprawling leaders, tumbling over them; the surge of twisted, contorted, bellowing brown bodies plunging from the precipice; the flailing of legs, searching in vain for purchase in the air as animals somersaulted from the precipice; the sickening thud of bodies slamming into the soft earth; the horrible bellowing of those first animals as they were hit again and again by more bison piling on top of them; the mound of thrashing, writhing brown bodies that formed beneath the cliff; the final wave of animals sailing into this mass of moving flesh, bouncing off, tumbling to the sides. It adds up to a pretty heavy night of ceiling staring.†

Palliser provides riveting testimony of the final moments of a mass bison kill. Marching with his 1857–60 expedition, he heard in the distance "the bawling and screaming of an immense [Indian] camp, all in a high state of excitement." Approaching, he discovered the Natives had succeeded in driving (curiously, during the night) a large herd of bison into a wooden pound and were now engaged in the slaughter. "The scene was more repulsive than pleasant or exciting," he wrote, for into the corral were "crammed more than 100 buffalos, bulls, cows, and calves."

A great number were already killed, and the live ones were tumbling about furiously over the dead bodies of their companions, and I hardly think the space would have held them all alive without some being on the top of the others, and, in addition, the bottom of the pound was strewn with fragments of carcases left from former slaughters in the same place.

Confined to the pound, the terrified animals "run round and round violently," Palliser reported, and noted with curiosity that Natives claim the animals always circled "with the sun," that is, clockwise (east to west) within the corral. Fifty years earlier Daniel Harmon noted the same curiosity, substantiating it with the assertion that this "I have frequently seen myself." Palliser then describes how "Indians, even mere boys and young girls," were stationed on the walls of the corral, "all busy plying bows and arrows, guns and spears, and even knives, to compass the destruction of the buffalo." Faced with a large kill, one can imagine how hunters ran low on ammunition. Palliser witnessed chilling efforts to retrieve weapons:

† Hind must have had some sleepless nights as well. Witness his harrowing account of the final, grisly moments of a bison pound: "A sight most horrible and disgusting broke upon us as we ascended a sand dune overhanging the little dell in which the pound was built. Within a circular fence 120 feet broad, constructed of the trunks of trees, laced with withes together, and braced by outside supports, lay tossed in every conceivable position over two hundred dead buffalo. From old bulls to calves of three months old, animals of every age were huddled together in all the forced attitudes of violent death. Some lay on their backs, with eyes starting from their heads, and tongue thrust out through clotted gore. Others were impaled on the horns of the old and strong bulls. Others again, which had been tossed, were lying with broken backs two and three deep. One little calf hung suspended on the horns of a bull which had impaled it in the wild race round and round the pound."

After firing their arrows they generally succeeded in extracting them again by a noose on the end of a pole, and some had even the pluck to jump into the area and pull them out with their hands; but if an old bull or a cow happened to observe them they had to be very active in getting out again.

At a buffalo jump, the plunge from the cliff is far from the end of the excitement. Once the waterfall of flesh had ceased, a bizarre scene faced the hunters waiting below; a mound of seething brown fur, moving like some giant organic pyramid. Many bison, of course, were dead on impact or crushed to death by those who followed them. But many, especially the later arrivals, survived the fall but were in varying stages of injury: some had broken limbs, some had broken ribs, necks or backs. Some, by the sheer luck of the draw, managed to land and roll in such a way as to avoid injury entirely. The scene below the cliff would truly have been one of controlled chaos. People running frantically around the mound of animals trying to kill the wounded and yet avoid being killed; bison stumbling, rolling, dragging themselves from the pyramid, and the few fortunate ones, dazed and confused, up and running for freedom. All this demanded immediate attention. Wounded bison had to be quickly dispatched to prevent injury to the hunters and so the butchering could begin. Unscathed buffalo had to be chased down and killed. No matter how big the kill, no matter how many animals already lay dead and dying, any survivors had to be pursued and killed.

Paul Kane's beautiful but inaccurate rendering of the final moments of a buffalo pound shows several hunters reclining restfully along the lanes and at the entrance to the pound as the herd thunders past. (Courtesy Royal Ontario Museum)

Overkill?

Nothing of the buffalo was wasted and every possible part was eaten even to the predigested vegetable food from the stomach and the soft inner part of the hoofs. – Regina Flannery, on the Gros Ventre, 1953

The savages wage a merciless war on [the buffalo]; it can be said that they waste a great many. For instance, the Osage leave from one hundred to one hundred and fifty pounds of excellent meat on every carcass. – Victor Tixier, 1840

One of the most frequent public enquiries I deal with has to do with the issue of Aboriginal hunters as the original ecologists. Were they careful stewards of the land and its resources, or wanton exploiters of its resources? Buffalo jumps figure prominently in this debate, because they are sometimes portrayed as examples of great waste on the part of ancient hunters. Surely there must have been times when many more bison were killed than were needed or could be used. When especially large herds were brought to the cliff, was there an effort to reduce the size of the kill, recognizing that not all the animals were needed and leaving some for future kills? Did the hunters try to stop the drive after a great number were already dead or, alternatively, let the survivors of the jump run to freedom? The answers to these questions are complex and require us to look at cultural values and beliefs in a way very different from that in which we are accustomed.

Most of us think of hunting as a matter of choice, that hunters can choose to shoot an animal or choose not to, with the decision hinging on a variety of immediate contingencies. For Aboriginal people living on the Great Plains, hunting wasn't a choice. It was the basis of life. This is why Native hunters went to such extraordinary lengths to orchestrate great communal kills, such as buffalo jumps. Most non-Aboriginal people living in modern society are divorced from actually having to hunt for a living and were raised with Western-based ideas of science and conservation. We are taught to separate the human from the animal and natural world, that humans stand alone at the pinnacle of the chain of life, that humans alone possess great cognitive powers, allowing us to appreciate and understand the world around us. Animals, plants, rocks, and water – the earth itself – lack these cognitive powers. People schooled in this fashion, which includes me, tend to think that this is the way the whole world is, just as we surely believe that all people on earth see the colour blue in the same way or count from one to ten just as we do.

It is no easy matter to appreciate that people all over the world, and for all time, have found and embraced different ways of perceiving the reality of the universe around them. It is a humbling experience to realize that other cultures have devised their own unique answers and solutions to the puzzles that have challenged humankind: thunder and lightning might be the voice of spirits rather than a discharge of energy; perception of colour can be conditioned by your culture; some natives of the Amazon jungle count one, two, and three, and no further.

The belief system of Aboriginal inhabitants of the Plains differs from that taught by Western science. Rocks, plants, animals, water, earth, and sky belong to one world, along with people. These non-human parts of existence have powers and abilities that are unknown in contemporary western teachings. Rocks, special ones in special places, might have their own power and be revered, respected, and included in the ceremonial world. Animals were viewed as having many of the same abilities as people: they were sentient beings, conscious and perceptive of the world around them, and most importantly, were connected with the spirit world. The survival of people, the success of future hunts, depended on maintaining a sense of harmony with the spirit world. This in turn had many implications for how hunts were conducted and how animals were treated. How many animals were needed at any one time to feed the people? The question is what was the proper way to conduct a hunt so that the spirit world was kept in balance, thus ensuring that future hunting efforts would be successful?

Perhaps the best example of putting these beliefs into practice came at the end of the buffalo jump, when wounded and unscathed animals were attempting to escape. At this moment, in the case of a large kill, the hunters could choose to ignore these surplus animals, letting them live for a future kill. But they did not. Universally across the Plains, bison-hunting cultures made every effort to kill all the animals brought to the trap, be it a jump, pound, or other type of communal kill. They did this regardless of whether or not they had just killed ten, one hundred, or one thousand animals. They didn't do this because they were bloodthirsty or wasteful, even if at times it meant that they could not use all of the slain animals. They did it because their belief system dictated that it had to be done. To the Plains hunters, bison possessed many of the same attributes as people. Buffalo were aware of the world around them, perceived the behaviour of humans, and recognized patterns of actions and their consequences.

Despite being well aware of their own wanton slaughter, many Europeans roundly condemned Plains Indians for overkill and waste.[†] Yet a few perceived that something more complex was at work. Alexander Henry, on the Plains at the beginning of the nineteenth century, wrote that at the end of the drive, "not one of the whole herd do they allow to escape; large and small, fat and lean, all must fall, to prevent alarming other herds." On the Plains at about the same time, John Bradbury came across a group of bison skulls that had sage stuffed into the eye sockets and nostrils. When he asked for an explanation, his Native guides told him this was done to "prevent them [the skulls] from apprising the living buffaloes of the danger they run in approaching the neighbourhood."

Native beliefs about hunting and killing may be best expressed by Thomas Woolsey, who, describing a buffalo pound operation in the mid-1800s, made a critical observation regarding hunters not allowing any animals to escape:

They could easily shoot such as they mean to take and let the rest go off again, but the Indians maintain that if this was done, the same buffalo could never be taken a second time and that they would also make known to others the deception that had been practised upon them.

As I have tried to convey in these pages, a tremendous amount of effort, and spiritual belief, went into planning, organizing, and executing communal kills. And a great amount of trickery and deception was employed in making sure the kill succeeded and that people were unharmed. All the animals brought through the jaws of the trap have now experienced this deception. They had seen how they were repeatedly tricked and, in the belief of the hunters, they were not about to forget it.

All the bison had to be killed because they now knew too much. They knew the secrets of the trap. Survivors would mingle back into other herds and spread the knowledge of how they had been deceived. Future attempts at driving bison to a kill were doomed to failure if survivors were allowed to escape and join up with unsuspecting herds. Plains hunters tried to kill all the animals brought to the jump

† Supreme in this regard had to be Edward Harris. He frequently referred to being "ashamed" and that he "regretted" his senseless slaughter of bison, adding that for one hunt "we had no means of carrying home the meat and after cutting out the tongues we wended our way back to camp, completely disgusted with ourselves and with the conduct of all white men who come to this country." Yet on the way back from that very hunt he joined in another because "the temptation was too strong." But a callousness developed, and he perked up with the realization that "ere long our consciences became pretty well scar[r]ed and we had no more feeling at the death of a Buffalo Bull than at the demise of a Towhee Bunting, such you know is human nature all the world over." John Audubon, travelling with Harris, likewise lamented, "What a terrible destruction of life, as it were for nothing, or next to it, as the tongues only were brought in, and the flesh of these fine animals was left to beasts and birds of prey, or to rot on the spots where they fell. The prairies are literally *covered* with the skulls of the victims." [emphasis in the original].

because they had to ensure their own future and that of the generations to come, and ensure that bison would continue to be successfully tricked into stampeding to the brink of a cliff. It was not an option, not a decision of conservation or waste; it was the crux of survival. The challenge is to respect the belief systems of people raised and taught in ways vastly different from ourselves and not to judge them by standards as remote from their culture as driving buffalo over a cliff is to ours. The killing continued so that the people themselves could continue.

There are also strictly practical reasons for hunters to kill all the animals at the great communal kills. Wounded, disoriented, enraged bison are not to be taken lightly. They posed a serious threat to men, women, and children stationed at the kill sites. Dispatching the wounded or panicked animals eliminated this threat. The situation during the final moments at a buffalo pound was quite different from those at a jump. Animals are fully contained in a pound, and it would have been impossible for the hunters to venture into the confines of the corral and commence butchering while angry, thrashing buffalo were alive. In 1857 John Palliser noted just this issue when he witnessed the killing of all the bison in a Cree pound, commenting, "The scene was a busy but a bloody one, and has to be carried on until every animal is killed to enable them to get to the meat."

Over thousands of years of communal bison killing, across the entire Great Plains, every conceivable scenario must have transpired. Some efforts to round up and drive bison failed completely. The missionary Robert Rundle watched as several attempts by the Cree to impound bison went wrong, the herds "rushing off in a contrary direction to that of the mouth of the pond [pound]." Sometimes the herd arrived at the cliff or pound entrance, only to break through the drive lanes and ranks of people. Audubon recorded, "It happens sometimes however, that the leader of the herd will be restless at the sight of the precipices, and if the fence is weak will break through it, and all his fellows follow him, and escape." Certainly there must have been times when people stationed along the drive route were trampled, wounded, and killed, and the herds ran to freedom. Sometimes the animals poured over the cliff and a few lucky survivors bounded up and quickly bolted beyond the reach of pedestrian hunters armed with bows and arrows. All these examples of animals escaping would later figure into explanations of why some kill episodes failed. Animals

who knew the secrets of the trap had spread this knowledge to previously inexperienced herds.

European eyewitnesses describe incredible scenes of bison herds escaping from attempted pounds and jumps (for sheer drama, failed buffalo drives must have been just as exciting as successful ones). None of these accounts are more evocative than that by Alexander Henry:

But this method sometimes proves dangerous; for if the leading buffalo, on coming to the edge of the precipice, is not entirely exhausted, she may refuse to make the leap, suddenly turn about, and break through the ranks, followed by the whole herd, carrying before them everything which offers to obstruct their progress. No effort of man suffices to arrest a herd in full career ... and thus lives are sometimes lost, as the natives standing near the precipice, to form the ranks and see the buffalo tumble down, have no time to get out of the way.

To Europeans, such occurrences were proof that conditions were wrong or that Native hunters had made some kind of practical mistake; to Aboriginal hunters, something had gone very wrong in their communion with the spirit world. Likely, the buffalo had become aware of the trap, survivors of previous drives had mingled back

George Catlin's painting of a Mandan village shows buffalo skulls on the roofs of many of the huts, signifying a spiritual connection between people and the buffalo that kept the herds from wandering too far. (Courtesy Smithsonian Institution)

into new herds and spread the alarm. So, whenever the killing could be done, it was done. The hunting strategy and belief system of the ancient people of the Plains was clearly a successful one; it supported their way of life for thousands of years without leading to a decline in numbers of bison.

Assertions that any group of people have always acted in a certain way should be regarded with grave suspicion. Plains hunters acted according to the contingencies of the moment: how many people were on hand to drive the game; how many animals were killed; how many mouths there were to feed; how many relatives would visit soon after the kill; what the weather was like; how far camp was; how many hands were available to butcher and transport the spoils of the kill. Certainly there were times when more buffalo were killed than could be used, and masses of food were sometimes left wanting. Many times, every scrap of every carcass was meticulously scrounged, hoarded, and savoured. Some Aboriginal and non-Aboriginal people believe it is a disservice to Native heritage to state that sometimes more bison were killed than were needed. In my opinion, such assertions show a lack of understanding of both the deeply spiritual and profoundly practical world of Aboriginal buffalo hunters of the Plains. It seems to me always a disservice to relegate rational and spiritual people to the status of robots, acting in machine-like fashion without regard to contingencies, deeply held cultural beliefs, and common sense.

The multitude of people who had worked to drive and contain the herd during the final stampede must have rushed to the edge of the cliff to view the results of their efforts. (Courtesy Shayne Tolman)

Drop of Death

Whilst the buffaloes were being driven in, the scene was certainly exciting and picturesque; but the slaughter in the enclosure was more painful than pleasing. – Paul Kane, 1840s

I once had the opportunity to work with an artist who was commissioned by the National Film Board of Canada to paint a series of images that described the operation of a buffalo jump from start to finish. It was a great opportunity for me, as I was able to have all my half-baked ideas about how events transpired fixed forever in a series of illustrations. It's funny how having your theories painted into a scene that is photographed and made into a production seems to lend credence to the story, as if this magically removes ideas from the realm of conjecture and puts them into some higher state of fact. As the artist and I worked through the story, we eventually arrived at the moment when the bison had finished pouring over the cliff. I knew what I wanted the next scene to be. So many times I had placed myself imaginatively at the edge of the cliff during those final dramatic moments and wondered what everyone involved with the drive would do. The answer seemed obvious. We'd all rush to the edge and peer over, to see the spoils of our actions and to watch the second stage of frenetic activity about to begin. So the artist painted a line of hunters staggered along the cliff, looking down on the writhing mass of bodies and the chaotic scene unfolding below.

Steeped in the belief that all bison had to be killed to avoid future failures, the action at the bottom of the cliff would have indeed been frantic. Wounded bison are not something to make light of. They are certainly aware that their lives are at stake and that the time to fight is now or never. While the healthy ones may still use flight as their prime defence, injured ones no longer have this option and will stand and fight to the death. Their massive heads and deadly horns make formidable weapons, so that even a stationary animal must be treated with extreme caution. Hunters probably gave the animals a wide berth, circling around them to loose arrows or hurl long stone-tipped darts into the vulnerable parts of their bodies. Getting an arrow or dart through the thick hide of a buffalo is no easy chore at the best of times (if there was such a thing). In many places the hide is over a centimetre thick, in some places closer to two. Great force and precision are required to place a shaft and stone tip in a spot where

Wounded bison were exceedingly dangerous and sometimes took revenge on men and horses. Note the arrow in the lower chest cavity of the bison and the archer aiming another in this vulnerable location. Painting by George Catlin. (Courtesy Bruce Peel Special Collections Library, University of Alberta)

† The difficulty of killing bison is legendary. There are many accounts like that of the Earl of Southesk who relates this story: "I fired both barrels of my gun right at the centre of his forehead. There was no result, no more than if a clod of earth had struck him: the bull continued in the same position, glaring at me with savage eyes; the densely matted hair on his thick skull had completely defied the penetrative force of a smooth-bore."

it will actually do any serious damage. Many shots could be wasted, hitting animals where the tip simply bounced off bones or where no vital organs lay hidden.† The favoured target was the lower front of the chest cavity, just behind the forelegs. The lungs are situated here, and when they are punctured the buffalo is suddenly unable to hold any breath and suffocates within minutes. Writing in 1840, Victor Tixier recounts how a wounded bison "vomits torrents of blood and falls to its knees before sinking to the ground."

How many people waited beneath the cliff for the herd to arrive is of course conjecture, just as it is with respect to the numbers involved with the drive. But reason suggests that hundreds would have been present on and around the bench beneath the cliff. Perhaps fifty men in their prime (between 15 and 30 years old) swarmed around the seething mass of bison, firing arrows and darts into those still able to stand or walk. Several hundred women, children, and elders waited in relative safety for the killing to cease and the butchering to begin.

Bison that plunged from the precipice and emerged relatively unscathed were perhaps less dangerous than the wounded, but in many ways they were more troublesome. These were the few, perhaps a dozen or so at each kill, that had landed on top of others, rolled and bounced in a fortuitous manner, and through sheer luck, suddenly found themselves standing at the sides of the pyramid of bodies. Initially disoriented and in shock, the instinct to run would soon have kicked in. Uninjured bison were probably the primary target of the waiting hunters, who knew that seriously wounded animals would not be going anywhere. As the dazed buffalo began to bolt from the kill site, the hunters knew they posed a serious threat to future hunts.† They must have run after them from many directions, trying to encircle them and prevent a full-blown gallop to freedom. Fifty armed men swarming around the kill site firing a barrage of arrows and darts had a pretty good chance of catching most animals most of the time. But undoubtedly there were times when a few escaped.

As the uninjured were brought under control, attention must have returned to the mound of carcasses. Animals too wounded to stand posed little danger and were likely dispatched with heavy stone clubs, made with grooved mauls tied on to long wooden handles. These were swung hard against the front of the skull, smashing in the bones and exposing the brain cavity – not only to kill the wounded beasts, but also to allow access to the brain, an organ much desired for the subsequent chore of tanning hides. Skulls are poorly preserved at Head-Smashed-In and are also conspicuously rare, but other buffalo jumps on the northern Plains clearly show this pattern of smashing in the skulls.

Many of the injured would pose a serious threat. Some would have been standing but, wracked with broken bones or internal injuries, would be unable to move. Others would have been capable of short movement, head-swinging, and kicking. All of these were probably killed from a distance, peppered with arrows or darts until they fell.

Eventually the great slaughter was over. The bodies of one hundred, two hundred, or more bison lay mounded up beneath the shadow of the jump. A few dozen others lay as dark spots scattered on the golden prairie, crumpled where they made their final stand. The dust from the thundering stampede and from the subsequent flurry of killing probably still hung in the air, swirling in the vortex of the cliff and then slowly drifting out over the plains. Blood, a rusty crimson colour, flowed into the dark earth, turning the slope into a sticky, soggy mess. Imagine the smells in the after moments of a great bison kill: the dank, churned earth; the pungent hide and hair; the stench of vomit and feces that erupted from the dying; the faint metallic smell of blood and death. I wonder if there might have been an eerie silence, at least for a few moments as the final buffalo expired. But I suspect this was short lived and was followed quickly by shouts, cheers, whoops, and the celebratory exclamations of people who know they have ensured their survival, at least until the next great herd is brought to the jump.

† While most accounts agree with Edwin James that the efforts of the buffalo "are to the last directed solely towards an escape from their pursuers," there are many harrowing accounts of bison fighting to the end. John Audubon reports that hunters are sometimes "trampled and gored to death" by wounded, enraged bison. Peter Fidler, in 1793, likewise asserts that bison "will run their horns into the Horse & kill it upon the spot" and that hunters are occasionally killed. Incredibly, Fidler recounts how some Native hunters "narrowly escape … by springing astride upon the animals back & there remaining until he either kills it with a knife, or until it is quite fatigued, when he jumps off and runs away as fast as possible."

Bones on Fire

The surrounding country is all on fire. – Daniel Harmon, 1804

There is a curious thing found at many of the buffalo jumps across western North America. For reasons still puzzled over by archaeologists, many of the layers of bones found at these sites have been burned. As you excavate down through successively deeper and older layers of buffalo bones beneath the cliff, the thick deposits of bones show clear evidence of having been burned. Sometimes the bones are charred a deep black colour. Sometimes they are so completely fired that they become almost pure white – what archaeologists call calcined. Heavily burned layers of bones are found at Head-Smashed-In and at the nearby Calderwood jump and many other mass kill sites. It is not true of all jumps, or of all layers at each jump, but it shows up enough to raise suspicion and generate questions.

There are two possible explanations. First, the bones may have been fired during the course of natural prairie fires. Wild fires were a constant part of the natural and cultural environment of the Plains. Raging prairie fires were lit by lightning, by campfires out of control, and also intentionally by Native people for a wide variety of reasons that had to do with sensible management of their environment. Undoubtedly, over the six-thousand-year history of Head-Smashed-In, fires swept across the landscape countless times.

Most of these prairie fires don't generate a great deal of heat. The wind whips the fire through the grassland at great speeds. The grass cover burns down to the stalks, essentially the end of available fuel,

Excavations by Brian Reeves at the Head-Smashed-In kill site revealed prominent white layers of burned bone in the walls. (Courtesy Brian Reeves)

and the fire moves on. Very little heat penetrates the ground. Even objects lying on the ground, such as bones, would not reach very high temperature during a prairie fire. Certainly, prairie fires were horrific for the animals roaming the Plains, yet it seems unlikely that a fire sweeping across the Plains could cause bones to combust and burn.

But the bone layers at Head-Smashed-In are not out on the open prairies. They are nestled up against the lee side of a high cliff, protected from the wind. The grass here is tall and luxurious, watered by the abundant seeps and springs that flow through the sandstone bedrock. The same water and protection has fostered a rich growth of Saskatoon berry bushes and other brush beneath the cliff. A fire here, especially in the dryness of autumn, might burn hotter and for much longer. Would it be enough to cause the fresh, greasy bones of a recent kill event to burn? No one knows. Certainly with bits of bison hair lying around, and the spilled contents of the guts and splattered fat, it might be ripe for catching fire.

There is a second possibility. The sheer frequency of burned bone layers at buffalo jumps suggests deliberate activity by human beings. Might fires have been intentionally lit and, if so, what was the purpose? The theory goes that the organic and grease-rich layers of a recently abandoned jump might have been purposely torched by the hunters just as they were preparing to depart the site. The reason behind this has to do with the overwhelming stench that must have emanated from any buffalo jump. Unless a jump was used in midwinter, within days the whole kill site would become a putrid pool of decaying buffalo parts. The stomach contents and guts of a hundred or more animals had been emptied into the dirt. Tufts of hair and bits of skin were everywhere. And, of course, thousands of discarded bones lay scattered around.

Bones may not look like very useful fuel for a fire, but they are chock full of grease and fat. Grease, as we all know, is highly flammable when brought near a fire. Although it was by no means a preferred fuel, there are numerous accounts of Aboriginal people burning buffalo bones as a source of heat, especially in emergency situations.[†] Bones, rich in fat and with chunks of meat still clinging to them, would have begun to putrefy soon after the butchering commenced, adding to the stench of the kill site.

So what's the big deal about a stinky site? It's hard to imagine that ancient hunters were especially sensitive to it; after all, they lived

[†] Camped on the open prairie, Maximilian, Prince of Wied, wrote, "There was no wood at all; but we threw fat and marrow-bones into the fire, by way of fuel." And for the Plains Cree, Mandelbaum reports, "On wet days a buffalo skull was smeared with grease and set afire. The skull kept an even heat for a long time."

† Once again, the literature helps inspire the imagination. In 1793 Peter Fidler passed a used bison pound said to contain the remains of 250 buffalo: "When the Wind happened to blow from the Pound in the direction of the Tents, there was an intollerable stench of the great number of putrified carcasses, &c. on which account the reason of our leaving it." Some sixty years later, Hind graphically described the residue of a Cree pound: "It is needless to say that the odour was overpowering, and millions of large blue flesh flies, humming and buzzing over the putrefying bodies was not the least disgusting part of the spectacle."

‡ The Assiniboine were known to leave special openings in the pound walls to allow dogs in to help clean up the mess. George Catlin reported an unbelievable one thousand dogs were on hand to clean up the carcasses at a bison pound.

their entire lives surrounded by the spoils of butchered animals that fed, clothed, and housed them. Archaeologists doubt that bison kill sites were torched because the noses of the hunters were offended. Rather, it has everything to do with cleaning up the site so that it might be used again in the near future.

The stench that comes from one or two massive putrid carcasses on the prairies is bad enough. The stench of dozens, possibly hundreds, of buffalo in a smallish space is unimaginable.† More important than the sheer number is the clumped effect of a mass kill. A single carcass on the prairie will be cleaned up in short order by wind, rain, sun, insects, birds, and coyotes. Within a few weeks there will be little left. But the remains of a hundred carcasses packed close together, especially in a protected area, such as the lee side of a tall cliff or the confines of a wooden pound, produce a cumulative effect that the elements and scavengers can't clean up as efficiently.‡ Body parts, hair, and guts will remain hidden, rotting, for months if not years. This probably won't win us many admirers, but archaeologists have actually studied this phenomenon, charting the long-term decay of massed carcasses killed in catastrophic events (such as drownings or lightning strikes). I'm almost embarrassed to admit that we know of what we speak.

Given that a mass kill site will continue to steep in its own fetid remains for months, possibly years, it is reasonable to speculate what effect this might have on future attempts to use the jump. True, the wind typically blows over the jump and across the mass kill, keeping the smell from swirling back into the gathering basin. But the wind doesn't always blow from this direction; sometimes it is just the opposite, coming from the east over the kill and blowing directly into the basin. Of course no Native group would attempt a buffalo drive on such a day, but imagine the effect it might have on herds grazing behind the jump. Likely it would cause herds to flee the area, abandoning precisely the ground where Native people want them for the next hunt.

Henry Youle Hind might have been alluding to this fact when in 1857 he noted that the Cree were constructing a new pound, having abandoned the old one "on account of the stench which arose from the putrifying bodies." I suspect that it was not the effect of the stench on the hunters that caused the Cree to move, but, rather, their knowledge that no more herds could be driven into the rank old one.

Two matching lower leg bones from a bison show heavy charring at one end but not the other. Presumably one end of the legs had been placed in a fire. (Courtesy Royal Alberta Museum)

At the Gull Lake bison kill site in Saskatchewan, the excavator Tom Kehoe observed a repeating pattern of heavily burned layers of buffalo bones capped by unburned layers, which in turn were overlain by deposits of soil without any bone in it. Kehoe advanced the reasonable hypothesis that the burned layers had been torched by hunters because they knew they would return soon for another kill, and the overlying unburned bones were the residue of their second kill. That the upper layer of bones was not burned was explained by arguing that the hunters intended to abandon this site and move elsewhere in their territory for a period of time, thus removing the need to go through the laborious process of torching the kill site. The overlying deposits of soil lacking any bone conform to the idea that the site was unused for an extended time.

The problem with a burned layer of bones at a buffalo jump is that there is ample evidence of burning but none to inform us of what lit the fire. We can't, so to speak, identify the smoking gun. We can only state with certainty that a high proportion of jumps and other mass kills exhibit deposits of bone that have been fired. It is possible that the grease-rich ground and thicker grass cover of the kill site caused a natural fire to burn more intensely, causing even the discarded bones to ignite. But more reasonable is the likelihood that Aboriginal hunters lit the whole hillside on fire, as they left the site. By starting an intentional fire, they could manage it by first lighting the grass and brush cover, then throwing bones into an already roaring fire. Our experiments in my field camp, discussed later, indicate that it is exceedingly difficult to simply light bones on fire, but toss them into an existing fire and they burn quite well. I suspect that this is what the users of Head-Smashed-In and other jumps did, and they did it in order to ensure that the site would be ready for use the next time that people came in search of the buffalo.

Let the Butchering Begin

The process of cutting up a dead Buffalo would rather astonish our butchers.
– Edward Harris, 1840s

All that had happened up to this point in our story wasn't so much the result of hard work as it was a careful application of craftsmanship and ingenuity. True, the buffalo runners had a strenuous job, and pursuit of escaping bison must have been an intense and often frustrating chore. But these tasks pale in comparison to that which lay ahead. As the several hundred people gathered once again as a single group, they would have gazed upon a mountain of brown carcasses with a certain amount of melancholy, knowing that the really hard work was still to come. At times, when a great number of animals had been killed, their butchering duties must have seemed overwhelming. For the mountain of flesh, bones, and hide that lay in a steaming pile had to be transformed into products not only usable but, most importantly, storable.

If an average kill consisted of about one hundred cows (and a few bulls), each weighing some 450 kilograms (990 pounds), and a mix of another fifty calves and juveniles with an average weight of 250 kilograms (550 pounds), the vast heap of carcasses would weigh in at about 60,000 kilograms (132,000 thousand pounds). That's about the weight of one and a half bowhead whales. Put another way, picture twenty-five full-sized pickup trucks in a tangled pile beneath the cliff. Some kills involved more than one hundred and fifty bison, some less. But whatever the total, there was a staggering amount of animal products. How would you even begin to go about disentangling and processing this enormous bulk?

Think of an assembly line. We are familiar with the meaning from our own culture, and the term denotes order, system, control, and process. At first blush it doesn't seem to be the kind of image we conjure up of ancient hunters faced with a throng of dead animals. If a movie was ever made of the event, the butchering would certainly be pictured as a primitive and bloodthirsty feeding frenzy – an orgy of gluttony as hunters swarmed over the mound, ripping bodies open, consuming still-beating organs, drenching themselves in blood.† It might make good cinema, but it wouldn't make any sense.

Of course there was some celebratory snacking just after the kill. People needed strength and nourishment in the aftermath of their efforts. Indeed fresh organs were among the choice pieces; they are, after all, loaded with nutrition. Most commonly mentioned as items consumed immediately, meaning raw, are the liver, kidney, stomach, heart, lungs, and marrow from the massive leg bones. "A hearty meal," Edwin Denig reported for the Assiniboine, included consumption of raw cow's nose. Colonel Richard Dodge reports, with his usual flair, that the lucky hunter "betakes himself to what is to him a most perfect repast. The smaller entrails go first, but he is not satisfied until bowels, stomach, liver, and not unfrequently, heart and lungs have all disappeared before his astounding appetite." While most immediate post-kill snacking was to satisfy hunger and provide quick energy, some was based on the practicalities of avoiding spoilage. As Buffalo Bird Woman told Wilson, the kidneys were eaten immediately "and while still warm, as they soon spoiled; indeed, they could hardly be kept over night."

These treats would have been a brief moment of indulgence, satisfying some initial cravings but contributing little to the overall need to render the mound of carcasses. That would come only with a concerted effort by all the people acting in an orderly, systematic fashion and driven by a single purpose – to get the most food and by-products from the heap of carcasses before it was too late, before the whole hillside turned into a stinking, rotting, putrid mess. An assembly line may be a concept of our industrial society, but I am convinced that it is also an apt description of what took place beneath the cliffs of Head-Smashed-In many thousands of years ago.

It is important to remember that buffalo jumps are communal kills. Hundreds of people came together to make these events a success. In our society, hunting is a highly individualistic activity. People

† No doubt the film-makers would seize upon descriptions such as Alexander Henry's: "Here I observed the filthy manners of these people in feasting on the raw entrails of buffalo. The paunch, livers, kidneys, fat, testicles, gristle, marrow-bones, and several other pieces, they hand about and devour like famished wolves, whilst blood and dung stream down from their mouths; it was disgusting to see them." They would likely ignore Lewis and Clark's description of their own men feeding on raw animal parts "which we are accustomed to look with disgust… one of [the men] who had seized about nine feet of the entrails was chewing at one end, while with his hand he was diligently clearing his way by discharging the contents at the other."

† The situation was somewhat different for solitary kills and those made by small groups of people. In these situations, individuals were more closely identified with specific carcasses. We know, for example, that arrows were often marked with personal designs. Yet even under these circumstances there was strong social pressure to share food. All families knew that their success one day might be matched by that of another family in days to come.

may go out with a few friends, but ultimately it comes down to a single hunter framing an animal in the crosshairs of his scope and pulling the trigger. Mano-a-mano is part of the appeal. It is an epic battle between the stalker and the stalked, and when it is over, individual credit and ownership are paramount. Credit for the kill is a matter of intense personal pride, having strong implications for who is entitled to what parts of the animal and also who does the work (or pays the costs) of butchering and transporting the carcass. If you shot the animal, these matters are your responsibility.

But there is no yours or mine at a buffalo jump. Hundreds of people collectively found the distant herds, tricked them into the drive lanes, stampeded them to the cliff, killed them below the jump, and butchered the remains. There is no individual stamp on any carcass, no crosshairs, no silver bullet. Communally they were rounded up and killed; collectively they were butchered and distributed. Given the extraordinary co-operative social organization that had to exist for the jump to take place, it would be absurd to think of the spoils as individual property, as if people could sort through the hundreds of carcasses and somehow say they were more responsible for the death of certain animals.†

Plains Aboriginal societies were known to be generally egalitarian in nature, meaning simply that there was equality between people. Things were shared, and no one person or group had some inherited or Creator-given right to more or less than anyone else. The buffalo carcasses piled at the base of the jump belonged to everyone. And everyone had to pitch in to turn them into usable food and materials for the good of the entire group.

There were some inequities. Various tribes had their own traditions of rewarding key people. Grinnell informs us that the Blackfoot divided up the results of the kill "among the people," but that "the chiefs and the leading warrior [received] the best and fattest animals." An Assiniboine informant to Robert Lowie reported that the buffalo runners received the fattest animals, and Henry (the elder) said that chiefs were given the tongues. There were acts of great generosity and magnanimity, with reciprocal expectations attached. Henry (the younger) wrote that Cree pound masters (ceremonial leaders of the event) partitioned out the spoils of the kill to all the people and "gives each tent an equal share, reserving nothing for himself. But in the end he is always the best provided for; everyone is obliged to send him a certain portion." If a family was unhappy with the share they received, the fluid nature of Plains culture provided a simple solution: "no one will complain," eyewitness Daniel Harmon records, but "should any be displeased with their share, they will decamp, and go and join another party."

In thinking about how the butchering must have been done, it seems reasonable to believe that there must have been an ordered system to dismembering the spoils of the kill. Random, idiosyncratic behaviour of individuals simply doing as they please just doesn't make sense. There are both biological and social imperatives that argue for the application of a common system to the butchering of the buffalo carcasses: biological in that there are critical attributes of fresh-killed animals that must be recognized and acted upon, social in that people shared a common goal of maximizing the return of their efforts. The two imperatives merged to suggest a method to the madness of butchering a mountain of slaughtered beasts.

A mound of a hundred or more dead animals must have been a staggering sight to behold. Just moments before, these buffalo had been grazing in the gathering basin, ingesting and ruminating, perhaps drinking from a local pond or stream. Although they are dead, not much has really changed. This may sound implausible, but think for a moment: their hearts have stopped beating and blood is no longer flowing through their veins, but other than that, little has changed. Their bodies are still composed of meat, fat, organs, bone, and hide. Their stomachs are still full of the last meal of grass, their intestines packed with digested food, their body temperature unchanged from just moments before. Adding to that, something we can call the "pyramid effect" (the fact that the bodies are piled in one great mound) creates a whole different set of biological relationships than would have been had the carcasses been strewn over a wide area. The most important of these relationships involves heat.

Bison Hide as Insulator

The skin is in some places of incredible thickness, particularly about the neck, where it often exceeds an inch. – Samuel Hearne, 1772

The body temperature of living bison is much like our own, about 37° C (98.6° F). But we, most decidedly, are thin skinned. When we die, our body temperature begins to decline rapidly, because (unless

† There are a number of chilling accounts of buffalo hunters, Indians and whites alike, surviving savage winter storms by gutting out bison carcasses and crawling into the protective hide covering (though they later faced the unpleasant task of trying to pry their way out of the frozen shell). Humans were not alone in seeking refuge inside a bison. John Audubon wrote of a Native hunter who approached a buffalo carcass only to discover, to his dismay, an angry grizzly bear hunkered down inside.

we are wearing a winter parka) there is little in the way of insulation to retain our body heat. Not so with bison. They have dense coats of hair and extremely thick hides that act as astonishing insulators.† A series of somewhat bizarre experiments were conducted at Elk Island National Park, where calves of several large mammals were put in a specially designed refrigeration chamber. The tests included yak, bison, and Scottish Highland cattle – all considered cold-adapted species – and Hereford cattle. Temperature in the chamber was lowered to -30° C (-22° F) and the metabolic response of each animal was measured. All but the bison showed a marked increase in metabolic activity; that is, subjected to extreme cold, they increased their metabolism to burn more energy in an effort to raise body temperature. We humans would do the same. Not bison. Incredibly, subjected to -30° C temperatures, buffalo showed a lowering of metabolism. As it got colder, bison slowed their metabolic rate.

What this tells us is that bison are supremely adapted to cold weather. They have evolved over countless millennia to save, rather than burn up, their body energy reserves. Animals that increase their metabolism to fight off a sudden cold spell are trying to get through the moment, hoping for better times to come; bison, by lowering their metabolism, illustrate an evolutionary adaptation to the inevitability of future cold spells, saving critical body reserves for the many difficult times that still lie ahead. It is an approach to life on the rugged Great Plains that has served the bison well since time immemorial. And it relates directly to how and why ancient Aboriginal hunters went about butchering the mound of flesh in the manner they did.

Here's an obscure fact to impress friends at cocktail parties: bison have about ten times more hair per square inch of hide than do modern cattle. Bison hair is thinner than that of cattle, but is much denser. The thick hide combined with this dense coat of hair makes bison an insulating machine engineered over millennia of evolution to conserve heat. Another research project at Elk Island National Park dramatically illustrated the insulating properties of bison hide. One of the wildlife biologists, Wes Olson, was using infrared (heat sensitive) equipment while doing an aerial census of park animals. It was winter, with sub-zero temperatures and fresh snow, and Wes was picking up the heat signals of moose and elk. But he hardly found any bison, despite a large herd resident in the park. He noticed, however, that the infrared screen was showing some amorphous, faint crescents

A bison's hide is such an effective insulator that it is common to see snow build up on the animals – not enough heat escapes the hide and dense hair to melt the snow. (Courtesy Johane Janelle.)

of heat. When he re-inspected these spots, he discovered they were bison lying in the snow. Their exposed bellies, the only parts, not covered with hair, were causing the faint crescent signals. The rest of the animal was not letting out enough heat to be detected by the infrared equipment.

Importantly for our story, none of the evolutionary characteristics of an insulating hide abandoned the buffalo as they lay dead on the slopes beneath Head-Smashed-In. The carcasses on the outer portion of the mound would have been exposed to the cool air of the season, but, even then, their amazing insulating properties would have prevented much heat loss. Those buried under the bodies of their colleagues would have been completely sheltered from any cooling effects and probably would have experienced virtually no loss of heat over the hours and even days that followed. The importance of this is that, as we all know, heat spoils food.

Lacking refrigeration, in the aftermath of the kill hunters faced a serious biological imperative. The mound of carcasses had to be fully butchered and processed into usable food in short order or else become waste through spoilage. If a great majority of the food supply were allowed to waste, the tremendous effort that went into orchestrating the kill would have been in vain. The pressing need was to counteract the awesome insulating properties of the bison hide.

I once witnessed first hand the remarkable insulating qualities of bison hide, only in a reverse kind of way – keeping the cold in. We were filming a movie that was to be shown inside the new interpretive centre at Head-Smashed-In and needed some dead bison. We had a frozen bison carcass delivered to us in a Budget rent-a-truck. It was September: gorgeous fall days of warm daytime sun and cool evenings. For five days we filmed with this animal, tossing it over the cliff, hauling it back up for an encore. At the end of the shoot it lay on the grass beneath the cliff, of no further use to the crew. A young Piikani man, Willy Big Bull, asked me if he could take the head. He was going to have it mounted.

We walked up the slope together, Willy armed with a large axe. Willy was a big, powerful man, muscular, and a black belt karate instructor. He took a mighty swing with the axe and struck the neck of the bison. Though this happened several decades ago, the image is still vivid. The axe hit the neck and stopped; it just stopped. The handle of the axe shuddered in Willy's hands, and he let go of his grasp, shaking his hands in pain. The sharp metal bit had penetrated the hide maybe a centimetre. Despite lying out five days in fine fall weather, the hide had insulated the carcass such that it was still nearly completely frozen. Willy wedged the axe free from the carcass, and we headed back down the slope together. There would be no more swings of the axe that evening.

The first order of business was probably cutting the hide off dead bison, to allow heat from the carcass to escape. (Courtesy Shayne Tolman)

Back to the Assembly Line

Willy Big Bull failed because the insulating properties of the hide and the dense coat of hair prevented the cold from coming out of the buffalo carcass. Conversely, ancient hunters needed to let the heat out from the bodies of the dead bison. This is why we think that they went about it in assembly-line fashion. If your approach to the task was to select one carcass at a time and butcher it completely, you would be spending a great deal of time doing a thorough job on a few carcasses, while others waited untouched. Those in the waiting queue sat stewing in their internal body heat, the hide and coat of hair ensuring that this heat escaped only ever so slowly.

A lot of internal body heat comes from the acids in your stomach, reacting with the food you eat, producing the heat that keeps us alive and warm. The dead bison at the base of the buffalo jump had not long before been grazing on the fine grasses of the gathering basin. The digestion of these grasses by stomach acids continued to produce heat long after the animals were dead, so to avoid losing a great deal of the catch through spoilage, the primary goal would be to stop the production of heat from within the bison carcasses and to release as much of the internal heat as possible. When bison hunting in the 1800s, Colonel Richard Dodge recognized, "These animals spoil very quickly if not disembowelled."

From a balloon hovering above, the scene at the base of the sandstone escarpment probably looked much like an anthill, with small hunters clamouring on and around the mound of massive carcasses. If our suspicions are correct, the first order of business would have been to pull that mound apart, separating the bodies so they could begin to cool down. Bison are much too heavy to drag very far, so hunters would have worked first on those near the edge of the kill. Breaking the peripheral animals into more easily moved parts made space for the next batch of carcasses to be pulled from the pile.

Of the animals that could be butchered first, we suspect that the priority was, again, to cool down each individual carcass. The best way to do this was to get the hide, that powerful insulator, off the body. Using sharp stone knives and the points of spears and arrows, the hide was cut through and peeled away from the underlying fat and meat. The naked bodies, streaked red and yellow from bloody meat and grizzled fat, were left on the splayed hides to keep the meat clean. Then the stomach cavity was cut open and the steamy contents spilled out onto the grassy slope. At this point, fresh, cool air could circulate around the outside of the flesh and through the inside of the chest cavity. These two steps, removing the hide and emptying the stomach, were most crucial in cooling down the carcasses, ensuring that the greatest possible amount of food was saved for future use.

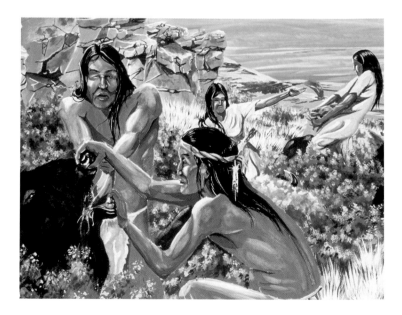

Tongues, the most esteemed part of the buffalo, were invariably removed early in the butchering process. (Courtesy Shayne Tolman)

Once a group of animals was exposed in this manner, the hunters probably returned to the kill pile to begin the same procedures with the next batch. Another group must have started butchering the exposed carcasses. Teams of people worked together, the chores being too strenuous and the parts too heavy for individuals. The prized ribs were chopped off with heavy stone axes. Huge legs were disarticulated at the joints. The massive head was severed and pushed aside. As the carcasses dwindled in size they became more manageable and could be rolled over. The pronounced hump of bison, formed by elongated spines of thoracic vertebrae, is composed of a delicious mix of meat and fat and was one of the most sought after parts of the animal. These were chopped off at the base of the vertebrae. Internal organs and the great balls of precious fat that surround them were sliced from the body cavity, some of them to be consumed immediately. Most importantly, the bluish-black tongue – the single most esteemed part of a bison carcass – was severed from within the jaws.† Tongues were so highly regarded that they were often saved for special post-hunt ceremonies and were presented as a sign of respect to revered elders and to those most responsible for the success of the hunt (ceremonial specialists, buffalo runners).

That Natives were highly skilled in the task of dismembering the game is to be expected. Edwin James observed, "In the operation of butchering, a considerable knowledge of the anatomical structure of the animal is exhibited, in laying open the muscles properly, and extending them out into the widest and most entire surfaces, by a judicious dissection." Father Lewis Hennepin witnessed buffalo butchering in the 1600s, before metal tools were widely available: "It was no small matter of Admiration to see these Savages flea [flay] the Bull, and get it in pieces; they had neither Knives nor Hatchets ... and yet did it dexterously with the Point of their Arrows." There are numerous accounts from European visitors to the Plains of the details of cutting up a buffalo carcass. A succinct version comes from Daniel Harmon:

The Natives generally cut up the body of an animal into eleven pieces, to prepare it for transportation to their tents, or to our forts. These pieces are the four limbs, the two sides of ribs, the two sinews on each side of the back bone, the brisket, the croup, and the back bone. Besides these, they save and use the tongue, heart, liver, paunch, and some part of the entrails. The head, they carry home, the meat which is on it they eat; and the brains they rub over the skin, in dressing it.

† The muscle tissue of the tongue is composed of about 20 per cent fat, far more than any other piece of meat in a bison carcass. Accordingly, Natives and non-Natives alike regarded it as the choicest piece of the buffalo. Palliser waxed eloquent on its savoury nature: "Well do I remember how these tongues addressed themselves to the feelings of us hungry hunters … They sent forth an appeal more eloquent than the language of a Demosthenes; true the tongues were silent, but they were fat! When well boiled they are delicious, the rind then peels off, and they become tender, plump, and juicy." Josiah Gregg was more concise: "But what the tail of the beaver is to the trapper, the tongue of the buffalo is to the hunter." Samuel Hearne astutely observed, "What is most extraordinary, when the beasts are in the poorest state, which happens regularly at certain seasons, their tongues are then very fat and fine." This explains many of the historic accounts of kills where the tongue alone was taken.

Slowly, methodically, the buffalo carcasses were taken apart. The hunters must have been a sight. Hands, arms, legs, and feet caked in sticky blood and slippery grease. There would hardly be any point in washing up; the race against spoilage dictated plunging immediately into the next available carcass. And so the work continued, probably around the clock, as much as the light from fires would permit. Like flesh-eating beetles, ancient hunters swarmed over the mass of hide and flesh, gradually picking the kill apart, spreading it further to the sides, reducing great carcasses to manageably sized portions. As the pieces piled up on the fresh hides, it was time for the operation to move to the next phase of work, and to a whole new place. It was time for the work to shift to the great camp that lay waiting on the immense prairie below the buffalo jump.

CHAPTER 7

Cooking Up the Spoils

The buffalo meat which the hunter roasts or broils upon this fire, he accounts more savory than the steaks dressed by the most delicate cooks in civilized life. – Josiah Gregg, 1837–38

T he extensive flatlands that stretch to the north, south, and east from the base of the slope beneath the cliff at Head-Smashed-In have been called by archaeologists the processing site. This is the place where the painstaking butchering of bison was conducted. It is not called the "butchering site" because much more than simply cutting up the animals transpired on this section of prairie. It was quite literally a processing of the entire buffalo carcass, one after the other, no doubt employing the labour of hundreds of people spanning days of time. The events that transpired at the processing site lacked the adrenalin rush of the kill event, but they were just as critical to the survival of the people, for you could successfully kill dozens of bison and the effort would all have been in vain if you didn't process the remains of the kill in a timely and efficient manner.

To be sure, the work settled into a more relaxed mode compared with the frantic, chaotic pace of the kill event. But it could hardly be called leisurely. Time was of the essence. Spoilage of the meat, fat, and hides began the minute the animals died, and many critical steps had to be taken to ensure the maximum amount of food was saved. The whole point of the great expenditure of labour and skill had not been so that the hunters could settle down to a two-day feast. Rather, it was to leave Head-Smashed-In with a huge quantity of food and hide that would help the people make it through the strenuous months ahead. Travelling among the Plains Indians, Colonel Richard Dodge noted that the great communal hunts of the fall were "made for the purpose of killing sufficient animals … to furnish dried meat for

† There is, however, a spectacular buffalo jump in Wyoming, the Vore site, where bison were driven and killed in a huge sinkhole in the prairie and then had to be dragged upslope for processing. You can still see the trails where hunters schlepped the carcass parts up the sides of the sinkhole.

the next winter's supply." The pace may have slowed, and, in comparison to what had come before, the work became monotonous, but it was no less urgent.

The Processing Site

The requirements of a landscape suitable for a successful buffalo jump don't end when a mound of carcasses lie at the base of the cliff. Processing the animals also has certain demands that must be met. For one thing, people need room to work. They must be able to pull the carcasses away from the heap and have space to spread them out and cut them up. There must be some adjacent land that can be used for butchering, and owing to the great weight of the animals (even the cut up parts) it can't be far away. Ideally, it should be on ground that is level to the jump or somewhat downslope, so as to avoid having to drag carcass parts uphill.†

From the base of the cliff at Head-Smashed-In, a moderately steep slope angles down toward the prairie below. After a distance of about one hundred metres, the slope levels off and the land becomes relatively flat. This gently rolling plain extends for several kilometres to the north and south, paralleling the trend of the bedrock outcrop. To the east, heading away from the cliff, the level prairie only persists for a few hundred metres before it again drops gently to a lower and much more extensive flatland that covers the entire region east of the Porcupine Hills. Processing the spoils from Head-Smashed-In took place on the flats below the cliff. Everywhere the land is roughly level we find the archaeological remains of bison carcasses and butchering activity. Where the land starts to slope, the soil is devoid of artifacts; you wouldn't camp and work on sloping ground when there is plenty of level terrain nearby. The extent of the processing site is massive, covering at least a kilometre from north to south and hundreds of metres to the east until the land begins to slope down toward the lower prairie.

Along with the requirement for space, buffalo jumps required water. Water was not only vital for the people to survive, it also played a key role in many of the food processing activities, the hunters were committed to spending at least several days in hard labour at the processing site, probably working around the clock. Writing in the 1850s, Schoolcraft said that butchering buffalo provoked an "inordinate

thirst" that when neglected, "the suffering is almost intolerable." When no water was available, Schoolcraft observed, "the means taken in some measure to assuage thirst, is to chew leaves, or even the cartilaginous portion of the nostril of the slain buffalo." Referring more to solitary kills, Daniel Harmon records, "When there is no water to be found, they at times kill a buffaloe, and drink his blood, or the water which they find in his paunch."

Water located a considerable distance from the kill placed a great burden on people to make constant return trips, hauling heavy water in hide containers and diminishing the size of the work force available for butchering.† There are a few buffalo jumps located a long way from water, but they are very rare. Almost every known jump is situated immediately at a water source or very close by. Another reason that jumps are near water is that bison, too, need to drink (typically once a day), so the prospect of finding herds to drive will almost always be greater near water sources.

A visitor today to Head-Smashed-In would think that there was no water to be had for a considerable distance. The Oldman River valley is located some five kilometres to the south. I once had an awkward moment when a Native elder who was unfamiliar with the

Below the cliff at Head-Smashed-In, the land flattens out to a gently rolling prairie where the carcasses were butchered and processed. (Courtesy Royal Alberta Museum)

† Availability of water governed much of Plains life. Searching out suitable campsites, Palliser said, "It is always water that determines the choice." Natives did transport water, using buffalo stomachs and skins from the heart, but it was a heavy burden and a temporary solution.

† There is a pattern to this. Seeps and springs emanate from many bedrock escarpments. Desperate with thirst on the Plains, Edwin James followed bison trails hoping they would lead to water. He recounts how the trails "converge from all directions to the places where water is to be found, and by following their guidance were soon led to a spot where was found a small spring dripping from the side of a cliff of sandstone.

specifics of Head-Smashed-In visited the site and, after surveying the area, informed me that we had made a mistake – this was not a buffalo jump; it could not be, for there was no nearby source of water. The old man was drawing on his knowledge that buffalo jumps were only located close to water. But there is water right at the site; in fact it flows from directly beneath the bedrock cliff right at the main kill location. There is a natural spring of pure, fresh water that seeps out from under the sandstone, and it has obviously done this for quite some time as there is a prominent spring channel cutting through the middle of the processing area.† This channel is now dry, but in the memory of the local residents it was a dependable source and was even dammed at one point and used to water cattle. When Boyd Wettlaufer excavated at Head-Smashed-In in 1949, his crew used to bathe and swim in this waterhole, and it was where he found the nine thousand year-old Scottsbluff spear point mentioned earlier. Water still flows from beneath the cliff; its path has just moved slightly below the surface. Take a shovel and dig a hole near the head of the spring channel and within a depth of fifty centimetres you will have water seeping into the pit.

We can presume that water was always available from this spring at Head-Smashed-In, and it formed a vital part of the story of processing the carcasses. It provided drink to the hundreds of people who slaved away at rendering down the carcasses, and, as we will see below, it was used in many ways in washing and cooking the parts of the buffalo. Without this natural spring, it's quite likely that Head-Smashed-In would never have been used as a buffalo jump. Early hunters would have turned instead to one of the other cliffs and embankments that border a permanent water source.

Day Fades to Night

Some of the events that transpired in the huge camp on the flats beneath the cliff can be documented with archaeological and historical evidence. Others can only be guessed at. Earlier I noted that archaeologists have devoted a great deal of effort to studying bison kill sites and very little to the remains that document how the drive took place. In like manner, historic observers have left us with gripping written descriptions of the tumultuous events that transpired at the kills; after all, this was the exciting part of the story. In the aftermath

Camps set up below the cliff would have been intentionally temporary. People knew they would soon be moving away, and business, not comfort, was the order of the day. (Courtesy Head-Smashed-In Buffalo Jump)

† The same applies to historic artwork. There are dozens of fabulous images of bison hunting that capture the thrill, danger, and excitement of the chase. But the great Western artists – Catlin, Kane, Bodmer, Miller, and others – moved on when the kill was over. There are almost no historical paintings or sketches of bison butchering.

of the kill, as the mundane and tedious days of butchering set in, many European eyewitnesses moved on. The written record of these events is paltry in comparison to those of the kill.† Archaeologists, likewise drawn to the excitement of the kill, have focussed their work on the rich bonebeds beneath the cliff, paying only cursory attention to the processing areas of communal bison kill sites. Yet by combining all sources, a reasonable picture of these ancient activities emerges.

We can be assured that the place would have been a beehive of activity: hundreds of people sitting, standing, or moving over an area of many hectares. It was a camp of sorts, at least in a temporary sense, but not in the usual sense of a place where people selected to live. It was an industrial site; it existed for the span of a few days, dedicated to a single purpose, and was then abandoned. I spent a good portion of my professional life digging into the soil of the Head-Smashed-In processing site, and as you can imagine I have often thought about what that busy place might have looked like.

Slowly, in the hours after the completion of the kill, the heavy carcass portions made their way down the slope from the cliff to the expansive prairie below. Hunks of bloody meat and slippery bone were probably heaped onto fresh bison hides and dragged by several people. The hides acted as skids, making the work much easier and helping to keep the food free of dirt. For a sizable kill, this task of transporting may have lasted several days. I imagine people worked long hours, from first light to late evening, not wanting to have any

† Although the men may have knocked off. There is ample reporting of butchering being mostly women's work. "At the time of the 'great fall hunt,' there was no rest nor excuse for her," Colonel Dodge observed. "She must work at any and all hours ... When the buffalo was dead the man's work was done. It was woman's work to skin and cut up the dead animal ... The women were obliged to work hard and fast, all night long before their task was finished." John McDougall, a witness to buffalo kills in the 1860s, said, "The life of an Indian woman in those early days was, indeed, an extremely busy one ... cooking, cutting up, drying and pounding meat, rendering grease, chopping bones to get out the marrow fat, making pemmican, stretching, scraping and dressing buffalo hides to make robes or leather – a long, tedious process." George Catlin witnessed a bison kill, "The throng of women and children ... had been assembled, and all of whom seemed busily at work."

of the meat spoil or to have scavengers help themselves. A night-time view from the cliff out toward the eastern prairie would have certainly been a spectacular sight. Yellow-orange flames from dozens of camp-fires would have sparkled across the flats like stars. A few conical skin tents, being nearly opaque, would have caught and reflected the light like strange cones piercing the night sky. All around, shadowy figures moved between the flickering flames of the fires, talking, laughing, and groaning with the continuing load of work, maybe occasionally breaking into a low, rhythmic chant.

To be sure, there would have been celebrations in progress, but probably not in the way we conventionally think. I doubt that everyone knocked off work and joined as one in a massive feast and ceremony.† There was simply too much work to be done, and for the sake of survival it had to be done quickly. Also, people would have been exhausted. Some, like the buffalo runners, had been at work since before sunrise or even longer. Instead, I suspect that celebrations were brief and spontaneous and probably sprang up among family groups centred at different tents and fires, perhaps prompted by the cooking of a massive roast or nutritious soupy stew. Frequent consumption of high energy foods would have certainly been required to keep people supplied with the nutrition they needed to continue slogging away at what must have seemed like an eternity of bison butchering. No doubt people took turns slipping into tents to catch a few hours sleep, although given the great number of people present, many may have simply lain down on the grass using old tanned bison robes as blankets. Children, spared the most strenuous work, must have had a glorious time, running between the fires, grabbing snacks, playing games with toy bows and arrows, and occasionally getting collared to settle down and do something useful.

Work was indeed the order of the day, and of the days and nights to come. Remember, the equivalent mass of twenty-five pickup trucks lay mounded beneath the cliff waiting to be converted into usable, storable food. With the exception of kills made in mid-winter (where cold temperatures helped chill and preserve the food), fresh bison meat and fat would only last for a matter of days before it started to spoil. Over thousands of years of dealing with the yield of bison kills, Plains hunters developed a number of clever ways to convert the fresh food into a commodity that could be stored, carried, and consumed for the months to come.

Dried Goods

Some meat was eaten fresh, but the bison hunt was primarily undertaken to provide a store of dried flesh. – Turney-High, on the Kootenai, 1941

About 65 per cent of the weight of bison meat is made up of water, so you can imagine that drying the meat would make the bounty from the kill far lighter and easier to carry. Of course, if you have no plans to travel anywhere, making the fruits of your hunting efforts light and portable would be irrelevant. But Head-Smashed-In wasn't a place where people would want to camp for long periods of time. Other than the mound of bison carcasses, there were no other significant food resources at the site, and water was limited to the small spring that flows from the bedrock cliff, a source that probably ceased as winter set in. More importantly, Head-Smashed-In is open to the fierce winds of the high Plains, had no local supply of wood, and would have been completely unsuitable for winter camping. If, as we suspect, autumn was the main season for buffalo jumping, then the coming of winter was a strong inducement for quickly moving to more favourable camping places. Reducing the weight of tens of thousands of kilograms of meat, fat, and hide became a critical matter. Drying food was the primary means of cutting down on weight.[†]

Huge chunks of meat, such as sides of ribs or the hams (from the upper legs), are too big to dry out. Only the outer surface of the meat would lose its moisture, turning to a hardened crust that actually serves to protect the bulk of the water remaining inside. Getting rid of the majority of moisture requires food to be cut into thin strips, thus exposing a great deal of the surface area to the drying effects of the sun and air. Days were spent using sharp stone tools to cut meat and fat into thin segments and then hanging them on simple wooden racks that were probably erected in the campsite on the plains below the cliff. No archaeological evidence of these wood racks has been found, but we can presume that they must have existed, as John McDougall witnessed:

[Meat was] cut into broad wide flakes, not more than a quarter of an inch in thickness. These flakes in turn were hung on stagings made of clean poles, and the wind and sun allowed free work at them. When dry on one side they were turned, and kept turned every hour or so during the day ... Thus in two or three days, according to the weather, the first lot would be ready for sorting ... Though only air and sun were utilized in the curing, still this was sweet and perfect in its effect, and the meat would keep for years.

[†] It's probably fair to assume that some of the meat from just about all large-scale bison kills was dried. Interviewing the Coeur d'Alêne people, James Teit reported, "Meat intended for winter use or to be carried a long way was invariably dried either by the fire or in the sun, or both, assisted by wind and smoke."

Hung out like socks on a laundry line, the strips of meat and fat were desiccated by the warming rays of the sun and the incessant winds of Head-Smashed-In. Evaporation of the water content by simple air-drying could reduce the weight of the food by as much as half, a massive difference in the load that people had to carry away from the jump.

Drying meat and fat not only makes it lighter, it helps preserve it. We are all familiar with beef jerky, flat strips of relatively hard meat that pulls apart in shreds as you eat it. You might see it lying in trays at the butcher shop or wrapped in plastic and hanging by the grocery checkout. It may not have occurred to you to ask why this particular kind of meat can sit in trays or plastic bags, unrefrigerated for weeks or months, without spoiling. Although the beef jerky we purchase today is treated with salts and chemicals, it doesn't have to be. Simply drying meat in very thin sheets converts it to a state that retards the process of decay. Meat spoils because of bacteria that take hold on the surface. Bacteria need water to survive. Drying meat leaves it with a dry, tough, outer crust that is inhospitable to bacteria. This is critical to preventing spoilage through insect infestation. Flies are attracted to fresh, moist meat and will happily lay their eggs on the soft surface, which leads to rapid spoilage. The hard crust produced by drying deprives flies and other insects of a suitable surface on which larvae can live and hatch.

Native hunters air-dried much of their meat and fat, but they also occasionally helped the drying process using heat and smoke from fires. Smoking helps to dry meat in two ways. First, heat from a smoky fire acts to drive off even more moisture from the food. Second, wood smoke is itself a preservative. Repeated experiments with meat and fish have shown wood smoke to be highly effective at preventing spoilage. The chemicals in smoke, primarily phenols, are both antioxidants, which help retard animal fats from becoming rancid, and antimicrobials, which slow the process of bacterial growth. Wood smoke does not impregnate the meat; rather, it forms a protective coating on it. Hides were (and still are) tanned and thus preserved by hanging them over a smoky fire. Many kinds of fish are also smoked, giving them not only a pleasing taste but also a much longer shelf life.

It would be difficult to smoke meat over an open fire on the Plains surrounding Head-Smashed-In Buffalo Jump. The wind would

simply blow the smoke into the far distance. Smoking could be better accomplished in some kind of enclosed structure where food could be suspended over a smoky fire, with the smoke lingering around the meat for a considerable period of time. We don't know much about the kinds of structures that hunters used for this purpose, but we know from early historic interviews that smoking of meat was common.† Tipis were probably used for this purpose, as were small hide structures, possibly consisting of no more than a hide thrown over a small wooden frame with a fire in the centre. The fire would have been kept intentionally smoky, rather than hot, by feeding it damp wood and grass and by cutting down on air with the hide covering.

Plain dried meat isn't the tastiest food. Here's why. Unfortunately for the Native people, drying meat didn't just remove water. It also removed a certain amount of fat. Most people think of fat as a thick rind that surrounds some of our favourite cuts of meat. This of course can be cut off and saved separately, discarded as waste, or for Native hunters to savour as a delicacy. But fat is also found within meat tissue itself. This is called intramuscular fat and is what gives meat its marbled appearance (which is the source of the juice and much of the flavour). Unless you are on an ultra low-fat diet, you don't want to lose this fat. Yet any drying of meat that involves heat (sun and fire)

The camp below the Head-Smashed-In cliff was probably dotted with tipis and many racks for drying meat. On calm days, outside fires were used to dry and smoke the meat. (Courtesy Head-Smashed-In Buffalo Jump)

† McDougall described meat being dried in a depression: "We made a fire and across the top of it placed willows, whereon we spread the meat." Referring to buffalo processing, Edwin James reported, "The meat, with the exception of that of the shoulders, or hump, as it is called, is then dissected with much skill into large thin slices, and dried in the sun, or jerked over a slow fire on a low scaffold."

† As Mandelbaum reports, they also sometimes tried to catch the melting grease: "Fat from shoulder and rump was placed before a fire and as it melted dripped into a hide container. This was called sasɪpmanpimɪ· (frying grease)."

will cause the fat to liquefy and drip from the surface. The net result is that dried meat tastes pretty much like the name implies. And, as we have already seen, meat without fat is of little nutritional value. Native hunters got around this problem in part by saving all other kinds of fat to add later to the dried meat, making it both tasty and nutritious.† Many kinds of fat were also dried, with sun and smoke, making them both lighter and longer lasting.

The dried meat and fat were stored in simple hide containers called *parfleches*. These were stiff, untanned hide satchels that folded closed, much like the brown banker's envelopes we use today. Food was tightly packed in the parfleches to keep out as much air as possible, thus reducing spoilage. Edwin James wrote, "The meat, in its dried state, is closely condensed together into quadrangular packages, each of a suitable size." Schoolcraft reported that the meat packages were about "sixty or seventy pounds weight" (about twenty-seven to thirty-two kilograms).

Properly cured and packaged dried meat could last for months and even years, depending in part on the weather (damp, warm weather would be bad for preservation; cool, dry weather would be good), and on how dry the food was when it was first stored. Fat is harder to dry than meat and couldn't usually be stored for as long a time. Thus, the future use of much of the stored dried meat depended on continuing to procure fresh fat to add to it. If the people were able to keep killing fresh animals, then of course there was no problem with a continuous supply of fat. But what if winter set in and hunting became difficult if not impossible? Was there a reservoir of fat that people could turn to in times of stress? There was, and it lies buried deep in the bones of the buffalo.

Grease is the Word

The large bones of the hind legs are thrown upon the glowing coals, or hidden under the hot embers, then cracked between two stones, and the rich, delicious marrow sucked in quantities sufficient to ruin a white stomach forever.
– Colonel Richard Dodge, 1860s and 1870s

Most people know that a fresh bone from just about any animal carcass is greasy to the touch. Fat is found throughout most bones in the body, and the best known fat is marrow, which occurs in hollow

Archaeological excavations at bison kill sites almost always reveal large leg bones that have been smashed to retrieve the rich marrow. (Courtesy Royal Alberta Museum)

cavities inside many bones, especially the long bones of the legs. Marrow, in a healthy animal, is almost 100 per cent fat and, accordingly, was one of the most prized parts of the buffalo carcass. During the laborious butchering process, big marrow bones were smashed with heavy stone hammers to extract the tasty and nutritious marrow, thus replenishing the energy of the workers. Marrow bones could also be saved for later use, although fat in the cavities of the bones would, within a relatively short time, start to putrefy.

Marrow was universally regarded as one of the tastiest and most nutritious parts of the buffalo. Edwin James called it "a most delicious repast ... a treat whose value must for ever remain unknown to those who have not tried the adventurous life of the hunter." Immediately following the kill, Natives and non-Natives alike often indulged in one of the most esteemed dishes. As Buffalo Bird Woman described it to Gilbert Wilson, "We cut the tough outer flesh ... leaving the more tender flesh still clinging to the bone, and this was laid near the fire, the two ends resting on two stones. When the meat was roasted and had been cut off, the bone was cracked open and the marrow pried out with a chokecherry stick and eaten with the meat." Thomas Farnham referred to marrow as "trapper's butter" and described how it was added to a pot of boiling water, mixed with buffalo blood, then stirred "till the mass became of the consistency of rice soup ... It was a fine dish; too rich, perhaps, for some of my esteemed acquaintances, whose digestive organs partake of the general laziness of their habits; but to us ... It was excellent, most excellent."

† These scavengers know
their subject well. I once
did a study of precisely
how much grease there
was in major bison bones.
I then looked at the
literature on scavenger
selection of bones from
carcasses. There was
almost a perfect one-
to-one correlation. If
you scatter bones from
a carcass in front of
carnivores, they will
quickly sniff among
the total sample and
then pick out the very
greasiest ones to eat first.

Marrow was also boiled or melted out of buffalo bones and the rich liquid fat saved to make other foods tastier. Indeed, there was a great deal of bone boiling going on at Head-Smashed-In and other bison kills. Some of it was for the purpose of extracting the rich marrow, but marrow was more easily acquired by smashing the massive buffalo bones in two and pulling out an entire plug of marrow fat.

Though bone looks to be solid, it is really more of a latticework of twisted strands of bone tissue interspersed with tiny spaces. This structure makes bone far stronger, better able to support weight, movement, and stress, than it would be if it were solid. The tiny spaces interlaced with tissue aren't empty; they are filled with small globules of fat. Called bone grease, it is a fat separate from marrow in that it is located within the bone structure itself, not the marrow cavity. Archaeologists may be just about the only group of scientists in the world interested in the question of how much grease there is inside the cellular structure of bone. Why anyone would care about this must seem like a pretty reasonable question. Wildlife biologists are very concerned with how much marrow there is in the cavities of big leg bones, such as the femur and tibia, because this tells you much about the overall health of the animal (marrow is one of the last fat reserves to be mobilized in times of nutritional stress, so an animal with low levels of fat in the marrow is a very sick animal).

But biologists draw the line at the contents of the marrow cavities. The fat contained in the actual bone that surrounds the cavities is essentially of interest to carrion bugs, wolves, coyotes, and archaeologists. The first three enjoy feeding on the bones, and since fat is tasty and good for you, these critters care a great deal about which bones have an abundance of fat and which are relatively lean.† Archaeologists care about this subject because ancient hunters also wanted to get all the fat they could from bison carcasses, and they too sorted through the bones in the body carefully and deliberately, selecting those with the greatest amount of fat. These bones could be processed to remove the bone grease right away after the kill, but the technique is very laborious compared with simply removing the other huge fat deposits of the body and the marrow. Also, the total amount of fat that can be recovered from within the bones is very small compared with the great amount of fat that comes from the rest of the carcass.

You wouldn't expect, then, people to try to render grease from bison bones unless they really needed additional fat. Logic dictates too, that, faced with massive food supplies in the aftermath of a successful bison drive, they did not. We might anticipate that prime grease-rich bones were saved for later processing, but sometimes evidence defies logic. Our excavations at Head-Smashed-In pointed to an astonishing amount of bone boiling going on at the site. During our years of work at the site, in the mid 1980s, little was known about how bone grease was extracted from the structure of the bone. We dug deeper into this cooking process.

High Plains Cooking

They make marrow fat, by cutting the joints of the bones, which they boil for a considerable time, and then skim off the top, which is excellent to eat with their dried meat. – Daniel Harmon, 1800–19

Lacking pots, pans, and stove tops, how did Aboriginal people cook their food? Pottery vessels did eventually make their way into the culture of the northern Plains groups, but only about two thousand years ago and only as fairly small pots unsuitable for cooking large amounts of food. If you can't cook by placing a big pot over a fire, the clever solution was to bring the fire to the inside of the container. From written descriptions, we know that Plains Indians had several methods for cooking up soups and stews, the most important of which

Wood and antler digging sticks were used to dig cooking pits in the ground, which were then lined with a fresh buffalo hide and filled with water. (Courtesy Head-Smashed-In Buffalo Jump)

These earthen pits were filled with water, then hot rocks from a nearby fire were added, and smashed bone fragments were tossed in to render the grease from the bones. (Courtesy Shayne Tolman)

† Another method of boiling water was to make an above-ground cauldron by suspending a buffalo stomach or piece of hide over a wooden tripod. The basin was then filled with water, and the water was heated by adding hot rocks. This method was not as effective in windy areas because the wind sapped the heat from the sides of the hide container.

was using pits dug into the ground.† Bowl-shaped pits, dug into the hard earth, were made watertight by pushing a fresh buffalo hide (fleshy side up) into the bottom of the pit. Water from the spring that flows from beneath the cliff at Head-Smashed-In was carried to the cooking pits. Once the hide-lined pits were filled, the water was heated by placing super hot rocks into the pits. Large, heavy cobbles were heated in a nearby fire and carried with a forked stick to the pit. As these rocks steamed, hissed, and lost their heat, another batch was being made ready in the fire. By continuously replacing the rocks, the water in the pits slowly got hot and food was added and cooked.

The process certainly sounds somewhat bizarre, but does it really work? My crew and I thought we would give it a try. First we needed the basic supplies for the experiments: pits, water, hide, rocks, and fire. We decided to do these experiments in our camp rather than at the buffalo jump so as not to create features at the site that might confuse future generations of archaeologists. Our camp was a beautiful spot near the Belly River, so rocks and water were in endless supply. Pits were easily dug to the approximate dimensions of the ones we were finding in our excavations at the buffalo jump. Fresh buffalo hides were hard to come by (and expensive), but cowhide seemed a reasonable alternative and readily available in cattle country. For the fire we gathered wood in the Belly River valley, but we also wanted to have fires like the ones of the Plains people, using that ubiquitous

Excavations at Head-Smashed-In Buffalo Jump uncovered many ancient pits dug into the surrounding sterile soil. The bison hide that lined the bottom of this pit has long decayed, but the stones used for heating and the buffalo bones remain. (Courtesy Royal Alberta Museum)

† Clearly this was a character building exercise: Milt went on to be a director in government; Caroline now holds a PhD in anthropology. I like to think my assignment left them well suited (and was perhaps even responsible) for their future career advancement.

supply of fuel that dotted the prairies for thousands of years: dried patties of buffalo dung. In the largely treeless prairies, dung, or chips, had been a universal source of fuel for both Native people and early European explorers. Getting dried buffalo chips for our experiments was going to be a little tricky.

Dried dung from cattle might be much the same as that from bison, but we thought we'd first try for the real thing. (Besides, un-like hide, how expensive could bison chips be?) A captive bison herd existed nearby in Waterton National Park. In what must have been a startling request, Milt Wright (one of my long-time colleagues) showed up at Waterton and asked the park ranger if we could collect a Sub-urban full of dried buffalo chips. It turns out collecting anything from a national park, including poop, requires a permit. Rather than filling out the required forms in triplicate and shipping them off for the long wait to Ottawa, Milt headed for a private bison ranch. The owner was only too happy (and no doubt amused) to part with half a tonne of dried dung. To this day I get a smile picturing Milt and his helper, Caroline Hudecek-Cuffe, streaking back toward camp with a Sub full of aromatic brown chips, wondering what the police officer would have said had they been pulled over.†

We now had everything we needed to make replicas of Native cooking pits, but we needed something to cook. Since our interest focussed not on cooking meat but rather on getting fat out of bones,

*After cooking meat and
bones in the pits, the food
was removed and the grease
skimmed from the surface
to be kept in hide bags.
(Courtesy Shayne Tolman)*

*After cooking meat and
bones in the pits, the food
was removed and the grease
skimmed from the surface
to be kept in hide bags.
(Courtesy Shayne Tolman)*

we wanted bones to boil up in our pits. Bones from freshly killed
bison were hard to come by, so again we settled for cattle. Loads of
fresh, greasy cattle bones were hauled into camp and dumped onto
the sun-baked prairie. We were poised to learn a lot about what a
mess it is to deal with fresh bones.

Another thing we knew about how Plains people cooked their
food was that bones were thoroughly smashed up before they were
boiled. The reason is simple. Hot water acts to melt the globules of
fat that reside in the tiny cavities of bone structure, sending fat into
the water where it rises to the surface. If you have ever boiled a soup
bone on the stove you have seen the glistening skim of grease that
forms on top of the water. However, to be effective, to remove the
majority of the fat, the hot water has to circulate around as much of
the bone surface as possible. Tossing a whole bone into boiling water
exposes only a very limited amount of the surface of the bone to the
hot water and would extract only a tiny fraction of the total fat content.
Smashing bones into small fragments allows hot water to circulate
around much more of the bone structure, driving out a much greater
percentage of the total grease content. A mound of fresh, slimy bones
lay in our campsite, needing to be smashed up and boiled. For this
seemingly ugly and thankless job we recruited one of the Blackfoot
people whom we had hired that summer, a wonderful woman named
Hazel Big Smoke.

Hazel Gets Slimed

Hazel Big Smoke was a middle-aged woman from the Piikani reserve, the boundary of which lies just a kilometre south of Head-Smashed-In Buffalo Jump. I always made a point of hiring Blackfoot people on my crews. I felt it was appropriate to offer employment to the local people whose ancestors had used the great buffalo jump. It helped them get in touch with their traditional culture, and it helped me and other non-Native members of my crew begin to understand a Native perspective of the world. It was immensely beneficial in both ways. But field archaeology is a science aimed at the young of heart and body. It is strenuous, back-breaking work, which at Head-Smashed-In was almost always conducted in ferocious winds and relentless sun. Typically, the crew I hired for this work included mainly people in their late teens or early twenties.

One year, after I had placed an ad for employment in the Band office of the Piikani Nation, I went down to conduct interviews. Among the respondents was a large, slightly heavy woman, probably in her late forties. I was a little shocked when she entered the room. I don't think anyone over the age of twenty-five had ever applied for one of my jobs before. I didn't quite know what to do with a clearly older, shy, demure woman who said she wanted to work on a dig. I did my best to discourage her, elaborating on the daily hardships: the wind-driven dust that packed every pore of your body, the aching of knees and back, the boredom of scraping away at baked earth, the sweltering sun, the minimal pay. Nothing worked. She wanted the job and was willing to start.

Hazel was a genuine person, honest, very shy yet strong willed, with an infectious smile (her standard answer to my endless reports of workplace atrocities was "Oh, geezze"). I was smitten, and so was everyone else who worked with Hazel Big Smoke. Besides, as we teasingly reminded her, she seemed to have the perfect last name for working with fires and cooking. By the end of the summer a grateful Hazel Big Smoke presented Milt with a beautiful pair of moccasins, me with a stunning pair of fur-lined winter mitts that I wear to this day, and many other members of the crew with handmade key chains and other gifts. Sometimes the world unfolds the way it should.

Hazel slaved away with the rest of the crew that summer, doing all the monotonous work the younger ones did (minus the back talk).

Hazel Big Smoke uses a sledge hammer to break up cow bones that were used in the boiling experiments. (Courtesy Milt Wright)

As the summer progressed, we continued to excavate more and more evidence of the smashing and cooking of bones in pits sunk into the ground. Milt, Bob Dawe (my other crew chief), and I became more interested in the whole question of how and why people might once have tried to get the grease out of the bones of bison. We knew that there were some relevant ideas floating around in the anthropological literature, but there were few details or specifics to help us understand what might have gone on in the days and months after the great buffalo drives. If you really want to know what might have gone on in the past, there is no alternative to trying something yourself. With our experiments we hoped to fill in some of the missing details of the bewildering process of cooking in a hide-lined pit. Knowing that it would be both ugly and fun, we enlisted Hazel.

Cow bones are much the same size and shape as bison bones; breaking up either is not as easy as it sounds. It's not just that they are very thick, dense, and large. It's that they are greasy, especially when they sit outside in the sun, which of course is why we, and Native hunters before us, were interested in them. Pick them up and your hands are immediately coated in a fine layer of oil, as are other objects you then pick up, such as the handles of the axes we used to smash the bones. Pretty soon everything gets a splattering of grease on it, including, most disgustingly, the people involved.

Starting our experiment, Hazel put the ends of bones on stone anvils, leaving the middle suspended in air, this midpoint being the target for first breaking the bone in half. That was the end of the easy part. After that, smaller pieces of bone had to be placed on top of flat stones and smashed with hatchets and hammers (to be really authentic we should have used stone hammers tied to wood handles, but we found that we were plenty inept with our own tools and decided to forego rigorous authenticity). Hitting curved, slippery chunks of bone is akin to grabbing hold of Jell–O. Half the time a blow was delivered, the fragments flew off the anvils in all directions. Hazel would let out an "Oh, geeze" and shield her eyes. Worse than the flying fragments was the splattering grease. Because we were working in the warmest part of summer, the bones were positively oozing. With each blow of Hazel's hammer, grease, albeit tiny amounts, would fly into the air. It landed on her hair, on her clothes, on her glasses, on everything. Because it was only a small amount each time, it took a while to notice it. Eventually you couldn't miss it. It was then that Hazel uttered one of my favourite lines of the summer.

Fed up and disgusted with the seemingly stupid experiments of a couple of white scientists, Hazel threw down her hammer and announced, "My ancestors never did this!" and retired to a nearby lawn chair. The rest of us rolled with laughter. We joked with her about how her ancestors simply went to the grocery store and got all the meat and fat they wanted, as opposed to the ignorant enemies of the Blackfoot who probably sat breaking bones on rocks and getting covered in grease. Not only was Hazel priceless to work with, she was probably right. The precious fat we were trying to recover was being lost on hands, rocks, tools, in the air, and on the ground. Bone chips were zinging around camp getting filthy. Our results were so unproductive that it seemed there must be a better way.

What we knew for sure was that the Native people who used Head-Smashed-In did indeed smash bones and boil them in earthen pits. Our excavation of literally millions of small bone fragments, stones used for boiling, along with the outlines of ancient pits and many fireplaces, confirmed these facts. But as we shared Hazel's frustrations in trying to replicate this activity, we knew we must be missing something. Although we never fully solved the mystery, it seemed likely that bones must have been spread over one or more bison hides to help catch the flying pieces. Perhaps the bones were even wrapped in hide before they were pounded, thus enabling capture of both errant pieces and the grease they contained. Working in cooler fall weather also would have improved results considerably.

† Josiah Gregg commented that it "is amusing to witness the bustle which generally takes place in collecting this offal." Edward Harris said he had a good laugh wondering what their friends back home would say if they could see him and the great naturalist Audubon carrying buffalo chips stacked up to their chins.

Despite the nagging feeling that ancient hunters who used the buffalo jump must have had superior methods to ours for breaking up bones, we pressed on with our experiments. With the bones eventually broken into thumbnail-sized pieces, we were ready to cook them up. Time to drag Hazel out of her lawn chair and into the next pleasant part of the task, firing up the buffalo chips. It is worth recording that all the staff coaxed into taking part in the bone-smashing activity were allocated a special privilege. The crew's regular cleaning up after a hot, dusty day digging at the site was to splash in the nearby Belly River. But grease-splattered staff needed heavy duty cleaning and were allowed to take the vehicle into the nearest town for a long shower with actual hot water.

Buffalo Chips

Since leaving Pembina River ... the plains were plentifully strewn with dry buffalo dung, which by also using as fuel we greatly economized the wood we took with us. This buffalo dung, the glow from which somewhat resembles that from coals, is a great acquisition to a camp fire. – Capt. John Palliser, 1857–60

For thousands of years, Aboriginal hunters used buffalo feces to cook up buffalo feasts. Dried buffalo dung was the standard fuel for all who resided on the prairies. Wood was the preferred fuel but was in short supply on the treeless Plains. Buffalo chips had the advantage of being everywhere; as John Audubon noted, chips were "so abundant that one meets these deposits at every few feet and in all directions." Of course, burning dung comes with certain baggage.† Schoolcraft commented that it "produces an ardent but transient flame, sufficient for cooking our daily food; but it evolves a smoke which, to the nasal organs of a stranger, is far from being agreeable." As expected, authors of the historic literature had some fun with the odor of the ordure. Yet there was consensus that, as Turnbull said in 1852, it "makes a grand fire."

At least it does as long as it is dry. All travellers on the Plains noted this important trait. "In dry weather it is an excellent substitute for wood," Josiah Gregg wrote, "but when moistened by rain, the smouldering pile will smoke for hours before it condescends to burn, if it does at all." Tixier experienced what must have been a frequent

occurrence, the inability to cook when the weather turned sour: "we had to use dried bison dung to make a fire. When the rain had soaked this fuel, we had to eat dried meat raw."

Our own experience was much the same. Patties of dried buffalo dung aren't as bad to work with as it sounds – just make sure they are really dry. The smell is mostly gone (except when you pile hundreds of them into a closed Suburban). You can stack them like poker chips, fling them around like Frisbees, all without feeling too slimed. But not Hazel. She wasn't interested in having much to do with chips of animal dung. Since this isn't the kind of thing you force on someone (after all, I had omitted this part from the job interview), Milt took over the experiment with Hazel as a keen observer.

It turns out that buffalo chips burn really well, and burn hot, as long as you meet a couple of criteria. First, it's hard to get chips burning from scratch. They are not like kerosene-soaked briquettes that burst into flame at the touch of a match. You have to get a small wood fire going first and then add the chips. Second, you need a breeze.

People using buffalo jumps and pounds would have spent a great deal of time gathering buffalo chips for fuel, possibly using hides to make collecting easier. (Courtesy Head-Smashed-In Buffalo Jump)

In dead calm, chips simply smoulder, smoke, and give off little heat. They require fanning from a stiff wind to burn with a steady flame and generate a reasonable amount of heat. Trying to cook on a calm night, Maximilian discovered the same: "[We] endeavoured to kindle a fire of buffalo dung in this place of general rendezvous; the wind was bleak, and we could not make our fire burn bright." Incidentally, a spin-off piece of knowledge gained from these experiments was the realization that buffalo chips would have made poor winter fuel, during a time when people were confined to living inside skin tipis. The lack of a breeze inside a dwelling would have rendered chips relatively useless and helps explain why winter camps were located in places like valley bottoms and wooded hills where wood was in abundance.

To our surprise, comparing the temperature of wood and chip fires, built side by side in the open air, showed very little difference. As long as the breeze was steady, chips burned just as hot as wood, sometimes hotter. One hundred and fifty years before us, Josiah Gregg proclaimed the same, saying that buffalo dung "even makes a hotter fire" than wood. Suddenly Hazel seemed a little more proud of the ingenuity of her ancestors for finding such a practical and valuable use for a renewable and abundant fuel nature had given to her people. With the fires glowing hot, it was time to add the rocks.

Hot Rocks

An old method of preparing food … entailed digging a pit which was lined with a green hide pegged to the ground around its rim. Meat and water were placed in the pocket and brought to a boil by adding hot stones. – David Mandelbaum, for the Plains Cree, 1979

The topsoil that blankets the prairie surrounding Head-Smashed-In has been blown in by the wind. All the archaeological materials that we excavated were contained within this windblown soil. Wind, no matter how strong, carries only small-sized particles such as silt and tiny grains of sand. Rocks can't be carried by any wind. Thus, all the rocks found in our excavation pits must have been carried in, and we found tonnes of rocks. Millions more remain buried in unexcavated portions of the site. Furthermore, of the literally hundreds of thousands of rocks we excavated, every single one of them was broken;

after ten seasons of digging at Head-Smashed-In we found not a single complete rock or cobble. What's going on here? How do we explain an almost solid layer of fractured rock packed into the topsoil on the prairie beneath the buffalo jump? Rocks, it turns out, are mute testimony to the enormous amount of cooking that went on at the site.

Boiling in earthen pits requires a huge amount of rock. In part this is because rocks have to be continuously heated so as to replace those put into the cooking pits. In addition, the rocks in use break into small pieces as a result of repeated heating and cooling. When you get a rock super hot and then plunge it into a bath of much cooler water, there are tremendous expansion and contraction forces at work. Cracks ripple through the body of the rock, and eventually the rock breaks along these crack lines. A typical rock used in boiling might be softball size to begin with. After a couple heatings these rocks might break into two or three baseball-sized pieces. If these are again reheated, they might end up being golf ball-sized chunks. We have reached the point of diminishing returns. The smaller the piece of rock, the less heat it is able to transfer into the pit of water. By the time rocks reached about golf ball size, they were regarded as essentially useless for boiling water and were abandoned.

Repeat this thousands of times over and you have an awful lot of rock scattered across the prairie surface at Head-Smashed-In. Our limited excavation of a small portion of the camp and processing area allows us to compute an estimate for how much rock would be recovered if the entire site were to be excavated. Based on this analysis, we figure that about four million kilograms of heating stones drape the soils at Head-Smashed-In Buffalo Jump. When nearly every one of these is golf ball size or smaller, that's a lot of rocks. Every single one has been intentionally brought out to the prairie for the purpose of cooking food. It's rather mind boggling to try to imagine the amount of human labour that must have gone into finding, transporting, and using all this rock. But clearly it did happen. The evidence reverberates up your leg bones every time you try to kick a shovel into the ground. Yet the most astounding thing is not the sheer amount of rock but what kind of rock it is and where it comes from.

As any photograph of the site reveals, the sandstone escarpment that forms the jump off at Head-Smashed-In is a massive feature of rock. For the hundreds of people who were busy butchering up the remains of bison carcasses, there was no shortage of immediately available rock. Yet they hardly used it or, rather, they used it for one highly specific purpose. Of the hundreds of thousands of rocks we excavated from the Head-Smashed-In camp and processing area, the overwhelming majority were not the local sandstone bedrock. Rather, they were fragments of quartzite cobbles – hard, dense, rounded stones that occur in limitless numbers in the creeks and rivers of Alberta. Deeper down in the soils around Head-Smashed-In, quartzite cobbles are found in great abundance, because they were dragged around and dropped by glaciers during the Ice Age. But you would have to dig for them, and in ancient times, with only simple digging sticks as tools, this would have been a great deal of work. Far easier would be to simply collect them from places where they are found on the surface, and for that you have to travel to the valley bottom of the Oldman River, about five kilometres away. Clearly this is what the ancient users of the jump did, and they did it in amounts and numbers that stagger the imagination.

Remember that the users of the jump had at their disposal only their own labour and that of their dogs. Try to picture, then, sinuous lines of humans and dogs tracing their way from Head-Smashed-In south to the Oldman, loading up with as many rocks as a person and dog could carry, and then retracing their path – uphill this time – back to the jump. This is not a precious cargo of bison meat for food or hides for winter blankets. This is people expending a huge amount of effort to simply move natural, round rocks from the river to the prairie beneath the jump. It was done in spite of the fact that millions of tonnes of sandstone bedrock lay right at the spot where the bison had been killed. Why on earth would people purposefully haul millions of kilograms of one type of rock over an uphill distance of several kilometres when an inexhaustible supply of another type of rock lay perched at their feet?

There was a pattern – the overwhelmingly dominant use of imported rocks as opposed to using the local bedrock – but we didn't know what caused the discrepancy. Clearly, there had to be powerful reasons to compel people to physically gather and transport distant rocks, and the only way to understand this seemed to be to replicate what they did with the stones. So when Hazel and the rest of us finally finished busting up the greasy bison bones as best we could, we began to cook them up in hide-lined pits of water. To bring the water to a boil we decided to use two types of rock, chunks of the local

Left, the circular outline of a boiling pit at Head-Smashed-In with an abundance of buffalo bones and fractured rock. Right, a similar pit seen from the side illustrates how semi-circular pits were excavated into the undisturbed surrounding soil. (Courtesy Royal Alberta Museum)

sandstone bedrock from Head-Smashed-In and rounded quartzite cobbles gathered from the Oldman River valley.

We heated both types of rocks in fires at our campsite and placed them in separate earthen pits filled with water and smashed bone. The results were dramatic and striking. Initially, both types of rocks heated up just fine. But as the experiments progressed, some glaring differences surfaced. Sandstone is a porous rock, full of spaces that form between the cemented individual sand grains. On first heating, sandstone gets extremely hot and thus transfers a lot of heat to the water when the rocks are first quenched. It would seem to be an effective heating agent. But these rocks lose their heat quickly in cool water and must be removed and replaced, and here's where problems start to develop for sandstone. When submerged in the cooking pits, the porous rock absorbs a lot of water in the spaces between the sand grains. When you move it back to the fire for reheating you also bring back a lot of water with the rock. We noted that sandstone rocks returned to the fire hissed as they were reheated as the internal water was driven off by the heat from the fire. Introducing water-saturated rocks into the fire acted to cool the fire, requiring more fuel and increasing the time it took to reheat the rocks. But there's a third problem; sandstone is, curiously enough, sandy.

Repeated heating and cooling breaks down the bonds between grains of sand in the rocks, causing sand to shed from the rock surface. This process is exacerbated by the bumping around rocks go through as you drop them into and then try to fetch them out of pits of murky water. Sand grains end up piled in the bottom of the pit, in the same place the food you are trying to cook is located. If you

Cooking in a hide-lined pit may have been authentic to ancient traditions, but it was also messy after a few warm, sunny days. (Courtesy Milt Wright)

are cooking meat, as in a stew, or boiling the grease out of smashed bison bones, you end up with the rather undesirable result of some very gritty food. It seems that there were three good reasons why the local sandstone bedrock was not a great choice for use in boiling water: it absorbs water and so takes longer to reheat, it cools down your fire, and it puts a lot of grit in your food. These factors must have been extremely important, for they led people to ignore millions of tonnes of sandstone at Head-Smashed-In and venture several kilometres away to haul by hand vast quantities of another type of rock, quartzite, uphill to the flats beneath the jump.

Quartzite is very different from sandstone. It is an extremely hard rock, very dense, and made up of extremely fine particles of quartz fused together. It doesn't have the loose grains of sandstone. In my early years as an archaeologist in Alberta, I worked exclusively in the Rocky Mountains where it can be cold at night (and even snow) in any of the summer months. A trick we all soon learned was to heat quartzite cobbles by the side of the campfire at night, wrap them in a towel, and place them in the bottom of our sleeping bags. It was a clever and successful way to drive some of the cold out of your bag and keep your feet toasty warm. The same properties that kept our feet warm made quartzite an ideal stone for Plains people to use when cooking food.

To be sure, quartzite also breaks up as you heat and cool it. There is no rock that would not. But it does so in a much more favourable fashion. Quartzite cobbles are so dense that they absorb a great deal of heat from the fire, giving them more heat to transfer to the water-filled pits. Their greater density also means that they do not absorb any water from the pits to bring back to the fire when being reheated. When immersed in cool water they of course also suffer great pangs of contraction and are typically riddled with cracks that radiate through the rock. After a couple cycles between the fire and water, the rocks split along these cracks, but when they break they fracture cleanly. No sand is left in the bottom of the container. The users of Head-Smashed-In had a very clear idea of what size of rock was still useful and what was considered expended. Of the hundreds of thousands of quartzite rocks we recovered from our digs, about 95 per cent of them were golf ball size or smaller. This was clearly the discard size, too small to warrant further heating and transfer to the fire because of the diminished amount of heat such small stones could hold.

It should be obvious why we didn't find a single large quartzite cobble in ten years of excavation. With an enormous expense of labour, every one of these rocks had been purposively carried from the Oldman River valley to Head-Smashed-In to be used in stone boiling. They had thus achieved the status of a precious commodity. To get more of them meant an arduous return journey, something no one could have looked forward to. So they were diligently used to the point of exhaustion, abandoned only when there was no more use left in them. We discovered vast clusters of shattered quartzite stones, all less than about ten centimetres in size, piled off to the side of the excavated boiling pits and fireplaces. They were clearly the discard piles of exhausted stones. In our early years of digging, before the pattern became apparent to us, we used these rocks to scare gophers away from our lunches and for backfilling excavations. On closer inspection, they revealed a remarkable story of intelligent recognition of the different properties of rock for cooking and the extent to which ancient people were willing to go to obtain the precise materials they deemed necessary to process the spoils of the kill.

Time for a Roast

The Indian is a great epicure; knows the choicest titbits of every animal, and just how to cook it to suit his taste. – Colonel Richard Dodge, 1860s and 1870s

Over the days that men, women, and children spent butchering the carcasses of the buffalo, they no doubt craved a succulent piece of cooked meat. Boiling up stews and fat from bones provided one variety of nourishment, but clearly some delicately cooked hunks of meat would have been a welcome change of diet. I say clearly, because archaeological digs at Head-Smashed-In have turned up unequivocal evidence of a unique and largely forgotten method of roasting parts of the bison carcass. First, let me note a method of cooking meat that just as certainly was used at the buffalo jump. It just didn't leave any trace in the archaeological record.

No doubt fresh chunks of bison meat were grilled over the many fires that would have dotted the level plain beneath the jump. How this was done is conjecture. Most likely, moderate-sized pieces of meat were skewered on sticks and angled into the flames. After turning or moving a couple of times, the sizzling steaks were ready to eat. Alternatively, chunks of meat may have been simply laid on hot rocks placed in or near the flames or placed on grids of fresh sticks laid down on a bed of coals. But a thousand or more years later, there is

Preparation for roasting food probably involved wrapping the meat in a protective cover and digging a hole in the earth. (Courtesy Shayne Tolman)

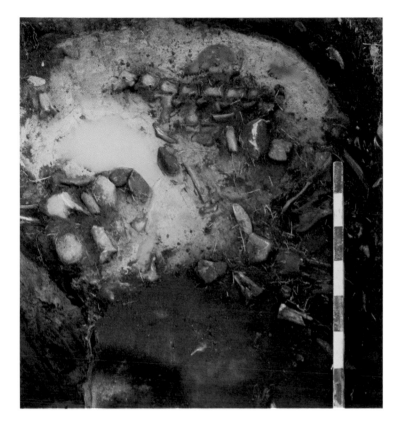

Excavation of a roasting pit at Head-Smashed-In. The dig is coming down on top of bones left in the pit, including several broken leg bones and, at left, an intact part of the backbone. The whitish colour comes from salts in the soil. (Courtesy Royal Alberta Museum)

nothing for the archaeologist to find confirming this type of cooking. More recent hunters certainly enjoyed food cooked this way. In 1840 Victor Tixier, armed with meat from a fresh kill, describes how "spits were put up everywhere; the short-ribs, the cuds, ribs, loins, the humps were being roasted over all the fires."

As tasty as a fresh-grilled steak is, there is a significant drawback to cooking meat this way, especially if you savour all the fats and juices that meat contains. All of us have grilled over an open flame (our barbeques), and so we know that the flame sizzles and roars to life as the juice and fat drips from the heated meat. This is inevitable when various fats contained in meat are heated to the melting point, and we don't mind so much because we are intending to cut off most of the fat anyway. But Aboriginal hunters minded. The fats and juices were life-giving sources of energy and nutrition for them. Grilling meat on a spit over an open flame was easy, quick, and took almost no preparation. No doubt it was done on a large scale at Head-Smashed-In.

However, to the Native hunters it was an inferior method of cooking that resulted in the loss of much of what makes meat so great to eat. As you might expect, over the vast time they processed up the remains of bison, they developed a sophisticated way to cook their meat and keep in all the essential fats. They roasted it in the ground.

This is something my crews and I never did try, but I met a number of ranchers who did and who attested to the supreme delicacy of the meat (it is not surprising that ranchers, surrounded by cattle, have explored many ways to cook meat, as did Native people). The method is decidedly laborious and time consuming. That it was done at all is evidence that the end result is a stunningly good feed.

It began with yet another pit dug into the earth on the prairie that skirted the buffalo jump. These pits were deeper and steeper sided than the boiling pits, averaging about seventy-five centimetres across and the same in depth. These had to be excavated into hard-packed soils with simple digging tools, such as antler tines or pointed sticks, so the labour investment was considerable. Then rocks were gathered to be used to line the bottom of the pit. While we knew this much from detailed historic accounts of how Plains people roasted food in earthen pits, when we actually found and excavated some of these features we were in for a surprise.

I have just finished describing the enormous effort that the users of the jump went to in order to obtain vast quantities of a particular type of stone, quartzite, from the Oldman River valley, with which to boil their water-filled pits. In the process, they ignored an endless supply of immediately available rock, the local sandstone bedrock. But as we began to discover and excavate additional pits identified as ones used to roast meat, we discovered that they contained almost exclusively sandstone rocks and hardly a single piece of quartzite.

Hard, dense, rounded quartzite cobbles were ideal for transferring heat from a fire into a pit filled with water, but the heating requirements of a roasting pit are entirely different. There is no heat being transferred. Rather, it is being reflected. The pit acted exactly like an earth oven, baking the food as it lay buried in the ground. The heat needed to be contained in the pit and reflected back to the meat that lay inside. Sandstone, made up of cemented sand grains, essentially pure silica, is highly reflective. If you need proof of this, work alongside a south-facing cliff of sandstone on a sunny day; you feel the heat radiating off the rock surface like an oven. I have painful personal

When completely excavated, the bottom of this roasting pit revealed a lining of sandstone slabs designed to reflect heat back to the buried meat. Note the charring in the lower right. (Courtesy Royal Alberta Museum)

experience. Working along a hot, sunny sandstone cliff in Writing-on-Stone Provincial Park, I discovered the power of both modern sun block lotions and of the reflective power of sandstone. My face, neck, and arms, lathered with a high SPF sunscreen, were well protected, while to my dismay I was sunburned through my clothes.

The towering cliffs of Porcupine Hills sandstone, of little use in boiling food, were ideally suited for the purpose of baking food in the ground. Furthermore, because the local bedrock was laid down millions of years ago in a marine environment, it has bedding planes, which cause the rock to break into relatively flat sheets. Flat slabs, not rounded cobbles, were precisely what were needed to form a reflective floor at the bottom of a roasting pit. Rounded rocks would have space between them where heat could escape into the lower soil; flat slabs of rock could be fitted together to form a nearly solid layer of basal stone. It was a perfect surface for radiating heat back to what lies above – large bundles of meat.

From historic accounts we know that when meat was roasted in the ground, a pit, shaped like an inverted bell, was lined on the bottom with a layer of rocks. Sometimes these rocks were heated before they were placed in the pit; sometimes a fire was built over the bottom layer of rocks to get them red hot. With the hot rocks in place, the meat was added to the pit. Usually, it was wrapped in a blanket of either hide or local vegetation (small branches of local willow, Saskatoon bushes, or conifers would have been ideal) to keep the meat from getting covered in dirt. Dirt was then piled on top of the protected meat and a fire was built over the pit. This fire was kept burning for many hours; some accounts say up to a full day or more. The long-burning surface fire sent heat into the earth below, through the meat, that was reflected back up again by the slabs of underlying sandstone. Finally, the ashes were pushed aside and the packaged meat was excavated from within the pit. From all accounts, both ancient and those of modern ranchers, meat cooked in this way is the most succulent, finest tasting you will ever have. Accounts of this type of cooking are rare, but Edwin James furnished us with a fine summary:

Cooked for dinner the entire hump of a bison, after the manner of the Indians; this favourite part of the animal was dissected from the vertebræ, after which the spinous processes were taken out, and the denuded part was covered with skin, which was firmly sewed to that of the back and sides of the hump; the hair was burned and pulled off, and the whole mass exhibiting something of a fusiform shape, was last evening placed in a hole dug in the earth for its reception, which had been previously heated by means of a strong fire in and upon it. It was now covered with cinders and earth, to the depth of about one foot, and a strong fire was made over it. In this situation it remained until it was taken up for the table to-day, when it was found to be excellent food.

From Mandelbaum's study of the Plains Cree we know that sometimes these roasting pits were made inside the tipi, dug into the floor, with the tipi fire providing the heat. Sometimes whole bison fetuses, plucked from their mother's bellies, were roasted in this way. So too were huge racks of ribs, and cuts from the massive hams of the rear legs. Meat, slowly roasted in deep, rock-lined pits, was literally baked in its own fat and juices, accounting for its delicious taste.

The original pits used by the Native cooks would nearly always be emptied of their contents by families eager to devour the fruits of their labours, and so we don't know what parts of the animal were placed in any one pit. But occasionally, for reasons lost to history (perhaps the appearance of enemies, the onset of a severe storm, or sheer forgetfulness), roasting pits were left with their contents intact. We discovered one such pit at the Head-Smashed-In processing site. The bones of what appeared to be nearly an entire fetus, or very young calf, were found tightly clustered in a pit and lying above a layer of sandstone slabs.

Since we discovered a number of these roasting pits during our years of excavating at Head-Smashed-In, it is clear that the ancient hunters were willing to go to the time and trouble of constructing and operating these impressive cooking features. Encountering the remains of a roasting pit is simple luck; there is no surface sign today of where they once were placed. Our discovery of a dozen or so, after having excavated only a tiny fraction of the entire site (much less than 1 per cent), suggests that hundreds if not thousands of roasting pits were used over the entire time that people processed the remains of bison at Head-Smashed-In Buffalo Jump. They are testimony to the great labour that ancient people were willing to expend to prepare food in the manner desired and to the recognition of the intrinsic properties of materials and circumstances (in this case, a sandstone-lined roasting pit to retain fat and juices) most suited to achieve their purpose.

Where Are the Skulls?

Round an isolated tree in the prairie I observed a circle of holes in the ground, in which thick poles had stood. A number of buffalo skulls were piled up there; and we were told that this was a medicine, or charm, contrived by the Indians in order to entice the herds of buffaloes. – Maximilian, Prince of Wied, 1832–34

One of the many really boring things that archaeologists do is count bones. We look for discrepancies in the counts that might guide us toward some greater understanding of what people were doing with the game they killed. One thing you can be sure of at any mass game kill is that bones will not be recovered in direct correspondence to the number of each bone in the body. That is, Aboriginal people were making very conscious decisions about what parts of the carcass they valued most. Thousands of years later, these decisions are still reflected in the widely divergent counts of different bones at bison kill and processing sites.

An inordinately high count of small lower leg bones at the kill site, for example, might indicate that these relatively worthless bones, with little meat or fat on them, were discarded immediately. Conversely, the ribs and the great spines of the thoracic vertebrae, known to be associated with some of the most favoured cuts of the animal, might have very low counts at the kill site, suggesting that they were nearly always taken away for consumption. Patterns in counts of bones recovered from the processing area are often a mirror image of the kill site: bones associated with the choicest cuts of meat should be recovered in great numbers (because they were moved from the kill to the butchering area), while bones linked to relatively poor parts of the carcass might be nearly absent (because they were abandoned at the kill).

Simple counting of buffalo bones from Head-Smashed-In reveals a very curious fact. There is a distinct shortage of skulls. Given that tens, probably hundreds, of thousands of animals were killed there over nearly six thousand years, there are not nearly as many skulls, or fragments of them, as one would expect, neither from the kill site nor the processing area. They are certainly not entirely absent from the site, but they are very much underrepresented in relation to all the other bones of the body.

Archaeologists always have to look at a wide array of factors to account for simple discrepancies in such things as bone counts. Some bones are much softer than others and will degrade more easily in the soil; thus you can expect harder bones (such as leg bones that had to support the great weight of the beast) to be better preserved and hence have higher counts. Some bones are more favoured by carnivores and scavengers (such as ones with more fat and marrow), so they might be preferentially dragged away and consumed by wolves, coyotes, rodents, and birds. Certain bones (like those from the hoof) are small, round, and easily rolled away by wind and running water. Others,

Skulls were found at Head-Smashed-In, just not in numbers consistent with the evidence for the number of animals killed. Skulls found in the spring channel tended to be better preserved because they were quickly buried. (Courtesy Royal Alberta Museum)

like the pelvis, are massive and angular and so resist almost any kind of movement. Even when all these factors are considered, skulls are very rare at Head-Smashed-In. Many of the great communal bison kills from the northern Plains show the same shortage of skulls.

There is not much meat or fat connected with the head of the bison. It's mostly a thick mat of hair and skin drawn over massive bone. Probably, the noses, eyeballs, and tongues were taken from every animal. There is little other food value associated with the head, so we can't explain their scarcity on the basis of people taking away a valued food source. And they are big and very heavy. You don't drag off something as massive as a bison skull unless you have a good reason.

Of course, skulls were the source of one very practical and necessary part of converting dead bison to useful products; they were the source of brains used in tanning hides. It just so happens that the chemical mixture of brains is almost exactly what is needed to tan animal hides effectively so that they don't rot. We know from both archaeological evidence and historic writings that skulls were routinely smashed (right in the centre of the head) and the brains were removed and saved for hide-tanning purposes. As a result, many of the skulls that are found show a distinctive crushing of the cranium. Even factoring these skulls into the equation, however, there is an inordinate shortage of skulls at the great communal kills. Something else was going on.

The answer may lie in the historic literature. Scouring the writings left by those who first studied the Plains Indians, it quickly becomes apparent that skulls figured into a wide variety of very special activities and beliefs, ones that did not pertain to other bones from the skeleton. Skulls, it seems, somehow represented, or embodied, the animal itself. It's as if skulls could stand in for the animals, serving as powerful icons that had the ability to mediate between real people and real buffalo. Perhaps most importantly, skulls could call other buffalo.

Studying the Teton Sioux, Frances Densmore told how a medicine man painted a buffalo skull with red and blue stripes. Then he filled his pipe and put both the pipe and the skull on a bed of prairie sage. "It was believed," Densmore reported, "that 'the skull turned into a real buffalo and called others.'" Pounds built by the Cree had a wooden ramp that the animals had to dash across before they plunged into the corral. A number of nations placed offerings underneath this ramp, presumably as gifts to the spirit world, in an attempt to ensure the success of the hunt. The Cree placed a buffalo skull under the ramp, hoping it would serve to call others of its kind. Maximilian, travelling through the Plains in the 1830s, observed the Assiniboine practice of building tall piles of stone "on the top of which is placed a buffalo skull, which we were told the Indians place there to attract the herds of buffaloes, and thereby to ensure a successful hunt."

In addition to rituals associated with calling the bison, skulls played a prominent role in many other ceremonies held by the people who subsisted on this animal. Bradbury, on the Plains from 1809 to 1811, encountered skulls that had been ceremonially decorated and was told that "it was an honour conferred by the Indians on the buffaloes which they had killed, in order to appease their spirits." In 1839 Thomas Farnham described an Arapahoe lodge in which the people "hang a fresh buffalo's head inside, near the top of the lodge … and the skin of a white buffalo, as offerings to the Great Spirit." Maximilian provides a wonderfully evocative description of how skulls were revered and cared for through the ages:

The buffalo skulls … are preserved in their huts, where they are everywhere to be seen, to be handed down from the father to the children. Many such heads are looked upon by them as medicine; they are kept in the huts, and sometimes the Indians stroke them over the nose, and set food before them. In general, the buffalo is a medicine animal, and more or less sacred.

Artist Karl Bodmer, travelling across the Plains with Maximilian, Prince of Wied, in 1883, discovered several of these stone cairns topped with buffalo skulls. They were said to be made by the Assiniboine for the purpose of encouraging the return of the buffalo. (Courtesy Joslyn Art Museum, Omaha, Nebraska)

In a previous chapter I made mention of how buffalo skulls were used in a piercing ceremony, attached by sinew to bone needles skewered through the skin of people making a pledge to the Great Spirit. The supplicants "are obliged to drag this heavy weight about," Maximilian observed, "with much pain." Such is their symbolic power that buffalo skulls also formed part of complex communication systems. In the early 1800s, Edwin James came across "a semicircular row of sixteen bison skulls, with their noses pointing down the river. Near the centre of the circle which this row would describe, if continued, was another skull marked with a number of red lines." Puzzled by this discovery, James inquired as to its meaning:

Our interpreter informed us that this arrangement of skulls and other marks here discovered, were designed to communicate the following information, namely, that the camp had been occupied by a war party of the … Pawnee Loup Indians, who had lately come from an excursion against the Cumancias, Ietans, or some of the western tribes. The number of red lines traced on the painted skull indicated the number of the party to have been thirty-six; the position in which the skulls were placed, that they were on their return to their own country. Two small rods stuck in the ground, with a few hairs tied in two parcels to the end of each, signified that four scalps had been taken.

Perhaps these records help explain why skulls are relatively rare at Head-Smashed-In and many other mass kill sites. The head of the buffalo was infused with power not shared by other skeletal elements. There is an important lesson here for archaeologists. We have a tendency to ascribe people's actions to straightforward, rational action, behaviour that is rooted in our notion of a common sense use of the resources that permeated their world. Certainly, much of my description of killing and butchering bison reflects this practical interpretation. For the most part, I have advanced a scenario whereby ancient Aboriginal people used the carcass of the buffalo in ways that maximized their return of nutritious, energy-rich food. The lesson of the skull serves to remind us that life is seldom that simple. In other cultures, people might refrain from eating meat on Fridays, avoid pork altogether, or even place a chicken "wishbone" on a shelf to dry so we can vie to be the one holding the greater part after snapping it. Cultures around the world have imparted deeply held beliefs to the foods that keep them alive; few, if any, do so more so than the Plains people did with the buffalo.

Packing Up, Among the Bears

We had not left the fort more than five or six miles behind us, when we fell in with an enormous grizzly bear, but François would not fire at him ... A younger man than he, who had his character to make, might have been foolish enough to have run the risk, for the sake of the standing it would have given him amongst his companions; but François ... would not risk attacking so formidable an animal with only two men. In fact, their enormous strength, agility, and wonderful tenacity of life, make them shunned even by large numbers, and few are killed, except by young men, for the sake of proudly wearing the claws. – Paul Kane, 1847

This pretty well covers the range of food processing activities that we know went on at Head-Smashed-In. Many parts of the story of what transpired at the processing site simply leave no archaeological trace and, except through speculation and the memories of elders, will remain unknown to us – the feasting, the prayers and ceremonies, the sending out of scouts to alert nearby groups of relatives to come to the jump, the daily exchange of conversation. But it would be a mistake to think that all the extraordinary hard work had come to an end. The

killing of a hundred or more bison at the jump put in motion a host
of longer term processing responsibilities. Some of these we believe
took place after hunters left the kill site, at the next camp spot.

There were a number of compelling reasons to depart from the
buffalo jump: the lack of protection, absence of wood, the unsuitabil-
ity of the place for long-term camping. But there was another reason
– the smell. Upwards of several hundred buffalo had been killed and
butchered at the site. Blood, guts, stomach contents, and stray bits of
fat, meat, and bone must have been spread everywhere. In the days
following the kill, this mess began to rot. The stench must have been
overpowering. We can't impose our own values on the ancient hunters
and assume that they found the smell repulsive. They may have been
much more accustomed to such situations than we could ever be. But
we can assume that the smell had another unwelcome consequence;
it brought in an array of bothersome visitors.

The wind-borne scent of the kill must have made its way to the
noses of a host of other animals that would have found it quite entic-
ing. Wolves and coyotes, virtually the constant companions of buffalo
herds, would have wanted to get at their fair share of the booty and
were probably a constant nuisance. Great flocks of carrion-eating birds
no doubt circled above the stinking mass, swooping down to pick at
the pieces. More ominously, the wafting smell might have attracted
the animal most feared by Native people, the grizzly bear.

We think of the grizzly as a reclusive animal confined to the
wild back areas of the Rocky Mountains, but before the development
and settlement of the West, they were much more numerous and
lived out on the open Great Plains. These fearsome beasts hunted
and killed anything and everything they wished. That they brought
down huge bison, including bulls, at full gallop is well documented.
In 1859, near the fork of the Bow and Red Deer rivers, Palliser told
of a companion of his who watched a band of buffalo emerge from a
river and ascend the opposite bank "when he saw a bear (previously
concealed in a deep rut) spring up and dash the foremost bull to the
ground, ploughing his sides with his monstrous claws and rending his
heart and vitals by a succession of tremendous blows." Edwin James
also attests to the enormous strength of the Plains grizzly, recounting how a companion of his shot a bison, "and leaving the carcass to
obtain assistance to butcher it, he was surprised on his return to find
that it had been dragged entire, to a considerable distance, by one of

Artist George Catlin drew
several scenes of ferocious
grizzly bears attacking
Aboriginal hunters.
(Courtesy Bruce Peel
Special Collections Library,
University of Alberta)

these bears, and was now lodged in a concavity of the earth, which the animal had scooped out for its reception."

John Audubon was told of a starving Indian family that had sought refuge on the gravel bar of a river. Desperate for food, the man spied a bison carcass:

The soldiers saw him walk to the body of a dead Buffalo lying on the shore of the island, with the evident intention of procuring some of it for food. As he stooped to cut off a portion, to his utter horror he saw a small Grizzly Bear crawl out from the carcass. It attacked him fiercely, and so suddenly that he was unable to defend himself; the Bear lacerated his face, arms, and the upper part of his body in a frightful manner.

More frighteningly, grizzlies hunted humans. James referred to the animal as, "without doubt, the most daring and truly formidable animal that exists in the United States," and he asserted that the grizzly "frequently pursues and attacks hunters." Thomas Woolsey, trekking across Alberta in the mid-1800s, recorded a female grizzly "nearly dragged one of the hunters from off his horse." But the most harrowing historical account of an attack on humans by a grizzly bear must go to David Thompson. Camped with the Peigan in southern Alberta, Thompson records how the silence of camp was broken by "the death cry." It came from a young man who had just returned with "one of his thighs torn by a grizled bear." It seems that three young men had come across the bear and decided to hunt him for the value of his hide and the highly prized claws. They had two arrows each, hardly an arsenal against a grizzly, and had the bad luck of having their arrows hit bones and non-vulnerable parts of the animal. Enraged, the bear "sprung on the first, and with one of his dreadful fore paws tore out his bowels and three of his ribs; the second he seized in his paws, and almost crushed him to death, threw him down, when the third Indian hearing their cries came to their assistance and sent an arrow which only wounded [the bear] in the neck, for which the Bear chased him, and slightly tore one of his thighs." Arming themselves, men from the camp headed out with the wounded hunter in search of the bear: "They found him devouring one of the dead … The first poor fellow was still alive and knew his parents, in whose arms he expired." When the bear was eventually killed, the wounded man asked to keep the enormous foreclaws but was denied.† The carcass of the bear was burned "until nothing but ashes remained."

Native inhabitants of the Plains were pretty much the lords of the land, the top of the food chain; they could and did kill virtually everything that roamed the prairies. But the grizzly bear was the one animal that hunted them (a pack of wolves may have taken the occasional solitary hunter, but this was probably very rare). Grizzly bears, being ferocious predators, were deeply feared but deeply respected by Native people. So strong was this respect that a number of Native groups were said to refuse to eat the flesh of the bear. While grizzly bears may have preferred fresh kills, they were not averse to scavenging carcasses. Lewis and Clark came across the largest grizzly they had ever seen, "devouring a dead buffaloe on a sandbar." The fear that the smell of rotting buffalo carcasses would attract grizzly bears provided a powerful incentive for people to vacate Head-Smashed-In as quickly as possible.

Thus, for a whole host of reasons, we suspect that the hundreds of people who had gathered at the jump were anxious to depart. They would head for a camp that was safe, secure, and more comfortable. They would leave behind a hillside and prairie flats stinking with

† The front claws of the grizzly bear (being much larger than the hind claws) were, as Paul Kane noted, "one of the most esteemed ornaments to an Indian chief." Edwin James tells how Native hunting parties went in search of the bears specifically to obtain the claws. They were, James records, "highly esteemed, and dignify the fortunate individual who obtains them. We saw, on the necks of many of their warriors, necklaces, composed of the long fore-claws separated from the foot, tastefully arranged in a radiating manner." I once recovered a complete set of grizzly bear foreclaws from an archaeological site in southern Alberta. Each claw had a drill hole for stringing, and each bore faint traces of red ochre paint. That the claws dated to 2,700 years ago attests to the great time depth of the Aboriginal belief in the power of the bear.

Front claws from a grizzly bear, 2,700 years old, found at an archaeological site in southern Alberta. Each claw has been drilled with a hole for stringing on a necklace. (Courtesy Royal Alberta Museum)

blood, spilled guts, and scraps of discarded food and bones – fodder for a plethora of scavengers, from bugs, birds, coyotes, and wolves to grizzly bears. Quite possibly, they set fire to the site before departing to clean it up and discourage scavengers.

Leaving Head-Smashed-In was probably not a single event. That is, it is very unlikely that at some point all the work was completed and the groups as a whole gathered up the spoils and quit the site. For one thing, there was simply too much stuff for everyone to carry. Departing the site was something that went on over a period of time, even as the butchering was still going on. Going home was a process, not an event.

CHAPTER 8

Going Home

Getting out of the Head-Smashed-In camp must have been a far bigger chore than getting in. People were leaving with tens of thousands of kilograms of bison products that they didn't have when they arrived, and it all had to be hauled away by the people themselves, and by their dogs, using a sled of crossed poles lashed together (a *travois*). It is inconceivable that the several hundred people who occupied the campsite could take everything with them in one trip. Given the tremendous loads that had to be carried, and the need to make the trip several times, where would these people go?†

Flowing west to east past the southern end of the Porcupine Hills and coming within a couple kilometres of the buffalo jump is one of the major waterways of southern Alberta, the Oldman River. It didn't get its name from the song but, rather, from the translation of the word the Blackfoot had given to the river. *Napi* means Old Man, in Blackfoot; the Oldman River is Napi's river. Napi is one of the most important characters in the spiritual world of the *Niitsitapi*,

† Father Hennepin remarked on the amazing strength of Native women, claiming that when moving camp they routinely carried 200 - 300 pounds of gear.

Packing up the spoils of the kill and moving off to better campsites would have been an enormous chore, which took hundreds of people several days. (Courtesy Head-Smashed-In Buffalo Jump)

This view looks southeast from the buffalo jump along one of the coulees connecting the jump to the valley of the Oldman River in the distance. (Courtesy Royal Alberta Museum)

† Many of the original names for Aboriginal groups across North America translate as "the people" or "the real people." This is true for tribal names such as Inuit, Beothuk, Innu, and Dene among many others. Names we are more familiar with were often given to the people by visiting Europeans, such as Sioux, Gros Ventre, and Nez Perce, which were named by the French. In contrast, Aboriginal groups tended to call their neighbours by less flattering, derogatory terms. After all, they were not part of the "real people."

the Blackfoot people; literally, the Real People.† Napi's river was the lifeblood of the Niitsitapi. It provided dependable water year round, an important avenue of transportation, shelter from winter, and trees for fuel, and it attracted game animals that the people depended upon. Most important to our story, it provided a close refuge from the buffalo jump, a place to retreat to with the spoils of the kill.

Recalling that we believe many of the great communal kills were conducted in the fall to secure supplies for the coming winter, the people leaving Head-Smashed-In would have been seeking a suitable winter campsite. The valley of the Oldman River offered everything the hunters required for winter survival. Best of all, it was exceedingly close. Round trips from the jump to the valley, even with heavy loads, could be completed in a couple of hours. Even while the butchering was still going on, men, women, and children carried loads on their backs, and every dog pulled a travois with piles of meat and hides. Seen from above it must have resembled a procession of ants - small, dark objects in sinuous lines connecting the source of food with the place that was to become the nest.

The valley of the Oldman has extensive flatlands where floodwaters have smoothed the earth. These flats offered an almost endless expanse of places to spread out in a large camp and to finish the business of converting the bison remains to food and products of hide. I can picture the dozens, perhaps hundreds, of bison hides stretched out

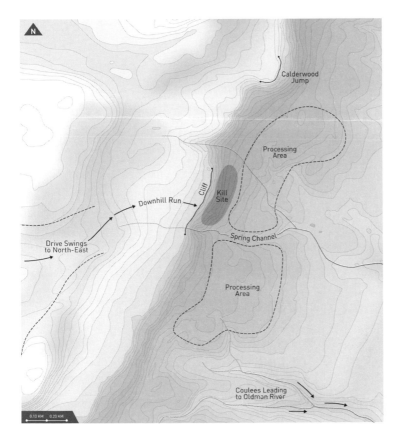

Just south of Head-Smashed-In are several prominent coulees. These protected valleys offered an easy route to the valley of the Oldman River about five kilometres away. (Courtesy Royal Alberta Museum)

to full size and pinned to the valley bottom with wooden pegs, looking like big brown scabs on the landscape. Dozens of tipis would have been pitched across the flats, clustered into small groups of closely related kin. Tipis might have been set close to the steep banks of the valley, using the surrounding high ground to protect people from the fury of winter winds and storms, or perhaps in amongst the cottonwoods that, serpent-like, hugged the meandering course of the river. In autumn, fires and cooking pits were scattered around and between the clusters of tipis, and the camp would have been a buzz of outdoor activity. But as winter approached, gathering wood began in earnest, and the chores of daily life moved indoors. A more perfect winter camp than the nearby Oldman River would be hard to imagine. Though we cannot yet prove the connection, all reason points to this place as the destination for the throngs of fully laden people making their way from the buffalo jump.

The valley of the Oldman River offers extensive flatlands for camping, protection from the winds of the upland prairie, water, and, most importantly, wood for winter fires. (Courtesy Caroline Hudecek-Cuffe)

† David Thompson was present when traditional shields were tested by a new weapon: "They had Shields of Bull's hide a safe defence against arrows and the spear, but of no use against balls."

Buffalo Hides

Whilst in the green state, [hides] are stretched and dried as soon as possible; and, on the return of the nation to the village, they are gradually dressed during the intervals of other occupations. – Edwin James, 1820

Imagine the loads that had to be transported! The hides alone from one hundred and fifty animals would have weighed thousands of kilograms. Yet hides were essential for making tipi covers, winter robes and blankets, mittens, caps, moccasins, containers for carrying possessions, and untold other products. The demand for tipi covers accounted for the greatest number of hides. A single tipi required twelve to fifteen hides sewn together, and they had to be replaced every couple years. Tipi covers, as much as the precious meat and fat, were essential for the survival of the people and were a major reason that great communal buffalo hunts were conducted. But here's the rub.

Autumn seems the ideal time for mass communal kills because bison were at their fattest and it allowed food to be stockpiled before winter. Indeed, archaeologists can demonstrate that many mass bison kills occurred in the fall. But autumn hides are generally unsuited for making tipi covers. In preparation for the greater insulation demands of winter, the hide of bison gets much thicker through autumn, which is true for both bulls and cows, though bull hides attain much greater thickness.† Since the fall kills captured mostly cows, it's possible that some of the younger cows may have had thin enough hides to work into tipi covers. But the hide of many of the buffalo would have been too thick to be effectively worked into lodge covers. It would be nearly impossible to sew hides that were one to two centimetres thick, and they would be staggeringly heavy to haul from camp to camp. While some of the ways Native people worked hide included thinning it, that required a great deal of work, and there was another, easier way, which was to wait until spring.

Changes in the nature of the buffalo hide over the course of a year were noted by early Europeans. The Earl of Southesk observed, "In buffalo robes the season makes a great difference." Bison hide gets progressively thinner through winter and is thinnest in the spring. This (and early summer) was the primary season when they were harvested for making tipi covers. While we know that many great kills took place in autumn, there must also have been mass bison kills in spring for the purpose of securing hides.

It is unlikely that fresh bison hides cut from the carcasses at Head-Smashed-In were scraped and tanned at the processing site. The traditional method of tanning hides involved spreading each one out to its full extent and staking it on the prairie to dry in the sun. The drying requires a great deal of flat ground, and it must be in a place where you don't need to leave any time soon. As already

Huge buffalo hides were stretched out, pinned down with wood or bone pegs, then scraped to remove adhering bits of flesh which were saved to be eaten as a tasty meal. (Courtesy Shayne Tolman)

Archaeologists occasionally discover bone pegs that were pounded into the earth. The purpose of these is often unclear, but they may have been used to hold down bison hides during the scraping process. (Courtesy Royal Alberta Museum)

noted, Head-Smashed-In was not an ideal winter camping place. The space requirement for working on hides was another reason for quitting the site. In addition, hides probably played an important role in transporting food to the campsite, acting as a protective wrap and, possibly, as a skid plate on which food was dragged.

Working a hundred or more hides at the winter campsite would have been one of the longest and most strenuous of activities in the aftermath of a buffalo jump. It is hard to overstate the difficulty of dealing with hide as heavy, tough, and large as that of bison. Indeed, it was these qualities that led to the near extermination of the great bison herds by hide hunters meeting the enormous demand for durable leather.

Exploring the central Plains in the early eighteen hundreds, Edwin James recorded the general method of tanning a bison hide:

The hide is extended upon the ground; and with an instrument resembling an adze, used in the manner of our carpenters, the adherent portions of dried flesh are removed, and the skin rendered much thinner and lighter than before. The surface is then plastered over with the brains or liver of the animal, which have been carefully retained for the purpose, and the warm broth of meat is also poured over it. The whole is then dried, after which it is again subjected to the action of the brains and broth, then stretched in a frame, and while still wet, scraped with pumice-stone, sharp stones, or hoes, until perfectly dry. Should it not yet be sufficiently soft, it is subjected to friction, by pulling it backwards and forwards over a twisted sinew. This generally terminates the operation.

James also notes that "for the convenience of manipulation," hides were almost always divided in half and then sewn back together with sinew once the tanning was completed.

Of course, not all Plains groups worked hides in the same fashion. Absent from James's account is the frequent reference to the smoking of hides. Among the more northern Cree (where the ground was less suitable for staking out hides), Daniel Harmon wrote that the hide was scraped and treated with brains, then smoked and soaked in water:

They then take it out and wring it as dry as possible; and a woman takes hold of each end, and they hold it over a fire, frequently pulling it and changing its sides, until it is perfectly dry. After this it is smoked with rotten wood, and it becomes fit for use. This last part of the process, is to prevent it from becoming hard after it has been wet.

Enormous labour was expended taking scores of fresh, greasy hides and converting them to life-saving articles of clothing, beds, and blankets. Without the thick hides of the buffalo for protection, it is unlikely that humans could have survived through a Great Plains winter. Days and weeks were spent wrestling with the huge and heavy skins. But even the thankless task of hide tanning had its occasional rewards. On his 1850 trip up the Missouri, Thaddeus Culbertson noted that the fine bits of meat and fat scraped from the inner side of the buffalo hide were cooked, mixed with dried berries, and eaten. The result was "esteemed," Culbertson proclaimed, "a most rare dish."

Astonishingly, bison hide was occasionally cooked for the express purpose of consumption and, furthermore, it was pretty good. George Bird Grinnell describes how the Cheyenne went about preparing this special dish:

The hide of the buffalo-bull was eaten. One way of cooking it was in a saucer-shaped depression dug in the ground, and lined with grass or leaves, on which were spread out large pieces of the fresh hide. Over the hide were two or three layers of green leaves, and on the leaves were placed a number of ribs or other flat bones to hold the leaves down. A layer of about four inches of clay was spread over this and was pounded down solidly and smoothed off, and on this floor of clay was built a large fire of dry wood which was kept burning for three or four hours. Then the fire was swept aside, the clay, bones, and leaves were removed, and the hide taken out. The hair slipped off easily from the hide, which was quite tender and very good.[†]

† Hide was also occasionally eaten in far less sumptuous circumstances. In the 1840s Robert Rundle described the arrival in camp of an Assiniboine man, woman, and their four children: "They had been 18 days without food excepting buffalo skins which they used as beds – old skins! Alas how can I describe them? They were in a miserable plight." Members of Bradbury's exploring team were reduced to eating the soles of their moccasins.

George Catlin's painting of a Native camp illustrates the process of preparing hide on the ground and on wooden racks. This image vividly conveys the great number of hides that would have been needed to supply tipi covers. (Courtesy Smithsonian Institution)

† In recent years, the staff at Head-Smashed-In did finally manage to have a small bison-hide tipi made for display.

Bringing to bear all the advantages of modern technology has done little to lessen the difficulty of working bison hide. Those of us working to build the Head-Smashed-In Interpretive Centre tried to commission both Native and non-Native people to tan and sew enough bison hides to fashion a tipi cover. Everyone who started the project gave up in exasperation. Eventually, we too gave up and made a tipi cover out of cow hide. Years later, wanting a more authentic display, we tracked down a group of Cree people who had made several bison hide tipi covers for another First Nations interpretive centre at Wanuskewin Heritage Park, near Saskatoon. These people flatly refused to consider another job, saying it was just too much hard work, regardless of the money.†

Ancient hunters had no such prerogative. Hides were critical to their survival. Eventually, over many days, the hides from the slaughtered animals made their way from the kill site to the winter camp. Here, people (mostly women, we believe) laboured over them for days on end, converting them to winter footwear, bedding to sleep on and blankets to pull over you, cape-like robes to drape over your shoulders, some heavy clothing, and a wide variety of containers like bags, satchels, shields, and drums. The amazing hide of bison had served the animal well in its lifetime, and so too it served the people who took it.

Pemmican

As the Indians use no salt in the preservation of their meat, the lean part is cut into thin slices, and hung up in their tents, and dried in the smoke, and the fat is melted down; and in this situation, it will keep for years. – Daniel Harmon, 1800–19

One of the final stages of converting the fresh buffalo meat to storable food was making pemmican, some of which might have transpired at the jump itself. Because of its time-consuming nature, my instinct tells me that much of this work would have taken place at the camps set up in the Oldman valley. But then my instincts also suggested that the laborious boiling of bones to extract grease would likewise be an activity better suited for the roomy expanse of the river flats, only to find abundant evidence of this activity at Head-Smashed-In. However, pemmican making doesn't leave the dramatic and unmistakable scars in the ground that bone boiling does (with its deep pits and mass of fractured rock and bone), so it's quite possible that we simply don't have the evidence to prove the making of pemmican at Head-Smashed-In. Whatever the location, the making of pemmican was one of the most crucial chores that ancient hunters faced, often spelling the difference between life and death during the coming winter.

Why attribute such critical importance to just one of the many products obtained from the mass kills? Because pemmican is food that can be stored for a very long time, making it is of tremendous significance to people who lived year in and year out wondering where their next meal would come from. Their livelihood, like themselves, was always on the move. It was impossible to predict when and where bison or other large game would be encountered. Although it is abundantly clear that early Native hunters thoroughly understood nearly everything about the animals on which they subsisted, some things were difficult to understand because they were by nature incomprehensible. Certainly, seasonal and long-term patterns of bison movement were well known to the hunters, but in the short term, nearly anything was possible. The historic record is replete with examples of bison hunters going to bed surrounded by vast herds of animals and waking up to find, as far as the eye could see, the prairies deserted.[†] Modern wildlife experts are equally at a loss to predict where a free-roaming bison herd will move over the short term. For ancient people, with only their own feet to propel them, this was a formidable problem.

† The patchy distribution of bison was a fact commented on by European travellers. Josiah Gregg recorded that "as they incline to migrate *en masse* from place to place, it sometimes happens, that, for several days' travel together, not a single one is to be met with; but, in other places, many thousands are often seen at one view." Edwin James camped on the Platte River with the Plains around him covered with "immense herds of bisons, grazing in undisturbed possession, and obscuring, with the density of their numbers, the verdant plain." Surveying the same territory the next morning, he remarked with astonishment that "upon all the plain which last evening was so teeming with noble animals, not one remained."

† Turney-High recorded just such an operation in use among the Kutenai: "In making this pemmican, a flat rock was covered with a soft tanned hide, which was kept for this purpose and not used for any other. The hide was folded over the meat to keep it from scattering, and then pounded with the common stone maul."

The vagaries of game movement made for a deeply uncertain life (accounting in part for the universal Plains trait of a heavy reliance on help from the spirit world). Stored food was the critical bridge to help weather periods of scarcity, and pemmican was the most storable food of all. Properly made and under ideal conditions, it could last for more than a year. At a minimum it provided months of dependable, energy-rich food, perhaps just what would be needed when bison herds, like the wind, simply vanished from the surrounding prairie.

The massive cuts of bison meat, lightened and preserved by slicing and drying, became the key ingredient of pemmican. Once the flat, jerky-like sheets of meat were thoroughly dried, they were suitable for storage or they could be converted into pemmican. For the latter, the jerky had to be mixed with other ingredients, and to make this possible the sheets of dried meat had to be pulverized into tiny flecks of meat. The meat was pounded with large stone hammers (mauls) tied to wooden handles and with blunt wooden sticks. For this you needed a flat, hard surface, and one that would keep dirt from mixing with the food. In all likelihood, bison hides were spread out on the ground to provide a clean working space. Flat slabs of rock, such as sandstone from the cliff of the jump, would probably be laid out on or under the hides to serve as anvils on which to pound the meat.† Once the proper space was set up, people settled into a routine of long hours and days of pulverizing the strips of dried meat.

Smashing strips of meat into small flecks allows the meat to dry even more completely than just making it into jerky, especially if the weather was sunny, warm, and windy. Greater drying of the pounded meat explains in part why pemmican was the most storable of food supplies. With the meat reduced almost to powder, it was then mixed with fat. Fats in game animals are often classified as either hard or soft (the difference stemming from which fatty acids form the bulk of the fat). Hard fats are found deep in the body cavity, such as around the major organs. These fats don't need to be very flexible. Soft fats include those of the legs and the subcutaneous fat just under the skin. These fats, located near the outside of the body, are more fluid (softer) in nature, otherwise they would become rigid in cold weather. If the fats of the legs (marrow and bone grease) were hard fats, the legs of the animal would become stiff in winter and inhibit movement. Soft fat was much preferred, as David Thompson noted, because "when carefully melted [it] resembles Butter in softness and sweetness."

Both hard and soft fats are well documented as being used in pemmican making. The choice of which probably depended on how much of each type was on hand and on the quality of pemmican desired. Not all pemmican was the same. Among the Blackfoot, Grinnell reported, "a much finer grade of pemmican was made from the choicest parts of the buffalo with marrow fat," that is, from the soft fats of the legs.

No doubt fat obtained from boiling large leg bones was one of the choicest fats used. Not only is this one of the softest fats in the body, if taken directly from the cooking pits it would have been in a warm, fluid state, making it ideal for mixing in with shreds of dried meat. Historical records indicate that warm grease or tallow was scooped from the cooking pits and mixed with the pulverized meat. The Blackfoot, according to Grinnell, constructed "a trough made of bull's hide" to hold the mixture and stirred the mash with a long wooden spade. The hands of the ancient hunters must have glistened with the sheen of warm, slippery fat. While this mixture of meat and fat could technically be called pemmican, and stored as it was, there was often a third, final ingredient, fruit.

Most accounts of pemmican-making from the northern Plains mention the inclusion of a type of berry or fruit into the mix. For the region around Head-Smashed-In, the berries of choice were the saskatoon and chokecherries. A pleasant cluster of saskatoon bushes grows at the site today, snaking up the side slope of the spring channel toward the cliff. We don't know if these would have been there a thousand years ago, but saskatoons and chokecherries are ubiquitous in the region and would never have been far away. Historic accounts of pemmican-making always mention improved taste as the reason for adding berries to the mix, and it is true that it is much more palatable with a healthy complement of saskatoons or chokecherries. However, there may be a more important purpose served by the addition of fruit to pemmican.

Many plants, including fruits, contain tannins (also called tannic acids). These astringent chemical compounds have well-documented antimicrobial properties. Tannins are part of the plant's natural defence mechanism against fungal and bacterial attack. They have long been associated with the process of turning hide into leather (hence the term *tan*, from the French tanin, and the colour of the same name comes from the appearance of tanned leather). Tanning is, of course,

Groups of people, mostly women, spent days and weeks after the kill making pemmican. They pounded dry meat, mixed it with fat and berries, then stuffed the result into hide bags called parfleches. (Courtesy Shayne Tolman)

essentially a process of preservation; fresh hides are converted to durable leather that will last for years. Although the specific tannic acid content of saskatoons and chokecherries is not well studied, it is almost certain that adding berry tannins to the mix of dried meat and fat furthered the cause of prolonging the life of the food by inhibiting bacterial growth. Whether or not the hunters were aware of this added benefit, or simply added fruit to pemmican for its pleasing taste, we can't know for sure. My hunch would be that it was no great mental leap for someone to recognize that pemmican made with berries tended to last longer than pemmican without.

Picture an array of brown hides stretched out on the prairie, workers kneeling to the sides and mixing together a mash of meat, soft fat, and crushed berries. When all the ingredients were thoroughly mixed, the mash was ready to be put in its final receptacle, heavy bags made of buffalo hide. Bags were made from several pieces of hide sewn together, forming large sacks that would typically hold between forty and fifty kilograms of pemmican, though perhaps smaller in the days before the horse. As David Thompson described, the pemmican bags were "about thirty inches in length, by near twenty inches in breadth, and about four in thickness which makes them flat, the best shape for stowage and carriage."

As air is the enemy of preserved food, it was essential that the mash was made as dense as possible, pounding and squeezing out all the air from the mix and from the hide bags. Aboriginal epicures were well aware of this requirement; Grinnell noted that pemmican was "shovelled into one of the sacks, held open, and rammed down and packed tight with a big stick, every effort being made to expel all the air."† The hide containers were then sealed, either by wrapping leather straps around them or at times by sewing them closed.

The completed product was a dense, nutritious, storable food that could serve as either a staple or as an emergency ration in times of shortage. Properly made and packaged pemmican had an enormously long shelf life. But the conditions the people would face in the months to come would likewise determine the fate of the stored food. As Daniel Harmon observed in 1800, "If kept in a dry place, it will continue good for years. But, if exposed to moisture, it will soon become musty, and unfit for use." It is known that Plains groups sometimes buried pemmican bags in the ground and tucked them into the banks of rivers. The intent was to help protect them from the elements and to lighten the load of the people when decamping. The intent also must have included plans to return to these valued caches.

That pemmican was an exceptional food substance is beyond doubt. Not only did it tide over Native groups for thousands of years, it proved to be the backbone of the exploration and fur-trade era in western North America. So rich and dense was the mix of meat and fat that it tended to fill the stomachs of even the hungriest traveller. David Thompson, with a slag to his canoe-paddling companions, commented that pemmican is "the staple food of all persons, and affords the most nourishment in the least space and weight, even the gluttonous french canadian that devours eight pounds of fresh meat every day is contented with one and a half pound pr [per] day." Naturalist John Audubon said that the men on the barges plying the Missouri subsisted almost entirely on buffalo meat and pemmican. The famed Arctic explorer Vilhjalmur Stefansson was deeply interested in the diet of hunting peoples, especially those, like the Inuit, who depended entirely on meat. To test the health of such a diet, on several occasions he subsisted for up to a full year on an exclusively meat diet, with pemmican making up the bulk of his consumption. At the end of these tests his doctors found him to be in perfect health.

† The desire to crush all the air out of pemmican bags reached almost comical proportions. Describing the Blackfoot, Grinnell said, "When the bag was full and packed as tight as possible, it was sewn up. It was then put on the ground, and the women jumped on it to make it still more tight and solid."

In the aftermath of a successful bison kill, hundreds of bags of pemmican must have been made. This represents an enormous stash of dependable food, giving people a security unattainable if they had to rely on fresh meat alone. It must have been a laborious and tiring job: continuous pounding and grinding of countless kilograms of meat until it turned to the consistency of powder, mixing in the fat and berries, stuffing into hide bags. Days and weeks passed before the pemmican making was completed, another reason why I suspect pemmican making was more an activity of the permanent camps rather than at Head-Smashed-In. Bone grease rendered at the kill site could have been re-warmed at the camp site before it was added to the meat mixture, but the archaeological record is silent on the location of this activity.

Fat was the key ingredient to the nutritional value of pemmican. For reasons discussed earlier, fat, not meat, was the essential food of survival to hunting and gathering cultures. Eating a mix of dried meat and berries was the path to certain death. Adding fat to the mix reversed your fortune to one of comfort and survival.

Plains people had made pemmican quietly and consistently for thousands of years. That we know a fair bit about it now stems from the importance pemmican took on in the early Euro-Canadian colonization of the West. Foreigners arrived with few of the life skills that the Natives had mastered and were to a very large extent dependent upon them for survival. The early settlers could ride horses and shoot bison with guns, but, at least initially, they shot the wrong animals and at the wrong time of year, ate the wrong body parts, and knew little of how to preserve any of the carcasses. George Catlin's first kill of the largest (hence oldest) bull he could find is a classic example of this initial folly.

The Aboriginal people taught Euro-Canadians about the differences between bull and cow bison, the changes in the animals over the seasons, the relative nutrition of different parts of the animal, and about pemmican. And the Native people made quite a business out of supplying pemmican to the foreigners in exchange for guns, horses, metal tools, tobacco, clay pipes, glass beads, and a host of other desired goods. It has been said that without pemmican there would have been no fur trade in the Canadian West.

Snow Falling on Cottonwoods

The beauty of an Indian camp at night deserves a passing word. It can never be forgotten by one who has seen it and it can hardly be pictured to one who has not. The top of each conical tent, stained with smoke, was lost in shadow, but the lower part was aglow from the central fire and on it the moving life inside was pictured in silhouette, while the sound of rippling waters beside which the camp stood accentuated the silence of the overhanging stars. – A.C. Fletcher and F. La Flesche, for the Omaha, 1911

Almost everything I have discussed in the past few chapters has a frantic pace to it. There was the pounding excitement of the drive and the kill, and the rush to process the immense mass of food and materials before they were lost. I can only imagine that during this time there were limited opportunities to sleep, eat, socialize, repair tools, bathe, recall the story of the hunt, procreate, dance, sing, and relax. Slowly, in the weeks following a great kill, life gradually took on a languid pace. All the parts that made up the complex and routine life of Native inhabitants of the Plains filtered back into their world. People feasted and celebrated the success of the kill, tempered against the omnipresent signs of the coming of winter. Ducks and geese cruised overhead on their migratory flights. Gophers retreated to their underground lairs. Leaves on the cottonwoods turned brilliant yellow, willows and wild rose flaming orange.

This hand-coloured photograph of Blackfoot tipis by Walter McClintock was taken in the early twentieth century and illustrates the beauty and serenity of evening camp. (Courtesy Yale Collection of Western Americana, Beinecke Rare Book and Manuscript Library)

As autumn weather sets in, people prepare for winter: camping in valley bottoms, gathering wood, and settling down to life inside the tipi. (Courtesy Head-Smashed-In Buffalo Jump)

Soon small, crystalline pans of ice began to flow down the Oldman River. Skiffs of snow came, angled wedge-shaped against rises in the land, and melted. But as the sun dipped lower in the southern sky, and the heat of the day diminished, eventually the snow held. The golden land of dried grass was blanketed with white sandy granules driven by the incessant winds. Tipi liners were hung from the inner sides of the poles to add an extra layer of warmth. Firewood, split with crude stone wedges and hammers, was stashed inside and outside the dwellings, sometimes piled on the outer edges of the hide tipi to help stave off the cold. People ventured out to search for fresh game on mild days and retreated to the safety of camp when temperatures plummeted and winds picked up. They told stories of the great hunt - of the near misses, the close encounters, the acts of immense bravery. They reaffirmed their faith in the all-enveloping power of the Great Spirit. They thought about the future, assured for the time being that at least there would be one. People hunkered down for another winter, awaiting the fresh grass of spring, buffalo cows dropping their calves, and the fattening months of summer.

CHAPTER 9

The End of the Buffalo Hunt

It is truly a melancholy contemplation for the traveller in this country, to anticipate the period which is not far distant, when the last of these noble animals, at the hands of white and redmen, will fall victims to their cruel and improvident rapacity; leaving these beautiful green fields, a vast and idle waste, unstocked and unpeopled for ages to come, until the bones of the one and the traditions of the other will have vanished, and left scarce an intelligible trace behind. – George Catlin, 1851

The air was foul with sickening stench, and the vast plain, which only a short twelvemonth before teemed with animal life, was a dead, solitary, putrid desert. – Colonel Richard Dodge, 1860s and 1870s

---

The serenity of smoke drifting up from the tops of conical tipis, wafting down the serpentine course of the Oldman River, and countless other sublime places on the northern Plains, was about to be broken forever. What Native hunters couldn't do in twelve thousand years – kill off the vast herds of bison – the inexorable westward spread of so-called civilization managed to do in the nineteenth century. A way of life, seemingly as timeless as the land itself, was about to come crashing to an end.

They had roamed the immense prairies of North America for hundreds of thousands of years, but they were doomed to come within a heartbeat of extinction. Bison, the great monarch of the Plains, the staff of life of Aboriginal cultures, were just too numerous for their own good. It was precisely their staggering numbers that in large part led them to straddle the thin line of extinction. How can thirty or fifty million animals be reduced, in the span of little more than a century, to perhaps a few hundred? It ranks as one of the most tragic and – very nearly – one of the most complete slaughters of

† Lewis Henry Morgan penned the following account of senseless slaughter on the Missouri: "We saw two bull buffalo standing on the edge of the river ... They had gone in after water and could not get out... There are over thirty men with rifles on board ... They had the first shot and dropped one of them, but he got partly up again. A moment after a volley from our boat brought down the other, but they both [buffalo] rallied, and they poured into them shot after shot, until they were finished. One of them got into deep water and along the boat ... As soon as he raised his fore quarter he was killed, and floated off down the river. The other was drawn with a rope and tackle on to the steamboat, not yet dead when the rope was put around his neck, but he was dead when they began to hoist him." On the same river, Edward Harris recorded, "On getting on board I found that Bell had been amusing himself with firing at this gang of Buffaloes, which then consisted of 7 and a calf, he fired 5 times, once with small shot at the calf which he wounded, and he also wounded badly a young bull ... He had to leave them, they were no doubt killed."

any form of wildlife in human history. It seems inconceivable. And that is exactly the point. For those who blasted away at the immense herds, it must have seemed impossible that there could ever be an end to the animal that blackened the prairies. If anything on earth seemed endless, it must have been the herds of bison. It was as if they would spring eternal (as many Native origin stories foretold) from the depths of the earth or from beneath the waters of great lakes. They were shot from boats to relieve the boredom of travel.† They were shot on hunts organized by the likes of Buffalo Bill Cody and Wild Bill Hickock to see who could bag the most in a day. They were shot from moving trains during events that were advertised as sport and for which people paid good money. They were shot for all reasons and for no reason.

At times bison were shot for no apparent reason other than to torment the animals and as a play activity for the hunters. There are countless examples of this senseless slaughter; the journal of Edward Harris provides one sad case. Writing in the mid-1800s, Harris describes how one of his European colleagues rode after a bull. He put two balls into the side of the bull, wounding it severely and bringing it to a halt. Harris and another man then ran to join the mounted hunter. The wounded bull had difficulty turning to face his enemy, a fact played on by the three hunters who "would jump aside and discharge our six-barreled pistols at his side with little more effect than increasing his fury at every shot." Harris then stood in front of the bull and put a bullet in its head, an act for which the bull almost managed to kill him. Figuring the animal was still dangerous, another round was put through his chest and lungs, dropping the bull. Adding insult to injury, Harris concludes, "He proved to be very poor [lean] and a bad skin and we left him for the wolves and birds of prey."

The Skin of the Animal

Most of all they shot buffalo for their hides, which were increasingly useful to a rapidly industrializing New World. Bison hides are as thick and tough as that of any animal in North America. Building the factories and industry in the east demanded belts to drive the new machines of the industrial age. There were no better, more durable belts than those made of bison hide. Countless millions of bison were slaughtered exclusively for their hides, the carcasses left

As the railroads pushed west, trains would stop so passengers could get out and shoot buffalo. Worse, passengers sometimes fired into herds while the train chugged along. (Courtesy Glenbow Archives/NA 1406-188)

to rot and stink on the prairies. Chronicling the slaughter, Colonel Richard Dodge succinctly charted the convergence of events leading to the demise of the bison:

The danger from Indians and the great distance from market had heretofore protected the buffalo from wholesale slaughter by whites, but by 1872 the buffalo region had been penetrated by no less than three great railroads, and the Indians had been forced from their vicinity. About this time too it was discovered that the tough, thick hide of the buffalo made admirable belting for machinery, and the dried skins readily commanded sale at three to four dollars each. The news spread like wild-fire, and soon the Union Pacific, Kansas

The waste was appalling. Millions of buffalo carcasses were simply left on the Plains to rot. (Courtesy Glenbow Archives/NA 207-68)

† For the three years from 1872 to 1874, Dodge estimated that trains from the west hauled away 1.4 million buffalo hides, 6.7 million pounds of meat, and 32.4 million pounds of bones. From these figures, Dodge estimated that "at least five millions of buffalo were slaughtered for their hides" in the three-year period.

Pacific, and Atchison Topeka and Santa Fé railroads, swarmed with hunters from all parts of the country, all excited with the prospect of having a buffalo hunt that would pay. By wagon, on horseback, and a-foot, the pot-hunters poured in, and soon the unfortunate buffalo was without a moment's peace or rest. Though hundreds of thousands of skins were sent to market, they scarcely indicated the slaughter. From want of skill in shooting, and want of knowledge in preserving the hides of those slain, one hide sent to market represented three, four, or even five dead buffalo.

Certainly meat was sometimes taken. Entire boxcars of ribs and tongues chugged off along the railway tracks to the eastern markets. Bones, too. Huge mounds of buffalo bones, like massive white worms, would line the sides of railroad tracks for several kilometres in each direction of a station, waiting to be shipped to the east.† Bones were valued in the sugar refining process, and their high phosphorus content was used to make fertilizer and gunpowder.

Mostly it was the hides that created an overnight, profitable industry. In the rapidly settling West, there was still little else a person could do to earn a living. Ever-increasing numbers of hide hunters flocked to the West to try and make their fortune. Many knew nothing about bison, hunting them, or skinning them. Many were outcasts, the dregs of their own culture whose only way to fit in was to leave. "They are usually the most abandoned and worthless among the

Although the vast majority of buffalo bones were simply left to decay, countless tonnes were shipped east by rail to be used for fertilizer, gunpowder, and in the sugar refining process. (Courtesy Glenbow Archives/NA 250-15)

whites who adopt the life of the wandering hunters," Edwin James proclaimed early in the 1800s, "frequently they are men whose crimes have excluded them from society." Many perished, lost on the vast prairie, caught in winter storms, stampeded to death by the very animals they sought, or killed by the increasingly angry Native tribes tired of watching their precious life source disappear. But the rumours of riches to be made kept the hide hunters coming. In some years, hundreds of thousands of bison hides were shipped east. Bearing in mind Dodge's comment that many more were killed than were shipped, it was a slaughter of unprecedented proportions, and it was one that could not be sustained.

Bison didn't just face wave after wave of merciless hide hunters and Natives riding horses and armed with rifles. They also faced competition for space and grass. The non-Native colonizers of the West brought with them millions of head of cattle and horses, and they built farms, ranches, and endless barbed wire fences to contain them. Bison had been the primary large grazers of the Plains; now they had to share that space with hordes of other large grazers. There was only so much room, and competition began to take its toll.

Bison fought hard against the westward expansion of civilization, as did Native hunters. Exceedingly fond of scratching themselves, and lacking much to rub against in the treeless prairie, they pushed over

Buffalo hides were the staple of the slaughter. The thirst for more hides was unsustainable and destroyed the bison population. (Courtesy Kansas State Historical Society)

† Bull bison in rut are of a single mind. Referring to the mating season, Lewis Morgan recorded, "It is at this time when the males are seeking the females that they stampede [wagon] trains which happen to be in the line of their march. At such times the herd press forward and carry everything before them."

telegraph poles, fence posts, walls of wooden forts, town buildings, and wagon carts. In newly formed western towns and forts, sharpshooters had to be on standby to fire into the massive herds whose only interest was in having themselves a good rub against something that suddenly appeared vertical in their environment. They routinely stampeded and trampled the endless waves of hide hunters that deluged the Plains, not out of conscious malice but because something foreign happened to be in their way.†

For the same reason, bison did not take well to the appearance of the railroad trains. As the first tracks cut a swath through the unbroken prairies, bison wreaked havoc on passing trains. Inexplicably, they seemed compelled to cross to the opposite side whenever a train approached. Hundreds of them would slam into the sides of passing trains, undeterred by the size and power of the machines, condemning themselves to death. As unfathomable as it seems, trains were routinely derailed by the sheer force of the mass of bodies – once two trains in a single week. Conductors were finally ordered to stop whenever a bison herd was sighted. It was one of the few concessions made in the otherwise iron-fisted push to settle the West.

The situation was not helped by the fact that Native people, too, killed bison in greater numbers than they ever had before. Why? Certainly not because there were more people to feed. Just the opposite was true. Europeans had brought with them to the shores of a new world a number of microbes to which North American Native people had never before been exposed. Foremost among these were smallpox, measles, and influenza. Because Natives had no time to build immunity, these diseases absolutely devastated indigenous societies. In some cases it eliminated an entire people from the face of the earth. More often it reduced them to staggeringly low numbers, often claiming up to 80 per cent or more of the population. Blackfoot, for example, are estimated to have lost some six thousand souls, or about 70 per cent of all their people, during the course of the nineteenth century.

Europeans also brought horses and guns. As these offered such superior hunting advantages, Native people did all they could to get plenty of both. Armed with rifles, especially repeating rifles, and straddling a fast pony, Aboriginal hunters were suddenly on par with European hide hunters in their ability to bring down great numbers of bison in a short space of time. While there were fewer Native people to feed than previously, remember that they subsisted year round on bison, unlike the mainly summertime European hunters. Natives also needed hides for tipi covers, winter bedding and robes, moccasins. In addition, buffalo had now become an important economic commodity for Native people. They still needed the meat and hides for their own use, but they soon realized that a surplus of hides could be traded to Europeans in exchange for more guns, powder, bullets, metal knives and axes, glass beads, and a great number of other exotic goods never before available to them. They occasionally traded for horses but preferred to steal them from hostile neighbouring tribes and from white settlers. Then they raised their own stock, eventually amassing huge herds of horses needing grass and water, which led to a major shift in patterns of Native camping and movement.

Caught up in a lucrative and seductive European-based economy, Aboriginal hunters at times killed more bison than needed for their own survival. They also probably became fussier about the cuts of meat they took from carcasses. Try to appreciate the magnitude of the change from twelve thousand years of having to devise clever and complex traps to capture bison to the sudden freedom of being able to swing over the back of a horse and ride out almost any time to shoot down an evening meal. This new-found freedom transformed Native culture, allowing them to roam great distances for war and hunts and to take only the choice cuts from the animals they killed.

There is no shortage of blame to go around. Many Europeans blamed the Indians; Aboriginal hunters blamed the white intruders. "In winter, there are periods of abundance during which they kill buffaloes just for their tongues and their skins," said Victor Tixier of the Osage people in 1840; "It is impossible to make these improvident people understand that to kill buffaloes in such a manner is to hasten their complete disappearance." Henry Youle Hind, having witnessed Aboriginal mass killing of bison, observed, "man in his savage, untutored, and heathen state shows both in deed and expression how little he is superior to the noble beasts he so wantonly and cruelly destroys." Yet Edward Harris, among many other Europeans, recounts the same for his people: "I am almost ashamed to tell you that we left our Bulls, and fine fat ones they were, on the ground for the Wolves, carrying away nothing but the tongues." Later, Harris adds a melancholy note on the nature of their behaviour: "We now regretted having destroyed these noble beasts for no earthly reason but to gratify a sanguinary disposition which appears to be inherent in our natures." Edwin James, early in the 1800s, laid the blame at the feet of his own people:

It would be highly desirable that some law for the preservation of game might be extended to, and rigidly enforced in the country where the bison is still met with; that the wanton destruction of these valuable animals, by the white hunters, might be checked or prevented. It is common for hunters to attack large herds of these animals, and having slaughtered as many as they are able, from mere wantonness and love of this barbarous sport, to leave the carcasses to be devoured by the wolves and birds of prey; thousands are slaughtered yearly, of which no part is saved except the tongues. This inconsiderate and cruel practice is undoubtedly the principal reason why the bison flies so far and so soon from the neighbourhood of our frontier settlements.

In a previous chapter I addressed the issue of Aboriginal hunters as overkillers of bison at the great communal kill sites. Understandably, the issue surfaces again in debates about the ultimate demise of the animal. My take on this has been that ancient Aboriginal hunters were first and foremost human beings, much like all human beings who have inhabited every continent since time immemorial. They were no better, no worse, and subject to all the spurts of rationality mixed with outrageous folly that has been the hallmark of our collective existence. I picture times of great privation on the Plains, perhaps induced by extended drought or disease, when many groups verged on starvation, some perishing completely. I further imagine a number of these destitute groups coming together to organize communal bison kills. If the effort met with success there would be great feasting in the community, thanks given to the spirit powers, and a dedicated effort to extract every possible ounce of edible material from every carcass.

But certainly there were opposite situations, when people and their neighbours were already relatively well fed as they set about orchestrating a great communal kill. A hundred, maybe two hundred, buffalo plunged to their death over a cliff or were slaughtered in wooden corrals. Did these people scrounge every scrap of the bison carcass – the stomach and intestine contents, hair, hoofs, ligaments and tendons, sinew, and every one of over two hundred bones in each animal? I suspect not. I think they probably exercised reasonable judgment and took their favourite parts, the most nutritious cuts, and left behind less useful parts of the carcass. I have asserted that it is a disservice to Native culture to argue that these hunters mechanistically used every part of every animal after every single bison kill regardless of such important contingencies as the degree of hunger, the number of people available to do the work, and the number of animals killed. It denies their humanity, their ability to make rational decisions, to exercise common sense when faced with differing conditions of life.

It is certainly true that Aboriginal people of the Plains used every part of the buffalo.[†] It's astonishing how seemingly useless elements were pressed into service for common, everyday uses. Tails were used as flyswatters and, whip-like, to flick water onto the hot rocks of a sweat lodge. Some of the outer sheaths of the hoofs were boiled to make a thick, gooey glue and others were strung together to make rattles.[‡] Bones were cut, drilled, and shaped into tools used to scrape the flesh off hides, straighten arrow shafts, and pierce hides for sewing. Bones from old carcasses were even sometimes piled up to make temporary dwellings. The people did at times eat the contents of the stomach and intestines. But to say that they used every part from

† For the Cheyenne, Grinnell stated, "They left nothing behind, but carried everything in. Even the bones were carried in, and the entrails, for the buffalo were hard to get and were only had occasionally, and the people felt that nothing was to be wasted or left behind."

‡ "They keep the Hoofs of those little Creatures," wrote Father Hennepin, "and when they are very dry, they tie them to some Wand, and move them according to the various Postures of those who sing and dance. This is the most ridiculous Musical Instrument that I have ever met with."

every animal at every kill relegates human beings to the status of unthinking creatures. They made sensible decisions based on the complexities of life that went with being a hunting and gathering people and with what their spiritual beliefs prescribed.

The Last of the Buffalo Jumps

It wasn't the near demise of the bison herds that brought an end to the age-old communal hunting methods of the Plains people. The mass-kill methods of jumps, pounds, surrounds, and all the others slipped slowly into disuse over the course of about a hundred years, from about the mid-1700s to mid-1800s. There were still plenty of bison around during these times. The abandonment of traditional techniques can be traced to the sudden availability of new technology in Plains culture: guns and, especially, horses. The introduction of these two elements into traditional culture spelled the end of the pedestrian-based hunting methods and brought about dramatic changes for the Plains groups.

Blessed with swift ponies, young men could sweep out onto the surrounding Plains and seek out buffalo that previously lay well beyond their grasp. They didn't need to kill hundreds at one time any more. They could kill a few any day and every day. They also had the awesome power of the horse to transport carcass parts back to camp that would have previously been far too heavy to carry on foot. Bison could be procured much more regularly and dependably with horse-based hunting than they could with the episodic, risky, and seasonal communal kills. It no longer made sense to gather together the hundreds of people required to outfit the drive lanes, find distant buffalo herds, coax them to the kill site, then kill and butcher the mass of animals. As the population of horses increased among the Plains tribes, and their skill in riding them grew, the incidence of the great communal kills waned.

The horse was the single most important element in bringing an end to laborious mass killing methods that prevailed on the Plains for thousands of years. It made the whole world of the Aboriginal people smaller. The availability of guns was likewise a factor, but a much less significant one. Native people already possessed a reliable killing weapon, the bow and arrow. To a large extent, Natives kept using the bow and arrow for buffalo hunting even after guns became

available. That they were extraordinary experts with this weapon is attested to in numerous eyewitness accounts from Europeans. In the 1830s Josiah Gregg provided the following:

The arms of the wild Indians are chiefly the bow and arrows, with the use of which they become remarkably expert. A dextrous savage will lay a wager, at short shots, against many riflemen. Indeed, there is hardly any more effective weapon than the bow and arrow in the hands of an expert archer. While the musketeer will load and fire once, the bowman will discharge a dozen arrows, and that, at distances under fifty yards, with an accuracy nearly equal to the rifle. In a charge, they are eminently serviceable; for the Indian seems to discharge his arrows with about as much certainty when running at full speed as when standing.

Zebulon Pike put nineteen balls into a bison before it crashed to the ground. The Cheyenne frequently killed bison with a single arrow, according to Grinnell, and, astonishingly, sometimes two animals with the same arrow: "Big Ribs, a Northern Cheyenne at Pine Ridge,

Hunting on horseback allowed Aboriginal people to be selective in ways that had never before been possible. Communal kills claimed the entire target herd; equestrian hunters could run alongside the herds and pick out the prime, fattest animals at any time of year. Painting by George Catlin. (Courtesy Bruce Peel Special Collections Library, University of Alberta)

and Strong Left Hand, at Tongue River Agency, are known each to have shot one arrow through two buffalo, killing both at a single shot." In about 1860 Lewis Morgan recorded the following interview:

White Cloud says that the Indians still prefer the bow and arrow to the gun for hunting buffalo. That the animal is easily killed, and the arrow does it with great certainty and that they can fire, or rather shoot, from the saddle much easier with the bow than with the gun. That the motion of the gun is liable to be unsteady, and therefore to shoot over, while with the bow they have no difficulty.

"An arrow kills more efficiently than a bullet," Tixier likewise reported; "If the arrow has not completely disappeared into its chest, the savage drives it in with his foot. Rarely is a second arrow necessary." Josiah Gregg, among the Indians in the 1830s, compared traditional weapons to the gun: "the Indian is apt to kill double as many with his arrows or lance."

These observations provide interesting insight into the practice of adoption of European goods by Aboriginal people. There is a common, and erroneous, perception that Native people simply abandoned all their ancient technology and practices as soon as European goods and methods were presented to them. This misconception stems in part from the assumed superiority of anything European compared with the presumed primitiveness of anything Native. To be sure, many European goods proved a vast improvement over ancient technology and were immediately adopted. The superiority of metal knives for cutting meat, and metal axes for chopping wood, were indisputable. Likewise, metal pots and kettles were immediately judged superior to heavy, breakable pottery vessels. Traditional pottery-making disappeared so quickly after the availability of metal pots that Native people in the nineteenth century had almost no memory of ever making it. Glass and ceramic beads, delivered by fur traders in bags by the thousands, put a quick end to traditional time-consuming bead-making from shell, antler, and bone. The list goes on, but these examples should not be seen as indicating that everything European was judged superior and immediately replaced its Native counterpart. The use of the gun in buffalo hunting is a case in point.

Certainly guns were highly coveted by Aboriginal people. When first exposed to them, people thought them to be magical implements. Early encounters with Europeans left Native people with the belief that it was the noise of the gun that somehow killed the target; after all, guns fired a projectile that was invisible as it flew through the air.† But they soon understood and mastered the use of rifles and recognized the new-found ability to bring down game animals or enemy warriors at great distances. But the early rifles traded to the Plains people were cumbersome muzzleloaders, requiring a great deal of paraphernalia to keep them operating.

Imagine equestrian hunters galloping across the Plains in pursuit of stampeding bison. In one arm they carried their rifles, in their mouths were perhaps a dozen lead balls, bouncing against their sides were horns of gunpowder. Wadding and ramrods were luxuries frequently done without. Attempting to reload these rifles while riding at full tilt was a frustrating and risky business. If powder and balls were added without wadding, the tip of the gun barrel had to be kept pointed upward to prevent the ball from rolling down. Even a slight roll led to an explosion in the chamber rather than a clean fire, and historic accounts testify that many young hunters bore terrible scars on their hands and faces from pulling the trigger just a few seconds too late during a frantic buffalo chase.

In stark contrast, hunters equipped with bow and arrows – the latter stacked in a leather quiver – rode and shot with ease among the pounding herds. Leaning forward on their most prized horses (the buffalo runners), both hands free of the reins, hunters loosed arrows in rapid succession. Deftly moving one hand back from the bowstring to the quiver, retrieving the next arrow, they could in a matter of moments let fly a dozen arrows or more into the sides of the buffalo. There were no misfires, no explosions at the side of your face. "Sometimes the young men mount their horses, and pursue them [bison] and bring them down with their bows and arrows," Daniel Harmon noted early in the 1800s, "which they find more convenient for this purpose than fire arms, as they can more easily take an arrow from the quiver, than load a musket, in such a situation." Despite the awesome power of the rifle, bows and arrows continued to be used by many horse-riding hunters long after guns had become common possessions. Native people rationally and deliberately picked and chose those parts of European culture that fit the lifestyle they desired.

Although arrows continued to be delivered with wooden bows, stone tips quickly fell into disuse. Perfectly functional for centuries, arrow points chipped from stone had been the preferred material

† In one of the earliest records, dating to the late 1600s, Father Hennepin wrote, "They heard the Report, but did not see the Bullets, and they thought it was the Noise that kill'd them … [They] cry'd out … this Iron does harm to Men and Beasts: We do not know how it comes to pass, but we cannot sufficiently admire how the Noise of this round Instrument breaks the Bones of the largest Beast."

Even after guns were widely available, hunters on horseback often preferred using the bow and arrow because reloading it was easy and fast, enabling more kills. Painting by Karl Bodmer. (Courtesy Edward E. Ayer Collection, The Newberry Library, Chicago)

with which to tip weapons. But rock is an unforgiving material. In a great many instances, arrows loosed at game animals missed their mark and sailed into the earth. Or they struck home and slammed into a large bone in the body. Either way, breakage was exceedingly common, as attested by the millions of snapped point fragments recovered from archaeological sites. Native hunters quickly discovered the resilient nature of metal, that it could bend and then be reformed to its original shape. Metal pots could get badly dented during travel and use but were easily pounded back into their approximate shape. The same was true of metal arrow points. Soon after the first metal goods were brought to Native camps, people began using fragments of worn out knives, pots, and barrel hoops to fashion their own metal tips. When these arrows missed their mark or hit a bone, the bent tip was simply hammered straight. European traders quickly noted this adaptation and began importing bags of perfectly manufactured metal arrow points to trade with the Indians.

The last of the buffalo jumps and pounds used on the Plains can include metal arrow points mixed with the stone artifacts and bones, but these are rare. Stone continued to be used because it was locally available at no cost and because the Native hunters possessed insufficient numbers of metal points. Also, metal was still a scarce commodity and greater effort would have been made to retrieve these points. But the primary reason that metal points are scarce at the great communal bison kills is that horses were becoming common at the same time as metal, and equestrian hunting soon made the ancient traps obsolete.

Rivers of Bones

As far as the eye could reach there were the bleached bones of the buffaloes.
– Maximilian, Prince of Wied, 1832–34

Earlier in this book I referenced the many inspiring quotations from Europeans who ventured out onto the Great Plains and witnessed the astonishing numbers of bison in their native habitat. But the land and its people were changing. Railroads bisected the country, barbed wire partitioned little squares of turf, towns sprung from the prairie, and new people arrived in ever-increasing numbers. Inexorably, relentlessly, settlement ground its way west. As it advanced it chewed up and steamrolled over a way of life seemingly as much a part of the land as dust itself. The once uncountable and indefatigable buffalo began to vanish. Their massive bones, once the lifeblood of a people, became the quarry of worms, bugs, birds, and coyotes. As the prairie winds swept aside the bones of the mighty beasts, so too went the culture of people who for more than five hundred generations had thrived on their bounty. With the Plains becoming white with bones, the journals of western explorers took on a harrowing and melancholy tone.

"The land was covered, in spots, with buffalo bones whitened by the dew and the sun. This camp was a sad sight," wrote Victor Tixier. On the Platte River, Turnbull observed "Buffalo Bones, & dung laying as thick as it can lay." Maximilian told of "bones and skulls, scattered

Where the prairies had once been brown with the hides of immense herds of bison, they turned white with the sun-bleached bones of their descendants. (Courtesy Glenbow Archives/NA 250-14)

Just as the numbers of bison on the Plains staggered the earliest European visitors, the rapidity and extent of the slaughter almost defies comprehension. As stunning as the mountain of skulls piled in Detroit is the realization that this is but a fraction of the tens of millions killed. (Courtesy Glenbow Archives/NA 2242-2)

all over the prairie." The Earl of Southesk, "constantly finding the skulls and bones of former herds" during his travels, continued:

The plains are all strewn with skulls and other vestiges of the buffalo, which came up this river last year in great numbers ... They are now rapidly disappearing everywhere: what will be the fate of the Indians, when this their chief support fails, it is painful to imagine.

Many Aboriginal people and whites alike saw it coming. The great John Audubon, his own team of men guilty of senseless slaughter, described the prairies as literally covered with the skulls of buffalo, "and before many years the Buffalo, like the Great Auk, will have disappeared; surely this should not be permitted." Schoolcraft cites a venerable old chief: "I fear we shall soon be deprived of the buffalo: then starvation and cold will diminish our numbers, and we shall all be swept away. The buffalo is fast disappearing. As the White man advances, our game and our means of life grow less; and before many years, they will all be gone."

Aboriginal buffalo hunters of the Great Plains had nowhere to turn – at least, nowhere that could provide the joys and substance of life as they had always known it. Flesh of the bison was "real food" as Flannery records for the Gros Ventre, "To those who had been brought up on buffalo meat, beef was a poor substitute. It was said, by those who experienced the change of diet after the disappearance of the buffalo in 1884, that many of the old people 'died of starvation' when deprived of buffalo meat."

Attempts to encourage Native people to engage in alternative means of support were nearly all disastrous. Only the immensely naive could expect people thoroughly immersed in an ancient way of life to abandon, in no more than the blink of an eye, everything they cherished and that had provided meaning to their lives and to embrace an entirely foreign and meaningless lifestyle. Even Alexander Ross, profoundly critical of Native culture, could see the passion with which they clung to the cornerstone of their lives:

There is no earthly consideration would make them relinquish the pursuit … so strong is their love for the uncertain pursuit of buffalo-hunting, that when the season arrives, they sacrifice every other consideration in order to indulge in this savage habit. Wedded to it from their infancy, they find no pleasure in anything else.

But the machine-like march westward of foreign peoples, cultures, and values was unstoppable and insurmountable. Before it, as Dodge wrote, "The buffalo melted away like snow before a summer's sun."

Final Abandonment of Head-Smashed-In

Despite the fact that the event is only about a century and a half old, we will never know the exact date of the final use of Head-Smashed-In. There was no one with pencil, notepad, or camera present to record the final plunge of bison from the cliff. Certainly the jump, and many others, continued to be used after horses were acquired. It must have taken several decades, at least, for the ancient tradition to fade. After all, much of Aboriginal ceremonial life revolved around ensuring the success of the communal kills. Most likely elders argued for the continuation of the great kills and the retention of all the spiritual significance they entailed. Young men, precisely those becoming the most skilled and enthusiastic riders, probably pushed for hunting by the new methods.

The transition to equestrian hunting was likely gradual, with communal hunts abandoned for increasingly greater periods of time. There was even a brief period where the two hunting strategies melded. The great fur trader and explorer Peter Fidler has provided us with one of the earliest written records of Native life in the Canadian West. He spent the winter of 1792–93 with the Piikani of southwestern Alberta, right in the vicinity of Head-Smashed-In. By the time of Fidler's stay the Piikani had acquired both horses and guns, although supplies for the latter were still in constant demand. To the best of my knowledge, Fidler is the only European who actually witnessed Aboriginal people attempting to drive bison over cliffs and who left us a written record. All other historic accounts of this activity were provided by people who either saw the kill sites and decayed carcasses of previous jumps (such as Lewis and Clark) or those who described how jumps worked based on Native informants (such as Edwin James).

Brought by Europeans, metal quickly replaced stone as the preferred material for arrow points. Stone would snap and break on impact whereas metal could be bent back into shape and reused. (Courtesy Royal Alberta Museum)

Fidler's journal records a number of attempts by horse-mounted Piikani to drive herds of bison over local cliffs, generally without success. On one day he records two such efforts. First: "Where we encamped yesterday was at a rocky precipice in a kind of Creek, but the rock was not very high. At noon the Men brought a herd of Buffalo to the rock but they all broke out at the outer end of the Dead Men & only one single one fell over the precipice & was killed." Later the same day he records, "the men brought another large herd, but they all broke out among the Dead Men as before. However, the Men killed several upon horse back by galloping after & shooting them with arrows."

Fidler was witness to the transformation of hunting methods, a hybrid of newly acquired horses and ancient techniques employing jumps. It is interesting that the hybrid failed the Piikani. The whole system of steep drops and drive lanes had been designed, planned, and predicated on the employment of people on foot. The accumulated millennia of knowledge and trickery that made traditional jumps work could not simply be pasted onto the new technology of the horse.

A decade later Alexander Henry wrote, "Horses are sometimes used to collect and bring in buffalo, but this method is less effectual than the other; besides, it frightens the herds and soon causes them to withdraw to a great distance."† We can only assume that use of jumps and pounds continued to fade as the 1800s wore on.

A few metal arrow points were found in the very upper (most recent) layers at Head-Smashed-In, though stone points still predominated, so clearly the jump was used in historic times. How often and at what date are unclear. For events as recent in the past as one hundred fifty years, radiocarbon dating of the upper levels of the site would be useless. The technique is simply not precise enough to establish actual years of site use. It is probably fair to assume that the site continued to be used, only very occasionally, until perhaps the middle of the 1800s. After that, I'd be surprised if it was used at all. By 1880 the bison were nearly extinct and the question becomes moot.

One clue we have is the earliest photograph of Head-Smashed-In. Taken in 1912, it shows a person standing on the side of the slope leading up to the cliff. Most apparent is the virtual river of bleached white bison bones sprawled across the slope. These must represent the bones of the final animals to be killed at Head-Smashed-In. That they are visible on the ground surface testified that no great span of

† Yet horses were occasionally used with success, at least when Native hunters continued to place humans along the route of the drive. Harmon provides testimony: "After this preparation, when a herd of buffaloes is seen at no great distance off, thirty or forty or more young men mount their racers, which are well trained to this business, and surround them; and little difficulty is found in bringing them, within the range of the stakes. Indians are stationed by the side of some of these stakes, to keep them in motion."

A view up the slope of the Head-Smashed-In spring channel in 1912 shows bleached white buffalo bones littering the ground, testimony that the last jump had not been very long before. (Courtesy Glenbow Archives/NA 4035-14)

time had passed since the last kill. If it had, the bones would have been largely buried or rotted away. The stark visibility of the bones in the 1912 photograph suggests that the last jump had taken place probably within the past fifty years.

Whatever the date, Head-Smashed-In was finally abandoned for good, bison hunters having turned completely to equestrian hunts and, eventually, to none at all. Though the site was deserted, it was certainly not forgotten. One of the most common questions asked is when and by whom was the archaeological site of Head-Smashed-In discovered. It was never in any sense discovered, because it had never in any sense been lost. People who had last used the jump, almost certainly the Piikani Band of the Blackfoot Nation, continued to live in the shadow of the jump well into the first few decades of the twentieth century. Many of the children of these people, and in turn the grandchildren and great-grandchildren, still reside within a few kilometres of the jump. The knowledge of its existence, and the lore of its use, were diligently passed on to successive generations. Head-Smashed-In Buffalo Jump may be an unknown curiosity to modern visitors, but it has never ceased being a proud piece of the past for the local Blackfoot.

With the coming of the first non-Native settlers in the late 1800s and early 1900s, knowledge of the jump's existence was passed on to a new culture. Nobody had to tell the ranchers and farmers about the buffalo jump; the bleached bones of the kill stood out like a sore thumb. It became a place for locals to gather, have weekend picnics, collect local berries, and poke among the dregs of the ancient kills for arrowheads and other curios. Several of the first settlers' families still live in the area, and nearly all of them have artifacts collected over decades of casual visiting to the site.

Over the years I have noted with interest a great concern for Head-Smashed-In among the local non-Native residents. Though completely unrelated to their own ancestry, the site tells a story that strikes a chord with them. It is one of understanding the land and its animals, of challenges and the struggle against the elements to survive. Modern ranchers know first hand the difficulties of making a living working the land, and they respect those who have done it before them. Land is everything to ranchers. They are fiercely possessive and respectful of it and feel a certain bond with other people, however different from themselves, who have done the same.

Natives and Europeans both wished that bison were unlimited and eternal. Sadly, they were not. Detail from Karl Bodmer painting. (Courtesy Joslyn Art Museum, Omaha, Nebraska)

The great drives and kills had come to an end, but Head-Smashed-In Buffalo Jump was never lost or forgotten. It entered a new phase of its existence, from a place of almost unimaginable drama and daring to one of silence and tranquility. The blood long dried and disappeared from the dusty soil, the bones weathered and cracked with age. But the story persisted. Head-Smashed-In ceased to be a place of valour, genius, and unbridled carnage. It entered the realm of memory. And imagination.

CHAPTER 10

The Past Becomes the Present

T he story of the great buffalo jumps should not be allowed to simply fade away. At least for Head-Smashed-In, it will not. It lives on in the stories of elders like Billy Strikes With A Gun, who carry the history of their people. As long as Blackfoot children and those of other First Nations continue to be taught the traditions of their ancestors, the stories of a glorious past will persist. Archaeological study of buffalo kills adds another layer to our knowledge of the past. More importantly, the story of Head-Smashed-In will stay alive for generations to come thanks to the presence of a stunning interpretive centre built directly into the cliff of the buffalo jump.

Sunk into the sandstone bedrock and prairie soil at Head-Smashed-In is a maze of huge concrete slabs that form an odd-shaped structure: a 2,400 square metre building that spans seven stories of elevation but is barely visible to a person standing outside. Welcome to the Head-Smashed-In Buffalo Jump Interpretive Centre. Located about twenty kilometres west of the town of Fort Macleod, Alberta, the

A part of the cliff at Head-Smashed-In has been transformed. A seven-storey high interpretive centre was nestled into the slope to blend with the bedrock and the surrounding land. (Courtesy Royal Alberta Museum)

centre has been open for two decades and has told the story of the great buffalo jump to two million visitors. That a ten-million-dollar project was dedicated to the telling of Aboriginal history is amazing in itself, and this book would not be complete without telling at least part of this story.

Beginnings

As with so many stories of wonder, this one begins with people of vision and persistence. You'd be hard pressed to find a person in Alberta more responsible for the public interpretation of heritage resources than Dr. William J. Byrne. A southern Alberta boy, Bill earned his PhD in Anthropology from Yale University, and as a student before that he excavated at many important archaeological sites on the Alberta Plains, including Head-Smashed-In Buffalo Jump. Soon after earning his doctorate, Bill took over as the director of a newly formed organization called the Archaeological Survey of Alberta. He brought with him a certainty that Head-Smashed-In would be a wonderful place to celebrate the story of what had transpired at the sandstone cliffs. But as part of a provincial government, his voice was a lonely one in the corridors of power. In the 1970s there were not many powerful people inclined to spend large amounts of taxpayers' dollars on the preservation and interpretation of what was then thought of as Indian history. Heritage development, for the most part, consisted of commemorating European settlement and the history of the province – a trend not restricted to Alberta, but one true for virtually all of North America. Dr. Byrne spent many a fruitless meeting extolling the virtues of Head-Smashed-In only to have his words fall on deaf ears. This all changed in 1981.

By the late 1970s Dr. Byrne began to toy with the idea that Head-Smashed-In Buffalo Jump just might be a worthwhile addition to the prestigious list of UNESCO World Heritage Sites. There were only a couple hundred such sites in the world at the time, including the pyramids, Stonehenge, and the Parthenon. It must have seemed unthinkable to many that a lonely stone cliff in the hills of southern Alberta, containing buried layers of buffalo bones and arrowheads, could share the company of the most famous works of human endeavour on the planet. But not to Bill Byrne. He hired Dr. Brian (Barney) Reeves of the University of Calgary to write the nomination package arguing that Head-Smashed-In should be included on the UNESCO World Heritage List. Dr. Reeves had directed archaeological excavations at Head-Smashed-In (of which Bill Byrne had been a member) and had written the most important scientific papers about the site. In 1980 the package was submitted to UNESCO, and the following year Head-Smashed-In Buffalo Jump was designated as a World Heritage Site.

Suddenly Dr. Byrne had some leverage to take with him into budget meetings. Power brokers not previously moved by the thought of developing an Indian site were forced to sit up and pay attention. The cachet of having a UNESCO site in your home province was simply too strong to ignore. Bill asked for ten million dollars to provide some form of public development at Head-Smashed-In, and, somewhat to his own astonishment, he got it. Thus began the next phase of the life of this remarkable place and with it the assurance that the story will never be forgotten.

A Beer-soaked Bar Napkin

Cattle, cliff swallows, marmots, arrowhead collectors, and archaeologists are about all that had disturbed the silence at Head-Smashed-In for the decades leading up to the 1980s. It had become part of ranching country. Land too rough to farm, suitable only for grazing of large herbivores, just as it had been for thousands of years. Ranching lays a gentle hand on the landscape. There are barbed-wire fences, a few dusty roads, houses scattered kilometres apart, and not much more. The land around Head-Smashed-In looks today much as it would have several thousand years ago. This was a key factor in the UNESCO designation and in the decision to put millions of dollars into the development of this site rather than one of the many other known buffalo jumps.

Soon after UNESCO designation and allocation of funding, Bill Byrne handed the Head-Smashed-In ball to Dr. Frits Pannekoek, then Director of Historic Sites Service of Alberta. From here, Frits managed the project. As if making a film, you could say Bill was the producer and Frits was the director. A team of people from the Alberta government was established – planners, project managers, researchers, display artists – and began to think about what could and should be done with Head-Smashed-In Buffalo Jump.

The first decision that had to be made was where to locate the new interpretive centre. Buffalo jumps by definition are characterized by considerable topography. This fact presented significant challenges with regard to the planning of such features as parking lots, hiking trails, handicapped access, bus drop-off areas, water and sewage, and other infrastructure demands. More fundamentally, the topography of the site was an essential part of the storyline. The final run to the cliff, the plunge from the escarpment, the butchering of carcasses below the jump, the camping on the lower prairie, all were components of one grand story. How could we interpret the site in such a way as to allow visitors to experience the major parts of the story of Head-Smashed-In?

Achieving this goal set in motion a series of meetings and field trips involving the planning team and consultants to examine prospective building sites. Architectural models were made of possible building locations on the prairie below the cliff and above the cliff back from the jump off. The former allowed hiking access to the kill and campsite area below the cliff but precluded the experience of standing at the brink of the cliff. A building on top of the bedrock escarpment permitted experiencing the final portion of the drive and the terrific view from the edge of the cliff but precluded access to the actual kill site and the lower butchering area. Both were highly desirable for public interpretation of the full story of Head-Smashed-In, yet the options seemed mutually exclusive. Like bison, the team was wallowing.

Honesty requires an admission that the solution to the dilemma of the location of the building site was arrived at one evening in a bar. I was enjoying libations with a friend and colleague, Charles Schweger, explaining to him the options that confronted and confounded us. As the night wore on, and glasses refilled, pens came out and bar napkins were scribbled upon. Ideas were debated, alternatives sketched, napkins crumpled and tossed aside. Eventually, though our memories of the evening are also sketchy, an idea emerged. What if the building could be sunk into the bedrock of the cliff, where it would straddle both the upper and lower portions of the site? If this could be achieved, access would be permitted to both the upper jump off viewpoint and to the lower butchering area. I regret that I didn't save the original bar napkin that roughly sketched a slanted, multi-storey building straddling the bedrock cliff of Head-Smashed-In. Surely it should be framed for posterity.

The seemingly bizarre suggestion was brought to the planning team for consideration. It was initially assumed that the blasting out of a huge hole in the bedrock and building a staircase-like structure on a steep slope would be either prohibitively expensive, technically untenable, or both. Surprisingly, neither was the case. When the architect priced out the options, the cost of constructing a building that straddled the cliff (about $6 million) was only about $500,000 more than the previous above-ground options. As the idea of a staircase design gained support, the next innovative idea was to bury the building into the cliffside. What better way to minimize the visual intrusion of an interpretive centre than to put it underground? A buried building would also result in savings in utility costs owing to it being sheltered from the extremes of weather.

The stage was set for what turned out to be one of the strongest selling features of the Head-Smashed-In project: the striking architecture of the interpretive centre. In total, only about 10 per cent of the total surface area of the building is visible. The remainder is buried into the cliff and covered with soil and vegetation. Clearly, the Head-Smashed-In building itself is a statement. It asserts the importance of not intruding on the landscape in which the story of the buffalo jump took place and the desire to convey to the visitors the nature of the vast, open prairies in which these remarkable events transpired.

Cranes on the Cliff

Armed with a dramatic vision of an interpretive centre, the next task was to figure out where to situate it so as to avoid the deep deposits of precious artifacts at the buffalo jump – the very resource that had given us the UNESCO designation. The architect, Robert LeBlond, walked the slope with us, scanning the rugged topography for a suitable building site. Though the project eventually brought him considerable acclaim, I can't help but think that there must have been anxious moments at the beginning when Robert wondered what he had gotten himself into. The approximate location of the main archaeological deposits was known, but not their full extent. The Head-Smashed-In team eventually picked a spot several hundred metres to the south of the main kill site, hoping this would prove to lie beyond the location where ancient hunters left their traces. My archaeology crew went to work testing and exploring the proposed building site. To Robert's great relief, the area was clear of the kill site, and we gave him the green light.

By 1985 huge cranes appeared on the cliff at Head-Smashed-In, explosions rocked the earth, and construction of the interpretive centre began. Built adjacent to the actual archaeological site, the Head-Smashed-In Interpretive Centre is a premier example of in situ interpretation of an archaeological resource in North America. The concrete was stained to match the colour of the local sandstone, and the portions of the building walls exposed above ground were etched with horizontal grooves designed to simulate the natural bedding planes of the sandstone. I still remember the day that Robert LeBlond drove his shiny BMW across the prairie and part way up the slope so that I could load a loose chunk of bedrock into his trunk, Robert hovering over me to ensure I didn't dent his precious car. The bedrock block was on route to Calgary for colour matching. Once the natural vegetation was re-established a few years after construction, the Head-Smashed-In Interpretive Centre became almost invisible as a feature on the landscape. Indeed, after construction was completed but before the road signs were installed, there were a number of complaints from people who had set out in search of the interpretive centre and, failing to see the building, had driven right past it. The centre has won a number of awards, including the prestigious Governor General's Award for Architecture, Canada's highest award in this field.

Unfortunately, it is not as easy to hide vehicles and parking lots. These ubiquitous features of any interpretive facility require careful planning. The initial proposal for the Head-Smashed-In project was to have the main parking lot on the level prairie below the jump. Aesthetically this was a poor solution, because the lot and vehicles would be highly visible from the cliff top and the centre. However, this was the only level ground anywhere around the building. As with all phases of the project, archaeological inspection of the area was required prior to construction. This time the architect didn't like what I had to tell him.

The entire level prairie proposed for a parking lot turned out to be a shallow and rich archaeological deposit thick with the remains of butchering and processing thousands of bison. I told Robert that none of this area (indeed none of the flat land anywhere around) could be used for a parking lot. Archaeology outweighed practicality. Robert was exasperated. Flailing his arms in the air he implored me to tell

Building the Head-Smashed-In Interpretive Centre required blasting a huge hole in the bedrock to situate the seven-storey building. (Courtesy Royal Alberta Museum)

him where the heck he was supposed to put one hundred cars and twenty RVs and buses? I surveyed the region and my eyes settled on the steeply sloping cliffside further south of the building location, a rugged zone that links the cliff top with the lower prairie. A worse place to park vehicles could scarcely be imagined. But as I knew that there was little potential for archaeological deposits on such a steep slope, I pointed to the hillside and told Robert he could have all of that area that he needed. Robert stared at me in disbelief.

In the end, this was the only place we could identify that lacked archaeological deposits. No doubt many visitors are befuddled by the layout of the parking area. It snakes for hundreds of metres in along the toe of the slope. If you are unfortunate enough to have to park at the far end, you are looking at a walk of nearly half a kilometre to the building, much of it uphill. While this formed a challenging but acceptable architectural solution for the parking, understandably it did not meet with the favour of some visitors. The walk from the parking area brought an initial rash of questions and complaints. These stopped almost completely when signs were erected informing the visitors that the parking lot was placed so as to avoid damage to significant archaeological materials. People will put up with seemingly unreasonable circumstances when they are told that valid and important reasons lie behind them.

A Rubber Cliff

The interpretive centre has seven levels, the upper two permitting access to hiking trails along the top of the cliff and the lower five composed of displays, administration, and service areas. The storyline proceeds from top to bottom, with the five display levels devoted to the topics of bison and the environment of the Plains, the culture of Blackfoot people, the operation of the buffalo jump, the coming of Europeans and the end of the buffalo hunts, and the archaeology of Head-Smashed-In. The centre also features an eighty-seat theatre, a cafeteria, and a gift shop. When first opened, it even boasted a well-equipped archaeological laboratory where my staff sat in full public

The signature display in the interpretive centre is a replica of the killing cliff with buffalo perched at the top and an archaeological dig at the bottom. (Courtesy Royal Alberta Museum)

view, cataloguing bone, examining artifacts, and answering questions. As envisioned on a bar napkin long ago, trails take the visitor out the top of the building to a spectacular view of the killing cliff and out the lower doors to trails that wind around the bonebed and the butchering area.

The Head-Smashed-In Interpretive Centre is a magical place. Staffed almost entirely by Blackfoot, it has a wonderful feel to it, like the past coming to life. The regional landscape is so unspoiled that you can still easily picture – and almost feel – the dramatic events of a buffalo jump unfolding much as it did hundreds of years ago. A walk outside is a crucial part of the visit. This is where the story unfolded, and there can be no substitute for getting connected to the land that ancient hunters once trod, land that echoed with the bellowing of wounded animals.

Certainly the signature display within the building is a group of three bison perched at the edge of a ten-metre-high cliff and an archaeological dig sunken into the floor below the cliff. So realistic looking is the replication of the sheer bedrock face and the dig beneath it that many visitors have gasped at the sight and remarked (I'm not making this up) at how ingenious it was to build the interpretive centre right around the actual cliff and the real archaeological dig, as if we had enveloped the UNESCO World Heritage site within the concrete walls. During the many years I strode the floors of the building in dirty jeans, running shoes, and T-shirt (looking, I suppose, like an archaeologist on his break), I can't count the number of times people pointed at the replica dig and asked what time the archaeologists went back to work, intending, apparently, to hang around with their families until we resumed our excavations.

There is one thing you might like to know. The cast of the cliff on display in the interpretive centre is not of the cliff at Head-Smashed-In. The display is a magnificent piece of work, and the genius behind it was an exhibits contractor named Ewald Lemke and his son Kurt. Ewald was for years a museum display designer, so he knew the importance of not disturbing real artifacts. And the cliff face at Head-Smashed-In is in a sense an artifact. Ewald explained that the process of casting the cliff would involve spraying a fine layer of latex rubber on the rock face, backing this with fibreglass to give it strength, and pulling the whole thing off. So precise is the technique that grains of sand and bits of lichen would come off the cliff and be transferred to the final cast. Ewald was concerned that pulling off the rubber mould might leave a cleaned stripe some four metres wide and ten metres long across the face of the bedrock. This different-coloured stripe would be visible to visitors for years to come. Ewald suggested we find another cliff from which to take our cast. Puzzled, I think I must have felt like the architect Robert LeBlond did when I told him he couldn't have his parking lot.

There's no shortage of rock in this region of the Porcupine Hills. But we needed a straight, vertical face that was ten metres high. Fortunately, I thought I knew just the place. One of the goals of our years of archaeological research was to scope out other important historical sites associated with Head-Smashed-In. This is what led to our study of the drive lanes, a nearby vision quest site, and other buffalo jumps. It had long been thought that all the drive lanes of the Head-Smashed-In gathering basin led to one paramount jump. Over the years, however, research by Dr. Barney Reeves and ourselves proved that there were several more kill sites in the immediate vicinity and that these were occasionally the object of the drives of buffalo herds coming out of the basin. One of these, named the Calderwood Jump after the local landowner, is situated about a kilometre north of Head-Smashed-In. Its distinct cliff, jutting out to a prominent point, is clearly visible from Head-Smashed-In. Our crew excavated a portion of this site to gain a better understanding of the scope of bison killing that took place along

Making the replica of the cliff was an arduous exercise, requiring a semi-trailer truck to reach the top of the Calderwood jump. Two sections of the cliff were sprayed with latex rubber and the pieces were merged together into a single cast. (Courtesy Royal Alberta Museum)

the cliffs of the Porcupine Hills. The cliff at the Calderwood Buffalo Jump is indeed impressive. It is even higher than Head-Smashed-In, and the slope below it is rockier, steeper, and more rugged.

Along with the Lemkes, we went to the Calderwood Jump and surveyed the cliff. It seemed perfect: high, foreboding, dangerous, and remote enough that if the casting pulled a clean stripe off the face, only us, the landowner, and some cattle would see it. But could we get a semi-trailer loaded with tonnes of gear to the Calderwood cliff? There were no roads, not even a trail, leading to the cliff. Approaching from below was impossible; the land is way too rugged and steep for any vehicle. Ewald surveyed the landscape, scratched his head, and said, let's try getting the semi in from the top.

So we did. As winter neared in 1986, an eighteen-wheeler semi-trailer, loaded with casting equipment, including massive aluminum scaffolding and heavy-duty tarps worth ten thousand dollars each, rolled across the prairie and low hills behind Head-Smashed-In. It was an unnerving sight, a tractor trailer perched at the edge of a high cliff in the Porcupine Hills. The scaffolding was erected against the cliff face, and the Lemkes scaled the framework going about their business like a family of monkeys. In freezing conditions, the crew sprayed a mist of latex rubber against the rock and tried to protect the surface with huge tarps. To remove it, they had to cut the mould into many small pieces, to be reassembled later on the floor of a giant warehouse in Calgary.

The cast of the Calderwood Buffalo Jump is the cliff face on display inside the Head-Smashed-In Interpretive Centre. And a fine specimen of a killing cliff it is, made all the better by virtue of the fact that it is from an actual buffalo jump.

And a Rubber Dig

Having the Lemkes' semi-trailer parked above the Calderwood Jump had a second benefit. Our excavation of that site was still in progress and the pits were left open over that winter. The interpretive centre was being designed to incorporate a mock-up of an archaeological excavation. The ground-level floor was to be recessed several metres deep to accommodate the dig. But there were no excavations going on at the Head-Smashed-In kill site, nor were any planned for the immediate future. What was I going to use to fill that two-metre-deep

I found it a harrowing experience, as an archaeologist, to watch a carefully excavated pit be covered in rubber, but the resulting detail of the reproduction was spectacular. (Courtesy Royal Alberta Museum)

pit inside the building? You can build a replica dig from scratch, creating fake layers of soil interspersed with artifacts. But they never look convincing; they look sterile and contrived, which of course is what they are. Far better is to replicate a real dig, getting an exact impression of the walls and floors of the pit with real rocks, bones, and artifacts in their actual place.

I was the one who wanted this exhibit. I thought we should have a view of the layers of bones, rocks, and tools found at the base of the cliff. After all, this is what the story of Head-Smashed-In is all about. The Calderwood Jump offered a handy and convincing solution. Our excavations at the base of the Calderwood cliff had exposed buffalo kill deposits that spanned several thousand years. The pits were about two metres deep, just what was needed. So the Lemke crew moved their gear to the bottom of the Calderwood cliff and commenced spraying latex rubber all over our excavation walls and floors. It was an arresting event for the archaeology crew: a milky white substance covering the ancient layers of a buffalo jump that had taken weeks of painstaking work to uncover. But my anxiety was worth it; the replica that emerged from the cast is extraordinary.

As with the cast of the cliff, the casting of the excavation pit had to be cut into pieces and then reassembled. I made many trips to the Calgary warehouse, crawling over the pieces of the cast, like a giant jigsaw puzzle, making sure that each section of wall and floor was

*When the pieces were
assembled, the replica dig
inside the interpretive
centre was completely
convincing. (Courtesy
Royal Alberta Museum)*

lined up with the appropriate joining piece. When the completed
display was finally installed, it was an exact copy of the real dig that
we had in progress a kilometre away. My crew then set about making everything around the replica dig look convincing. We raided
our own supply of battered metal buckets, dirty trowels, rusty tape
measurers, broken line levels, clipboards with dirt-smudged sheets
of graph paper, crumpled brown paper bags, beat-up backpacks – the
stuff you would see were you to drop in on any ongoing archaeological dig. The realistic look of the dig inside the Head-Smashed-In
Interpretive Centre accounts for the many tourists who have asked
when the archaeologists are going to scale the glass barrier and get
back to work.

In fact, we did occasionally hop over the wall and clamour around beside the replica dig. Since we had robbed our own gear to supply the replica, when extra crew or volunteers showed up, we occasionally found that we ran short at the real one outside. So, much like a real dig, the equipment scattered throughout the replica excavation moved around and changed from time to time, with no grand design or purpose and oblivious to the concerns of exhibit designers, which is the way I think it should be.

The Blackfoot Get Involved

I would be remiss not to mention the important role the Blackfoot people played in the development of the Head-Smashed-In Buffalo Jump Interpretive Centre. When the idea to construct a centre was first hatched, it was assumed that the project would be orchestrated and executed by the team of government workers and consultants, all of whom were non-Native. But this view did not last long. We knew, even in the early 1980s, that consultation with local Aboriginal people would be required. Head-Smashed-In is located just a few hundred metres from the boundary of the Piikani reserve, and the site was known and revered by this group and other members of the Blackfoot Nation. At first we thought we needed permission of local Native people, but it quickly became apparent that we needed a lot more than permission. We needed their support and their help. This job, and a daunting one it was for a young archaeologist with little experience working with living Native people, fell to me. It was a task that changed my life.

Members of the Piikani Nation recount stories of the buffalo hunting days during interviews for the development of Head-Smashed-In. (Courtesy Royal Alberta Museum)

Sheepishly, having no idea what to expect, I began attending band council meetings at the Piikani tribal council in the town of Brocket, the headquarters of the Piikani people. This was in the early 1980s. Up until that point I had excavated many sites, often in remote locations such as the Canadian Rockies, where an entire summer could pass with no more contact with the outside world than the checkout clerks at the local grocery and beer stores. Not with Aboriginal people. It may seem archaic to people today, but traditionally archaeologists in North America were not taught to interact with the people whose heritage they investigated. This is a recent, and welcome, trend. I entered the Head-Smashed-In project with all the training of a scientist who studied the dead and none of the preparation needed to deal with the living. The learning curve was steep and sometimes rocky.

I began discussions with the Piikani filled with enthusiasm. After all, what archaeologist wouldn't be wildly excited when faced with the opportunity to spend ten million dollars planning and interpreting a UNESCO World Heritage site. Surely, everyone else would be just as excited. This assumption proved to be a trifle naive. While I knew a fair bit about the more ancient aspects of Blackfoot history, I knew next to nothing about the contemporary situation on reserves, especially with respect to dealing with representatives of government. My first big shock was the discovery that I was a representative of government.

I thought of myself as an archaeologist and anthropologist, one who happened to be employed by the government of Alberta. Since my chosen field of study was the ancient Native culture of western Canada, I assumed there would be some bond between the Piikani and me. But when the band council meetings got around to my item on the agenda, it was announced that "The guy from the government wants to talk about the buffalo jump." Nobody learned my name, nobody knew what my title was, nobody cared that my training included knowledge about their own history. I was that guy from the government, not just for the first meeting or two but for several years of meetings. It took me a long time to figure out what was going on, but eventually I think I did.

First, I came to realize that these people's lives had been filled with representatives from government showing up and excitedly telling them that a plan was afoot that would be really good for their people. There had been a parade of such guys with such plans. Most plans either never came to pass or turned out to be not really good at all for the Natives. They had developed a healthy and experienced skepticism for anyone from government showing up and announcing they had something good in the works for them. I was just another government guy with big promises.

Second, I quickly learned how transient most government people were in the lives of Native people. Often they saw someone once and never again. Occasionally, a person stuck around for a few meetings, but rarely did anyone hang around in their world for any length of time. This added a further element of skepticism for the messages brought by government agents and also accounted for the general reluctance to bother learning your name or what you did. I knew little about these trends when I started meeting with Native people. But that works both ways. They knew little about me. As they would eventually find out (and I would eventually get known by my name), I was in this for the long haul.

Meeting with the Piikani

The whole story of the Blackfoot involvement in the Head-Smashed-In Buffalo Jump project is not just long and complex. It is ongoing. The Niitsitapi continue to play a major role in the operation of the site, holding the great majority of jobs inside the centre, including all of the jobs as site interpreters. Indeed, they are the only interpreters the site has ever had; this has been something on which all parties have insisted. Blackfoot people interpret their own history and culture.

Once I started attending Piikani band council meetings, it soon was apparent that my major contact would not be with the political elements of the band but with the elders. Repeatedly the councillors told me that the elders were the ones who would have to speak on the issues I raised. I was directed to meet with staff of the Piikani cultural centre, where the elders regularly came for meetings, and I was told that I would be appointed an elder as my senior working colleague. I had no idea if I would get a say in who was directed to work most closely with me, but it hardly mattered because at this point I knew no one in the Piikani community. Since I knew that this could be an important decision, I thought I would try to get some advance information just in case I had a voice in the matter. I placed a call to Hugh Dempsey.

Hugh Dempsey is a distinguished scholar of the Blackfoot people and their history, and the author of many books on the topic. First, I asked Hugh if he thought I would have a voice in appointing an elder to work with. His response was a quick and unequivocal "No." He explained that this would be a decision out of my hands. Second, just to humour me, I asked Hugh whether, in the unlikely event I had a say in the matter, could he recommend some names of Piikani elders I might mention as preferred working partners. Hugh thought for a while and then began to rattle off some names of senior and respected elders. Many of these were followed by comments such as "But he's probably too old now," "He might have passed away recently," and "He moved to Montana." In the end he listed a few individuals who he said would be good. Of these he singled out Joe Crowshoe. "Get Joe Crowshoe," Hugh said; "If you have any say in the matter, get Joe."

On my first day at the Piikani cultural centre, a group of elders and I sat around in a circle, me talking about the project, an elder translating into Blackfoot. It was still common in the 1980s (and, rarely, even today) for elders not to speak English. There was lively discussion about the possibility of having a major interpretive centre built just around the corner of the reserve at the buffalo jump. Most thought it was a good idea. A few voiced concern that we might mess things up. But all agreed on one point. If we do this we have to do it right. This was a phrase I was to hear many times over the coming years, and I learned it had a special significance to these people.

Doing it right to the Niitsitapi was nothing remotely like what a young and idealistic archaeologist thought it meant. I was treated to a litany of instances where museums had gotten it wrong: artifacts placed facing the wrong direction; artifacts placed next to each other in a way that would never have occurred in their culture; where the music played in a gallery was wholly inappropriate for what was on display. The list went on. It was a list of which I was completely unaware. It told a story of a people who had been excluded from decision making about the telling of their heritage, a people who could only look in from the outside and shake their heads at the mistakes made, and who, quite reasonably, must have wondered why someone simply didn't ask them.

In those days, no one asked. I hoped that Head-Smashed-In would be different, and I tried to assure the elders that we would want to do this right, in their sense of the word. There was a lot of talk in Blackfoot that excluded me, and you could tell they were debating the pros and cons of what amounted to a very big decision. Should they co-operate with a planned government development of the great buffalo jump that was so emblematic of their proud past and so revered by people of the day? Hoping, I suppose, to court their favour, I informed them of the council's decision to appoint a senior elder to work with me on the project. As there would be a regular salary involved, I assumed that this perk would result in someone in the room being designated. More discussion in Blackfoot ensued. A spokesperson announced that the group was still somewhat skeptical of the whole idea, but they agreed that I should work with an elder to further develop a plan. And the person I should work with was Joe Crowshoe.

I looked around the room. I didn't know who Joe Crowshoe was, but I assumed he must be present. I was wrong. As I found out later, Joe never came to these meetings. In fact, he was openly critical of the regular elders meetings, stating that the criteria for who was considered an elder were too lenient (he once told me with a laugh that anyone who can make a pair of moccasins was considered an elder). As I thought back about this later, I was deeply impressed by the decision of the elders committee. I was at their mercy. They could have appointed anyone as my co-worker – a relative, a friend, themselves – and secured a monthly government salary. Instead, they chose someone who not only wasn't there that day but who also was something of a black sheep in the elder community. They chose Joe because they knew he was the best person for the job. They were right.

Joe Crowshoe

It would be hard to overestimate the contribution Joe Crowshoe made to the Head-Smashed-In project. In a very real sense, I'm not sure we would have been able to pull this off without his support. He greased so many wheels, spoke to so many people, interviewed so many other elders, logged so many miles on the road, and spoke forcefully in favour of the project. I soon met with Joe and his incredible wife, Josephine. I liked them both immensely. They were, at the same time, both intrinsically good people and folks who wanted to improve the lot of fellow Blackfoot. We discussed the idea of developing the buffalo jump and how the Blackfoot people might be involved. Joe was immediately supportive and wanted to get to work. I couldn't spend the necessary time in southern Alberta away from my office, so I contracted an anthropologist from the University of Alberta, Roger McDonnell, to work with Joe in the early days. Together they hit the road, talking to other band councils and interviewing elders, all in an effort to do it right.

In the mid-1980s Joe was already a man of considerable influence and respect. Once he dropped in on a Blackfoot band council meeting wanting to discuss our project. Typically, Joe had made no provision to be on the agenda that day. But quickly and silently people in the room began making sign language regarding Joe's desire to speak (sign language is still widely used), and in short order, without a word said, the chair recognized Joe and he rose to speak in favour of the Head-Smashed-In project. Few other Blackfoot could have commanded this attention.

Joe's reputation was a formidable boost to the Head-Smashed-In project. I soon learned that the degree of respect other Native people gave an elder was closely related to how much that person knew about the traditional culture of the Blackfoot. It was common knowledge on the various reserves who the great keepers of the historical information were. When any of these people were present in a situation where traditional culture was discussed, all the others would inevitably defer to him or her: "Let so-and-so tell it," they would say, "He [she] knows the real stories." Joe's reputation was such that others frequently deferred to him. But the other advantage of having Joe on the project was he knew practically all the other Blackfoot who were widely regarded as the keepers of the most authentic information. Many were personal friends; those who weren't knew and respected Joe's reputation. Joe could call up just about anyone and say he wanted to come over and talk about the old days, and off he would go.

Although Joe's involvement served as a great promotion for the project, this was an ancillary benefit; promotion was only one of his interests. Equal in Joe's mind was the opportunity to gather information about the old days, especially buffalo hunting, from precisely those people who still remembered the most about it. He didn't care who the person was, what group of Blackfoot they belonged to, or where they lived. He wanted the best people who spoke with the greatest authority. This was an ideal opportunity for Joe. Someone else provided the car, paid the gas, bought meals, worked the tape recorder, and provided small honoraria to the speakers. All Joe had to do was talk and ask questions of his esteemed colleagues about subjects that interested him deeply. Many of the people Joe interviewed in the mid-1980s are dead now, as is Joe Crowshoe. But their stories have been preserved as a precious record of traditional Blackfoot culture. Some of them are told inside the Head-Smashed-In Buffalo Jump Interpretive Centre. Also inside the centre is a room used for education, especially of visiting school groups. After his death, and in memory of his importance to the project, it was named The Joe Crowshoe Lodge. I was honoured to be asked to write the text for a small plaque that hangs in the room, recounting the enormous contribution this man made.

During those years, and many that followed, Joe and Josephine became my friends. I shared coffee at their kitchen table, attended Blackfoot ceremonies as Joe's guest, stood with him at speaking events, and was adopted into his family and given a Blackfoot name. Once Joe asked me if I wanted to go with him down to the Pine Ridge Reservation in South Dakota. The Sioux were bringing back the traditional piercing Sundance ceremony where young men put skewers through their chests and then tore them from their flesh. Joe, one of the most respected medicine men on the northern Plains, was asked to come do the piercing. I was a little queasy about witnessing the piercing, and more queasy about being a white guy showing up on the Pine Ridge Reservation, a place that was having considerable trouble at about that time. I declined. Although I have since attended other piercings and Sundances, I regret that I didn't take that trip with Joe. I'm sure it would have been an incredible experience.

A Painted Skull

As Joe and Roger McDonnell conducted the research interviews, it became apparent that we would have permission from the relevant Native groups to move forward with the project. Many other pieces of the puzzle started to fall into place. As people began working on the building design, I began cobbling together the outline of a story to be told inside the building. Major consulting firms were brought in to further develop these and to plan and orchestrate the entire project. Throughout, the Blackfoot stayed involved. As ideas developed for possible displays, I would run these by the elders at the Piikani cultural centre. The same was done with the text as it was produced and artifacts that were slated for display. Most of the items on display are replicas of real artifacts, many of them made by Blackfoot people. While it might seem a simple thing to make and display replicas of real artifacts, I discovered this was far from the case.

As I have tried to convey in previous pages, many things in Blackfoot culture have, for lack of a better word, power. Their traditional world was a spiritual place, and many inanimate things in it were (and still are) infused with spiritual power. There was spirited debate among the Blackfoot elders about what kinds of stories and artifacts stemming from the spiritual world could be used in the building. On the one hand, they wanted visitors to the site to know that they were spiritual people, not pagans as some stereotypes portray. On the other hand, they didn't feel it was appropriate to put powerful artifacts out on display. Stuff of the spiritual world was not meant to be ogled at by tourists. Initially it seemed that making replicas of these objects was the obvious solution. But here's the rub. The elders were adamant that it would only be acceptable to replicate a powerful object if the person replicating it had the spiritual authority to do so. For example, Joe Crowshoe was a medicine pipe bundle owner, so if a bundle were to be replicated, a bundle owner (Joe) would have to do it.[†] Just as I thought we had come to some agreement, someone spoke up: "If a real bundle owner makes a replica bundle then isn't it a real bundle?" Well that sure got a lot of discussion going.

It seemed at times we were back to square one. The process turned in ways I could never have imagined but that never ceased to enlighten me. In the end, replicas of powerful objects were made by people with the recognized authority to do so. They became, de facto, equivalent to real objects. In this respect, nothing was more important than a painted buffalo skull.

There is a buffalo skull on display at Head-Smashed-In that was painted by Joe Crowshoe with traditional designs in black, red, and yellow paint. It is one of the most powerful objects in the building. Although Joe painted it expressly for display purposes, the skull is now indistinguishable from one that would be prepared and used at the annual sacred Sundance and other vital Blackfoot ceremonies. As required, sweetgrass is stuffed into the nasal cavity of the skull, and, as required, the glass case is occasionally opened and the sweetgrass

[†] Bundles are the most powerful objects in the Blackfoot ceremonial world. They are wrappings of buffalo hide, which contain items such as pipes, that are used in specific ceremonies. They exist for the good of the people and are not so much owned by someone as they are cared for by the people who have them. Of the many different kinds, the medicine pipe bundle is one of the most powerful.

Elder Joe Crowshoe painting a buffalo skull for use inside the Head-Smashed-In Interpretive Centre. (Courtesy Royal Alberta Museum)

replaced. The skull itself has been removed and taken to local Sundances for blessing. When this happens, only people possessing proper authority are permitted to lift the skull from the case.

Once a film crew working for the government of Canada showed up and wanted to film the skull. They were making a commercial to be shown in Europe promoting travel to Canada. They didn't want to film through a glass case; instead, they wanted the skull placed outside on the windswept prairie. They were told in no uncertain terms that this would not happen, that no one was around who could handle the skull, and that even if there was, such a use of the skull would not be permitted. The film crew was sent packing.

In many ways, this painted skull serves as a metaphor for the buffalo jump. It tells of times past but uses the present to do so. It reaches deep into Blackfoot culture, but is a bridge to the modern world. It evokes a fierce and unwavering connection to tradition. With Joe's permission, the image of the skull became the centrepiece of the poster for the jump. It is, in my opinion, one of the most stunning posters for any site, museum, or centre I have ever visited. It is simple, powerful, memorable. Which is why Joe's son, Reg Crowshoe, and the Aboriginal staff of Head-Smashed-In gave their permission to use the skull as the cover of this book. No other image would do.

The skull also serves to remind us why Head-Smashed-In is such a unique place – because it remains an object of reverence but also one of controversy and debate. Some Aboriginal people feel it is too powerful to be on display. Others feel it is appropriate for display but not for other uses. Still others see a wider, more public role for the skull as acceptable. While the skull has been the poster image for twenty years, it has never (despite being by far the most striking image of the site) been featured on a T-shirt. You have to appreciate that T-shirts are the top-selling souvenir of almost any visitor centre, and this beautiful painted skull on a shirt would be a certain hit. So why is it never seen on a shirt? When asked about this, I recall Joe Crowshoe's words: a poster is like an art object; people hang it on their walls and appreciate it. A T-shirt could be worn by anyone to do anything – rob a bank, commit other bad deeds. If the skull were to be seen in this context, it would bring great disrespect to the power of the skull and shame on the people who let this happen. So the skull has never been on a T-shirt, and never will be.

Once there was considerable debate among staff at the site as to whether or not it was appropriate to use the image of the skull on a highway billboard promoting the buffalo jump. To help resolve this debate, I was asked to write up a short history of Joe's painting of the skull and his words regarding its use. The issue was debated among the Blackfoot staff, and it was decided that the image of the skull

The buffalo skull painted by Joe Crowshoe was initially made for educational and display purposes but over the years has become emblematic of the deeply held Aboriginal traditions that are kept alive at Head-Smashed-In. (Courtesy Royal Alberta Museum)

hanging on a billboard was similar to one hanging on your wall. For me, this brought home the message that Aboriginal people continue to care deeply about matters of their traditional culture. They alone made the decision regarding the billboard, not government communication officers. This is all part of what makes Head-Smashed-In an intensely interesting place to work and be associated with. The power of the painted skull continues.

Where Are the Blood?

Up till now I have mentioned only working with the Piikani band of the Blackfoot people. This certainly seemed the logical place to start, since one corner of their reserve begins just a few hundred metres from Head-Smashed-In. But there are two other bands of Blackfoot in Alberta: the Siksika (Blackfoot) located on a reserve about eighty kilometres east of Calgary, and the Kainai (Blood), whose home reserve is about fifty kilometres southeast of the buffalo jump. I had not thought to include either of these two groups in my initial meetings and conversations about developing the jump. I simply assumed that, because of proximity, the Piikani were the one relevant band to talk to. This was perhaps the biggest mistake I made in my years working on the Head-Smashed-In project, and it was one that cost me considerable good will.

Here's an illustration of how important these matters are to Native people, and how memories of transgressions are long lived. In 2005, a full twenty years after my discussions with the Piikani were completed, I was meeting with respected elders of the Kainai Nation, a group called the Mookaakin Foundation. I was there on a matter unrelated to Head-Smashed-In, but it did involve participation of the Kainai in the public development of another important heritage site. During the meeting, one of the elders, Pete Standing Alone, launched into a discussion about the importance of meaningful involvement of his people. He started to tell the story of Head-Smashed-In. He talked about how for several years the Kainai were left out of the whole development process, how some government people continued meeting with the Piikani, and so on. At this point I raised my hand and stopped Pete. I told him I was that government guy who had only talked with the Piikani. I told him it had been a mistake. Everyone was quiet for a moment. Then there was a good laugh all around the room. Enough time had passed; we were all different people now, and we knew that despite transgressions a greater good had been served. But twenty years before it was no laughing matter.

The Siksika are the most northern Blackfoot, with their reserve situated along the Bow River, east of Calgary, Alberta. As I eventually discovered, they felt less attachment to the Head-Smashed-In area, conceding this region to the two southern groups. As I also found out, however, the Kainai felt strongly that their traditional lands and culture had very much included the region of the Porcupine Hills. They believed that their people had built and used the buffalo jump every bit as much as the Piikani (long ago, all the different Blackfoot groups may have been one people). Reserves are like small towns. There are no secrets. It didn't take long for the Kainai to hear about the dealings with the Piikani, about Joe Crowshoe's interviews, about the Piikani elders providing advice to people proposing to develop the site. And it didn't take long for a pickup truck full of some of the biggest Kainai people I had ever seen to descend on the site one day asking who was in charge. Unfortunately, I was.

It was summer. I was at the buffalo jump running an archaeological dig as well as continuing work with the Piikani. Construction of the building had just begun. I was the only government representative on site. A good portion of my crew that summer was Blackfoot, including some Kainai, a fact I thought might help me when the truck full of angry looking Kainai rolled in. It didn't. The visitors wanted to know what the heck I thought I was doing, who had given permission for this, which of their elders had been consulted, and on it went. I had a pretty wide strip torn off me. Clearly, people were quite angry. I was in a bit of shock. I had no idea that I had offended anyone so deeply. It was certainly not intentional, but it was a big mistake nonetheless.

The aftermath of this was an invitation for Kainai elders to visit the site. The group of us walked around the big hole in the ground where the interpretive centre would eventually be placed. I started explaining the plans we had developed for the storyline that would be told in the building. This of course had all been done in consultation with the Piikani and not at all with the Kainai, and none of it was lost on the elders. As they spoke in Blackfoot I kept hearing the word Piikani in their conversation. They were remarking on all the things that had been discussed with and approved by the Piikani, and not with them. Obviously, they were not objecting to consultation with the Piikani but to the exclusion of themselves.

The other members of the Head-Smashed-In project and I found ourselves in a tough spot. Planning had progressed a long way. The building was basically designed, the storyline developed, displays were being researched and produced, text was being scripted. The Kainai had been excluded from nearly all of this. Do we form a new partnership with the Kainai and put all of this material on the table for review, or do we go with what we had? In the end we chose the latter, although we did try to solicit input from the Kainai on certain topics and displays. Something of a truce was reached. While the Kainai were not happy with the course of events, they recognized that we had been advised throughout by their close relatives – the elders of the Piikani – and that they respected (though not always agreed with) the voice of their fellow traditionalists.

Hollywood North

A major video to play in the theatre had to be made. The script called for a re-enactment of an actual jump for which Blackfoot in period outfits were to be the actors. We had to find herds of live buffalo we could film, and, most importantly (given that live animals were out of the question), some dead buffalo to throw over the cliff at Head-Smashed-In. The latter is not a commonplace demand and required some inventive searching. Eventually we obtained two carcasses. One became available just before filming and so was still soft and fresh. The other was obtained several months in advance and was kept frozen until the time for action. To my knowledge, no one before us (or since) had thrown any dead buffalo – let alone a frozen one – over a cliff. As you can imagine, there was a fair bit of guesswork as to how this would be accomplished and what was going to happen.

It turned out to be one of those events laced with terrific memories. More than a hundred Blackfoot people, gathered on the slope below the cliff, whooped with delight at the sight of bison sailing off the cliff and slamming into the earth. Remember, no one had seen such a sight in a good one hundred fifty years. They called for an encore, and got their wish, since everything in Hollywood has to be done many times over. As the buffalo fell from the cliff, the loud noise of so

Making a film required throwing dead buffalo over the cliff, an event not likely seen anywhere in a century and a half. (Courtesy Royal Alberta Museum)

many clicking shutters completely stymied the sound man's attempts to record the thud of its impact. Needing some kind of audio of buffalo hitting the earth, the sound man and I returned to the cliff one evening. While I threw sandbags off the jump, he scurried around with his boom microphone dodging sandbags and getting the sound we needed.

Of course, no one knew what a frozen buffalo would do when thrown off a ten-metre-high cliff. It turns out that it makes some horribly unpredictable bounces – once careening wildly towards a half million dollar movie camera and crew, sending the latter scattering across the hillside. To simulate the fall from a buffalo's eye view, we packed an old, beat up camera in a box full of styrofoam, cut a hole for the lens, and repeatedly tossed it off the cliff. The camera survived; the footage was priceless.

In the same way Hazel Big Smoke had been with our bone breaking experiments, we discovered that modern-day Blackfoot were not quite so enamoured with bloody buffalo carcasses as were their ancestors. The script called for butchering the carcasses after the plunge from the cliff. Since we couldn't make a dent in the frozen one, only

The film needed an authentic looking Native camp beneath the cliff, a considerable challenge when so much is unknown about camp life a thousand years ago. (Courtesy Royal Alberta Museum)

the thawed one could be used, and by now it had travelled up and down the cliff several times over several days. To be kind, it was getting a little rank. Cutting into the thick hide revealed a repulsive green colour rather than a cherry crimson. Fake blood was brought in by the litre and poured over the hands doing the butchering. Only they weren't Native hands. The actors drew the line at putting their hands into a rancid carcass, and the archaeologists (who are known to possess no scruples) were enlisted as stand-ins.

An authentic looking tipi camp had to be erected on the flats below the cliff. Reg Crowshoe was his father Joe's principal acolyte in the practice of ceremonial Blackfoot culture. Like his father, Reg is well schooled in the traditional ways of his people. He provided competent direction in assembling the camp and dictating where the fires would be placed, where the poles for the travois would be stacked, and where the war shields would be hung. The biggest problem was that ancient tipis would have been made from buffalo hides, something nearly impossible to replicate today. We made all the tipis but one out of canvas and lit smoky fires to try and hide the fact. The one tipi used for close-up filming of the interior was made of cow hide. So realistic and powerful were the iniskim (sacred buffalo stone) ceremonies held inside the cow-hide tipi that the woman performing the ceremony quit a few days into filming. She was uncomfortable having to put herself, even in an acting role, in the position of handling the sacred materials. This was another lesson for me of the degree to which sacred ceremonies associated with the buffalo hunts are still remembered, of the power associated with them, and of the ongoing belief that only certain individuals possess the authority to journey into the sacred world.

Opening and Aftermath

The time leading up to the grand opening of the Head-Smashed-In Interpretive Centre was chock full of special and unique moments, ones that won't be replicated no matter what we do with the rest of our lives. The juxtaposition of all these players and circumstances – Native elders, archaeologists, government senior managers, architects, politicians, band councils, display fabricators, film-makers – will never come to pass again. There had been nothing like it in the generations leading up to it.

It was also a time of considerable panic and excitement. The grand opening was set for 27 July 1987. The Duke and Duchess of York, Prince Andrew and Sarah Ferguson, were coming to cut the ribbon, so the opening date was immutable. Yet we were clearly behind in getting the displays installed and the building ready. As the opening drew near, my archaeological crew, which had been digging out on the flats of the processing area, was called inside to help pound nails and lay carpet. Senior civil servants showed up to sweep floors, clean glass, and hang displays.

One of my Blackfoot crew members, Clayton Blood, had a fondness for setting off small firecrackers. Out on the deserted prairie, where our digs were located, it was harmless, so I ignored it. As the grand opening approached, given that Royalty was to officiate, we were swarmed with British and Canadian security people. They combed the building, scouring for possible sources of trouble. My office, located deep in the bowels of the building and lacking windows, was selected as the safe house to which they would bring the royal couple in the event of trouble. I was turfed out, and the sniffer dogs were brought in. Suddenly there was a great commotion. I was escorted, at a spirited step by people who wore sunglasses inside and who talked into their shirt cuffs, to my office to explain why a German shepherd had gone ballistic sniffing one of the small backpacks used by my crew. With the SWAT team hovering, I dug into Clayton's backpack to reveal the firecrackers. Security forces, having had the obligatory humourectomy, were not amused.

You may recall Willy Big Bull. He's the Blackfoot who made the mistake of taking an axe to the head of the frozen buffalo used in the film. Willy showed up for the grand opening carrying a mounted, stuffed head of a buffalo to present as a gift to the royal couple. With at least a hundred members of the international media whipped into a frenzy, Willy carried the stuffed head onto the plaza of the interpretive centre and handed it to Sarah Ferguson. She actually held it in her arms for a few moments, smiling with delight, and the cover photograph for newspapers across Britain the next day was a done deal.

Five thousand people came to Head-Smashed-In on opening day. It was the biggest crowd the site has ever had. My crew was outside digging, as we were part of the great interpretive experience. But my senior assistant, Bob Dawe, and I got to lurk inside the building and rub shoulders with royalty. Six years of planning, thinking, discussing, negotiating, compromising, working, building, sweating, and guessing had come to an end. Head-Smashed-In Buffalo Jump Interpretive Centre was open to the public.

Of Time and Tradition

The greatest food-getting enterprise ever devised by the human spirit and intellect has not been forgotten. Head-Smashed-In Buffalo Jump is there for you to see and experience. Through three-dimensional displays, a theatre, several video productions, and real and replica artifacts, the story of the buffalo, the Plains cultures, and the buffalo jump are kept alive. Blackfoot guides tour you through the building and their history. Much of what they present is personal anecdote, something I could never do, no matter how many years spent at the site. Let me give an example.

Once my crew was excavating the remains of a well-preserved dog from the butchering area of the site. It was well known that dogs were a common feature of the ancient camps, so these remains were not unusual. One of the Blackfoot guides was leaning over the wooden railing watching us. He told me a story of how he and his father had once

Tens of thousands of visitors each year come to the interpretive centre to experience the story of the buffalo jump. (Courtesy Head-Smashed-In Buffalo Jump)

been riding horses above the jump when they were hunting deer. Their trusty dog had gotten carried away with the hunt, and in the panic of chasing down some deer the dog had run over the cliff and plunged to its death. I looked down at the bones of the dog that I was excavating with new meaning and with the knowledge that Native people, not archaeologists, should be the ones who interpret this site.

It is a special place with special stories about the past, but also about the present. It is a place that Blackfoot people, despite government ownership, have come to claim as their own. It has been the site of weddings, funerals, medicine bundle openings, meetings of elders, and many other ceremonies that reflect the esteem in which the place is held. When two tourists died of heart attacks within the first few weeks of opening, staff insisted that the whole place be closed to the public (not an easy task at a government-run facility) and cleansing ceremonies held. This was done, and, incidentally, no visitors have died in the intervening decades.

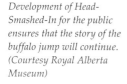

Development of Head-Smashed-In for the public ensures that the story of the buffalo jump will continue. (Courtesy Royal Alberta Museum)

When staff feels so inclined, the place literally shakes with the drumming and chanting of the Blackfoot who gather round a huge drum on the main floor. Visitors are positively transfixed by the ethereal Blackfoot singing as it reverberates through the seven-storey

concrete building. A Blackfoot janitor, hired to sweep and vacuum, took up the craft of chipping out stone tools. When not cleaning the building, Ronald Four Horns would sit down in front of split glass doors that open into the public gallery and chip out arrowheads, explaining his work to the passing visitors. The same janitor acted as the head ceremonialist for the site, blessing each new season of work and the crew recruited for the task. The head of the interpretive staff, Lorraine Good Striker, books off a couple weeks each summer to head out to the hills and conduct her vision quest – four days of fasting in a remote, windswept spot to seek help and guidance from the spirit world.

For me, it is a place from which I will never walk away. Stepping back from the edge, I was unprepared for the force that such a facility exerts not just in my own life but in the lives of Native and non-Native people inhabiting small, rural communities. As an academic, I began the project with the excitement of having a permanent structure devoted to the subject of Native culture and archaeology, of the chance to build exhibits and tell stories about the past. If you are lucky, such a project comes along once in a career. Yet for some in my field these are passing projects; they move on to other research, their lives turn in different directions.

But the local community doesn't move on and doesn't go away. People involved in planning and developing historic places are not trained to see years down the road and imagine the social, economic, and cultural impact such a place can have on the lives of those who live every day, year after year, with the fruits of our handiwork.

There is a small roadside motel in Fort Macleod that I always use as a base when visiting the site. It is now run by Connie and Don Hunter, the daughter and son-in-law of the couple who operated it when I made my first visit more than twenty-five years ago. They know my favourite room and where to hide the key for my late arrivals. Twenty years ago Native culture was something located down the highway on the reserve. Now the cramped lobby of the Sunset Motel is packed with Native crafts for sale and brochures and maps of Head-Smashed-In. Cow and buffalo skulls hang on the walls, and staff are well versed in the promotional spiel they have delivered to thousands of visitors. You don't build a facility of this importance to the local people and simply walk away. You are not allowed to. You become woven into its fabric forever.

The story of the great buffalo jumps and kills is only partially told. It is incompletely known from the voices of knowledgeable elders, from biased but priceless accounts of the final witnesses to these events, and from archaeological evidence that has been ravaged by the relentless forces of time. We can only imagine the fury of the chase, the taste of dust in the mouths of hunters as they trailed the pounding hoofs of a stampeding herd. We imagine the easy camaraderie and placid banter of men and women as they peeled away the blood-soaked hides of the slain animals. We imagine the chants of praise and thanks to the spirits, the songs that once echoed off the sheer cliffs, and the voices that will never be heard. Imagine how much is still untold.

Just a Simple Stone

Last Summer

A young hand holds the pointed metal trowel. It is a woman's hand, the skin is tight and free of spots and wrinkles. A fine layer of dust settles over the hand as it sweeps the trowel back and forth across the earth floor. The hand is experienced, knowing when to slow the sweeping motion and to pick carefully at the sudden appearance of a strange object. Punctuating the monotony of her task, a glassy clink rings out against the metal edge of the tool; Lisa quickly picks up a small paintbrush and begins to clear the area where the sound came from. Grains of dirt are brushed aside, and the outline of a tiny triangular stone is revealed. An old dental pick is used to probe the edges of the stone and then to lever it out of its ancient resting place. Dusty fingers lift the stone from the ground and, at the same time, jab the dental pick into the earth to mark its location. Rubbed between the thumb and forefinger, the dirt falls away from the stone and the outline of an exquisitely crafted arrowhead is revealed.

A cry of discovery from Lisa brings the other crew members to the side of the square hole where she kneels. Ancient tools are only rarely discovered, and each one is significant. Lisa extends her hand toward the crew with the tiny arrowhead nestled in the cup of her palm. A cascade of dirty fingers probe it, flip it over, trace its outline. The crew exclaims its praise and admiration, for this is the first point found today. Except for Bob. He's the competitive one, acting up bitterly when someone else makes an important discovery. Bob notes the flaws – a slight chip off the tip, a minor asymmetry to the edges of the blade. With a disgruntled face, Bob announces that he'd be embarrassed to admit to having found such an ugly point and that Lisa had better get back to work and find the rest of it, the part she probably broke off while digging. The crew laughs as they return to their own pits. The mood is upbeat now; the day is looking better, and Bob has performed to expectations.

Lisa flips a metal pail upside down and uses it as a seat at the side of her pit. She pulls a clipboard onto her lap and makes the necessary notes about her discovery. A small, brown paper bag is retrieved from her backpack, and she scribbles on it the information about the location of the point. The work is routine, and on most days Lisa would drop the point in the bag and return to digging. But it is still morning; she is feeling fresh and alert, unlike later in the day when the oppressive heat infuses a great lethargy. The wind is from the west and there is still a sublime coolness to it, a refreshing change from the hot blasts that cascade down the Porcupine Hills onto the parched prairie. The pleasure of the morning discourages routine. Lisa closes her palm around the arrowhead, announces she's on a break, and walks off toward the cliff.

Saskatoon bushes grow thick where water seeps out from under the bedrock escarpment. Other than that, there is not a shred of tall vegetation to be seen, nor any relief from the relentless sun. Lisa ducks under the shady side of a Saskatoon bush and sits facing out the expanse of prairie. She uncurls her fingers and looks intently at the tiny arrow point. So thin, so delicately made. It's hard to imagine that human hands using only crude tools could fashion such an exquisite piece. Yet she knows they did, thousands of times over. Lisa picks the point up with her fingers, turning it, examining it, first admiring its beautiful craftsmanship and then imagining the intangible realm that spurs people to be curious about the past. She wonders about the person who made this arrowhead. She stares intently at the artifact in her hand, as if sheer concentration might open a portal to the past.

A human being made this about a thousand years ago. Was it a young man exercising his skill as a hunter and proving himself as a provider? Was it a revered elder who had mastered the trade and supplied finished points to his people? What happened on the day this point was used? Had it brought success to the owner and claimed the life of a mighty buffalo, or had it missed its mark and sailed into the earth never to be reclaimed?

Lisa knew she would never have the answers to these questions. But she did know this: she was the first human to hold this arrowhead since a thousand years ago when the maker lashed it to a thin, wooden shaft and fired it at the thrashing body of a wild buffalo. That was all she needed. A connection. A bond between her and the ancient arrowhead maker and the mysterious and exotic world in which he lived. This is what gave her purpose, provided meaning to her work. This is why she knew she would go on investigating the past. The ancient craftsman could no longer speak, but he had provided the future with a tiny piece of his life. And now that tool would speak for him. It was both humbling and empowering.

Lisa closed her fingers around the point and headed back toward the excavation pit. This land, the plains around her, truly had no limits. The sky, stretching from the horizons, enveloped her in a radiant glow of blue light. Ground squirrels, protected from predators by the archaeologists' presence, scurried across the shortgrass prairie, diving into their maze of holes. She smiled as she watched them. They had grown almost tame now that the crew shared the crumbs of their lunches with them. Lisa disliked the way the squirrels disturbed the artifacts under the earth, rooting around and moving them out of their proper position, but she also envied them. They lived in the underworld, nestled in among the fragile vestiges of an ancient way of life. Sometimes she wished she could make herself impossibly small and join them, living in the dank, musky sediments where the mysterious people once lived.

Knowing she was sensitive, Blackfoot members of the dig crew loved to tease Lisa. Using small snares of string, they would catch ground squirrels as they emerged from their holes and then laugh uproariously as Lisa lunged to release them. They gave her an honorary Blackfoot name: Naapissko, Gopher Woman.

A Thousand Years Ago

The hand looks impossibly old, more like leather than skin, sun-baked brown in colour, gullied with deep lines, like the trails of ancient rivers. The fingernails are streaked with cracks that show as faint yellow lines, but the fingertips glisten with a bright red substance. As does the small odd-shaped stone that they hold.

Smoke from the burning bundle of grass forms a tiny ribbon, rising in a thin twisting wisp. An overpowering sweet smell fills and lingers inside the buffalo-skin dwelling. A long braid of sweetgrass rests on the edge of a ring of rocks. The leather brown hands twist and break more dried grass from the braid and sprinkle the shreds onto the red-black coals. For a moment the coals seem ineffective, extinguished, but a steady breath blows across the embers and a bright, orange glow sparks through the shredded grass. The dried sweetgrass crackles and a fresh wave of pungent smoke rises straight up toward the opening at the top of the conical tent. The red-tinged fingers grip the small stone and move it into the plume, holding it for a few seconds enveloped in the smoke, then pulling it back. Again. And again. Four times into the smoke.

The voice is cracked and aged, but still husky. It is the voice of Ipii Miistip Kipitaapii, Far Away Old Woman, named for having been plucked as a young bride from a tribe living west across the mountains. But she has lived most of her life in this country now, and she is one of the Niitsitapi, the Real People. As she chants, the fingers of Far Away Old Woman hold the sacred Iniskim, the buffalo stone. The Spirit Beings leave these for the Real People to find, scattered thinly across the land. She knows she is lucky to find one. Shaped like the mighty buffalo, the stone is a sign of power and good fortune. And it must be treated with great respect, rubbed all over with the brilliant red mineral pigment. Only then, and in the hands of a person who has earned the right to lead the ceremony, can the Iniskim be brought forward into the smoke, for the lives of the Real People depend on it.

The chant is rhythmic and hypnotic, as if conjured not from within Far Away Old Woman but from within an entire people. It is a chant of continuation, like the people themselves:

Spirit powers, we honour you with this smoke. And we call for your help. Let this smoke fog the eyes of the buffalo, so that they are blinded to the trap that lies ahead. Let this smoke cloud the minds of the buffalo, so they do not know we are coming for them. Let this smoke bring success, so that the Real People are fat with food. Let this smoke keep the Real People safe from harm, so that we may honour you again another day. Spirit powers let the spirit of the buffalo give itself to us.

The hands of Far Away Old Woman shake with age, but she reaches with purpose toward the curling smudge of sweetgrass. She cups her hands around a wisp of smoke and brings it to her head, which she bows as she passes a hand to each side, infusing her hair with the cleansing aroma. She prays for her ancestors. She reaches again and this time brings the gathered smoke to the left side of her body, washing it over her shoulder then down her arm and leg until she finally plants a palm on the beaten grass of the tipi floor. She prays for her parents and her brothers and sisters. A third time she cups the smoke and cleanses the right side of her body, asking the spirit powers to protect the elders and medicine people who surround her in the tipi. A final time she reaches into the smoke, bringing the last handful to her heart. She clasps her hands and for the first time looks around at those seated to each side of her. Hun Yaah, she says. It is good.

The half dozen or so men and women sitting along the back edge of the tipi now reach toward the thin wisp of smoke. The smudge of sweetgrass is nearly extinguished. Their reach is symbolic, the smoke much too far away to grasp, but they pull their hands back and clasp their chests, reciting in a low voice their own special prayers. A few voices linger, people who have more to ask of the spirit world. Everyone sits quietly until the last voice fades, and then Hun Yaahs are heard all around and people begin to shift their positions. All in the tipi this day are old, the ones who know the proper words and actions; today is not a day for teaching the young. That will happen on leisurely days in camp, when less depends on it.

Getting up is an effort. Everyone is stiff. They groan and complain as they slowly rise from the soft matted hair of the buffalo hides that have been spread across the ground. But there is laughter and chuckling as they tease each other about being so old. The mood is good; they know the ceremony went well. Everyone can feel it.

Far Away Old Woman leads the procession out of the tipi, circling clockwise like the sun around the fireplace, then throwing open the leather flap covering the east-facing door. A brilliant flash of sunlight streams in and casts a radiant glow into the opaque dwelling, like a candle inside a gossamer shell. The old woman steps into the blinding light and, still carrying the Iniskim, she again circles with the sun in front of the Real People who have waited outside in the camp. There are no speeches, no announcements. The ceremony needed to be done, and now it is finished. The woman opens a small leather bag – it too is deeply stained with red pigment – and places the Iniskim inside. Then she walks off toward the cliff.

The sheer sandstone wall shimmers with a golden hue in the drenching light of the sun. The sky above a cobalt blue, so deep it seems three dimensional, as if you could fall into it. Far Away Old

Woman stops to watch a red-tailed hawk gliding far above in the winds that sweep over the cliff. It soars in slow motion, almost hovering, then folds its wings and plummets toward the earth. Like a stone dropped from the cliff, it dead-falls as if it will crash headfirst into the solid dirt of the plain until, impossibly, at the last moment the legs are thrust out and the talons open like the jaws of a vise. A ground squirrel stands upright, perched on the small earthen mound above the subterranean opening to home and safety. It scans the prairie for signs of threatening movement, oblivious to the predator rocketing out of the sky. Just before the hawk slams into the earth, the wings spread to slow the descent and the talons reach for the squirrel. The rodent is smashed into the ground; locked firmly in the claws of the hawk, it is immediately lifted into the air, squirming, squeaking a high-pitched squeal. The red-tail stretches its wings to their full extent, labouring with the weight of her burden in the still air below the cliff.

Squinting into the bright light of the sky, Far Away Old Woman watches the hawk slowly climb with its trophy. The predator has its prey and will eat well tonight. She smiles, nods her head with resolution, and resumes her slow climb toward the cliff. Today the Piskun will earn its name, Deep Kettle of Blood. It will be a good day.

Three Months Later

Lisa kneels on the baked prairie, gathering up the small excavation tools: dental picks, grapefruit knives, paint brushes, tape measures. She drops them into a dented metal tool box, slings a small backpack over one shoulder, and rises, for the last time, from the outline of her excavation pit. Around her lies a lattice of empty dirt squares, a patchwork of brown set against the waving prairie grass. It's time to give up life on the high plains and head back to life in the big city.

The rough fescue grass has turned brown and brittle in the drought of late summer. It crunches and breaks under her boots as she walks across the Head-Smashed-In prairie. The air is a little cooler, laced with a freshness that hints at a change of season. Gophers are scarce now, only a few make their final forays across the plains to pack the last bits of food into their underground dens. Soon snow will blanket the ground, sealing in gophers and most other prairie life for another winter of retreat. The archaeologists mimic the natural world. Naapissko, Gopher Woman, is heading home.

Lisa is tired and sore. Ending the dig is always the hardest part. Long days and nights stack up on each other as the end of the season draws near. There is so much to do at the end – pits that are not quite finished, walls of dirt that must be sketched and photographed, artifact bags to be labelled and packed, notes to be finished before memories fade. And then the dreaded backfilling: Putting all the dirt back into the square holes, minus all the artifacts, bones, and rocks that were removed, and minus vast clouds of dust that blew from the shaker screens as each bucket was sifted. There is never enough dirt to fill the pits. Lisa pitches in with the crew as they scrounge the area for rocks, or dirt to place in the excavations, hauling seemingly endless wheelbarrow loads. Unlike the careful digging of the site, there are no rewards to this work; it is simply back-breaking labour.

Empty pop cans are tossed into the soft earth as the pits are filled. The littering is rationalized. The cans will serve as markers for future archaeologists, a way of saying that the area has already been dug. The wind and dust have sucked the moisture from Lisa's skin. She relishes the refreshing taste of the pop. She tosses the empty can on one of the backfilled pits and crunches it under the surface with her boot. A poor person's time capsule, she muses, as she heads off toward the waiting Suburban.

Leaving a site where you have spent months of your life, digging up the remains of those who lived there before you, is harder for some than for others. For some, the work is simply a step on a career path, an unemotional job that yields material for a thesis or dissertation. For Lisa it was an experience for which she now realizes she was unprepared, the experience of being immersed, simultaneously, in both the past and the present. The past is expected, lying at your feet every moment of every day. It's the present that catches her off guard.

She had not anticipated the extent to which she and the project would figure into the lives of seemingly unconnected people – the rural community that eyes you first as a curiosity and, eventually, as a part of them. Staff at the town pool where you swim and shower regarding your inconvenient evening arrival with mild annoyance but, over time, coming to sit by the edge of the water to talk about what you have been finding. Shopkeepers, distrustful, at first, of running accounts for strangers but then learning your names and wondering what they can order in for your project. Local teachers, reading the stories of the dig in the community paper, asking to bring their classes to the site or to have you come to school with artifacts and engaging stories of times gone by. Ranchers, people with whom you thought you might have little in common, inviting you for huge steak dinners, during which you discover they respect the land in the same way as the people who came before them.

Lisa knows that she is transient on the landscape; as she prepares to leave, the community stays behind. They hunker down through another winter and relive the residue of your impact on their lives, wondering if you are coming back, calling long distance to enquire if their children might be part of next year's crew. It is a burden that Lisa takes seriously, even relishes. She has learned that the work is important to the people of this small town, and, by extension, she is important. She thought she came to study only the past but found herself immersed in the present.

The dust swirls furiously through the air. Two red-tailed hawks hover overhead, their wings motionless in the fierce wind. The crew is milling around the Suburban and the equipment trailer, alternately packing and seeking refuge in the lee of the vehicle. Aluminum lawn chairs, bent and barely usable, are tossed in. Huge plastic coolers, their lids filthy from having served for months as lunch tables, are packed full with digging gear and kitchen stuff. Lisa joins in packing the daily artifact bags into cardboard boxes. This is where the goodies are kept: stone tools, precious charcoal for radiocarbon dates, bones of the slaughtered buffalo. As they sort through bags from the numbered squares, Lisa suddenly remembers the small bag in her backpack.

She rummages though her pack and pulls out the crumpled, worn brown bag. Inside is the exquisite arrow point that Lisa found early in the summer. She has kept it with her all this time as one of the prime show-and-tell pieces, items the crew keep handy to show visitors what they are finding. Lisa slides it out of the bag one last time, nestling it in her palm. The point glistens now, rubbed by many fingers. She flips it over, admiring its near-perfect symmetry. She remembers her joy at first finding the piece, wondering about the person who made it so many years ago. But in the ensuing months, Lisa has come to appreciate a new importance to the arrowhead, not what it tells her about people from the past but what it means to the future.

The finely crafted arrow point has come out of its bag time and again to show the curious visitors. Lisa remembers especially the children. Busloads have come from the nearby Piikani reserve. At first it was a game to the kids, running around chasing gophers and playing in the dirt at the screens. But when Lisa pulls the artifacts from her pack, she suddenly has their attention. The kids gather and press close to her, staring wide-eyed at the point held between her fingertips. She talks to them about an ancient hunter who made this piece a thousand years ago and shot it at a massive buffalo. She asks them if they could pick a simple rock from the ground and chip out something so perfect and beautiful. Then she calls one of the youngest boys forward and asks him to hold out his hand. Lisa tells the group of the great skill the maker must have had to craft a piece so fine that it is still sharp today. And with that she reaches out and gently pokes the tip of the point into the outstretched palm of the child. Thinking back to these moments, Lisa smiles to herself, loving the memory of what became such a predictable routine.

Pandemonium breaks loose. The child shrieks, clasps his palm closed, and jerks his hand back. But the child is smiling. For just a moment all the other children are stunned, and then, in a flash, a dozen other hands are thrust toward Lisa, like tentacles of a giant octopus, each child begging to be poked. Methodically, she works the crowd, poking each kid in turn, with each response the same as the first young boy's. Eventually, the game over, Lisa hides the arrow point and settles the children down. Then she kneels on the ground to be at their eye level. Again she holds up the point between her fingers.

We don't know the name of the person who made this, she says, but it was someone from long ago. Maybe he was one of your own ancestors. We do know he was a person of great skill and courage, someone who faced wounded and enraged buffalo with this tiny arrowhead. That person, and those who lived with him, only left us a few precious objects to tell the stories of their lives. So, Lisa asks, do you think we need to protect these things from the past so that those stories can be remembered? Heads nod all around her. Should we not, she says, show respect for things like this, because by doing so we honour and respect the people who made them? Lisa looks out at a sea of young eyes gazing back at her.

Three Days Later

Several men of the Niitsitapi are taking down the few remaining tipis. They remove the slender bone pins that hold the huge sheets of hide together and let them slide to the ground. While women disassemble the separate pieces of buffalo hide that make up the tipi covers, men begin slinging the long, straight poles into stacks on the ground. Tipi poles are precious to the people of the treeless prairies, and they will be dragged to the nearby winter camp. The Real People are moving on.

Dogs run freely now, finally set loose after days of being tethered. They were tied and muzzled during the buffalo drive to prevent their spooking the herd and then were restrained during the days of butchering to keep them from being a nuisance around the carcasses. Now they tear across the prairie, gripped in a feeding frenzy on entrails, fresh bones, and scattered bits of meat. The dogs run off the flocks of crows and magpies that have settled on the debris on the outskirts of the camp and snarl at the skulking coyotes that try to duck in and steal off with a juicy bone. Far Away Old Woman watches the dogs with amusement, thinking they too need to have their moments of pleasure. Soon enough they will be harnessed for the strenuous work of moving camp.

The camp resembles a military operation, with groups of weary hunters engaged in their pre-departure tasks: binding sets of poles to form travois, stacking up parfleches of dried meat, collecting bones that will later be boiled for their grease, cutting handholds in hides so they can be loaded with goods and dragged across the prairie, retrieving countless tools scattered across the ground. The crisp air of autumn helps keep them cool as they strain against the burden of a hundred buffalo carcasses. The cobalt blue sky envelops them. Despite their exhaustion, the mood of the Niitsitapi is high. The kill and the butchering have gone as well as anyone could have hoped. The Real People will be fed, clothed, and housed for many months to come. The spirit of the Creator has smiled on them.

Far Away Old Woman sits at the back wall of her tipi, reclining against the woven cane backrest. In front of her is the fireplace and next to it a small altar made from clumps of sod turned over and painted half red and half black. Her tipi will be the last one taken down, a sign of respect for her as the Holy Woman of the people. She tosses the last scraps of wood on the fire, thinking they will only go to waste once the tipi comes down. She might as well enjoy a final burst of heat before giving up her shelter and heading off on the march to the winter camp.

Far Away Old Woman puts the palms of her hands down to the floor and runs them over the soft hair of the bison robe on which she sits. Even years after this buffalo gave its life to the Niitsitapi, the hairs still glisten with a bright sheen, as if sprinkled with droplets of oil. The Old Woman knows this means it was a fat buffalo that gave up its life. The hairs of the hide are cool as she works her fingers through them, until she lets her palms rest for a moment in one place. Then she feels the warming properties of the hide begin to work. Her aged hands are often cold now, unlike when she was young, and she knows the time will not be long before she passes on to the Great Sand Hills. She lets her hands linger on the hide, the warmth rising through her flesh, and just for a moment her skin is soft again.

Such a small thing, she thinks, this great warmth that the bison has given to her people. Just a tiny part of all that the buffalo provides, yet one that helps keep the Niitsitapi alive through the harshest winter. As she has so many times before, Far Away Old Woman shakes her head in wonder at the wisdom of the Creator. Who but such a power-ful and benevolent spirit could have imagined a creature that gives so much to one people? She rubs her hands again through the dense fur and knows that the Niitsitapi are truly blessed.

The midday wind is starting to come up. She hears it growl under the stones that hold down the bottom edges of the tipi cover. The walls of the tent shudder, the fire leaps and retracts in time with the vibrations. She knows she must get moving. Soon the wind will make it difficult to take down the tipi. Her cloudy eyes survey the piles of belongings inside: the packs of dried meat, the rolled backrests and buffalo robes, a bundle of her clothes and moccasins, a wooden tripod that holds the war shield of her late husband, Weasel Tail. The taut hide of the shield is finely decorated with the emblem of his great power, the pelts of one of nature's greatest hunters, the weasel. The Old Woman stirs, lingering on the memory, then lets it slide away. It is time to move on.

The wrinkled hand of Far Away Old Woman reaches for the Inis-kim that lies on a soft bed of blue-green sage beside the fire. She holds it in her palm for a few moments, thinking about the enormous power of such a little piece of stone. Then she pulls open the drawstrings of a small hide bag and places the Iniskim inside. The pouch is coated red inside and out, for the Iniskim must always be steeped in the sacred paint. She bends down and places the pouch alongside the other contents of her powerful medicine bundle and carefully ties the bundle closed with thongs of rawhide. All the sacred items are now secure, ready for the next time help from the spirit world is needed.

Far Away Old Woman scoops the medicine bundle into her arms and circles clockwise, with the sun, around the inside of the tipi. She throws aside the hide flap of the door and emerges into the brilliant sunlight. Battered by a fierce wind, she cradles the bundle tightly against her chest. Through the bundle's hide covering she can feel the hard buffalo stone pressed against her thin flesh. She feels its presence and wonders, as she has so many times before, about the small buffalo-shaped rock's connection with the spirit world and how it lures great herds to the deadly cliff. Far Away Old Woman knows she will never understand the power of the Iniskim. But she knows that the sacred stone has, since the beginning of time, made it possible for the Niitsitapi to survive on this endless expanse of prairie. And that it always will. As long as the buffalo roam.

Sources to Notes

FOREWORD

xiii "is needless to say," Hind 1971, Vol.1:357.

CHAPTER 1: THE BUFFALO JUMP

1 "vast and worthless area," Daniel Webster cited in Morgan 1959:14.

1 "These great Plains appear," Glover 1962:181.

2 "A dreadful scene of confusion," Hind 1971, Vol.1:359.

Communal Buffalo Hunting

8 "Now ye manner of their hunting," Henry Kelsey cited in Ewers 1955:303.

9 "the nucleus for," Mandelbaum 1979:77.

10 "We have little apprehension," James 1905, Vol.3:174.

10 "The traveller who shall," James 1905, Vol.3:174.

10 "The prairie is not congenial," Morgan 1959:42.

10 "In fact, those Indians," Harmon 1911:81.

11 "as we are now in the land," Glover 1962:310.

11 "Here we halted and dined," Lewis 1966, Vol.2:338.

12 "even now speak with enthusiasm," Grinnell 1962:230.

Not Just Any Cliff

12 "In some part of its course," James 1905, Vol.2:281–82.

13 "So much do these people," Coues 1897, Vol.2:725.

For what makes some sites best suited for a buffalo kill, see Frison 1970 (The Glenrock Buffalo Jump), 1970 (The Kobold Site), 1973, 1987, 1991, 2004.

The Site

14 "Twice I have seen buffalo," Weasel Tail as told to Ewers 1968:166.

For popular articles describing Head-Smashed-In, see Brink 1986; Darragh 1987; Fagan 1994; Pringle 1988, 1996; Reeves 1983; Reid 2002; Sponholz 1992; Thomas 2000.

The Cliff

16 "On the north we passed," Lewis 1966, Vol.1:234–35.

18 "not killed or entirely disabled," Coues 1897, Vol.2:725.

How Long Have Buffalo Jumped?

18 "The usual manner of hunting," Lieutenant Bradley cited in Ewers 1968:162–63.

For the debate about Bonfire Shelter, see Dibble and Lorrain 1968; Bement 2007; Byerly, Cooper, Meltzer, Hill, and LaBelle 2005, 2007.

Blood on the Rocks: The Story of Head-Smashed-In

For more on the name Head-Smashed-In, see Dawson 1885.

For more references on communal buffalo hunting, the archaeology of other buffalo jumps and Head-Smashed-In, visit www.aupress.ca

CHAPTER 2: THE BUFFALO

27 "The American bison, or...buffalo," Catlin 1851, Vol.1:247.

27 On Ewers listing the great number of uses of the buffalo, see Ewers 1958:14–15.

29 "The activity of Buffaloes," Audubon 1960, Vol.2:142–43.

29 "most surprising speed," Audubon 1960, Vol.2:62.

32 "lumbering awkwardness of his action," Southesk 1969:85.

32 On the speed of bison, see Lott 2002:41; McHugh 1958:9.

32 "When wounded and mad," Audubon 1960, Vol.2:144.

Is it Bison or Buffalo?

33 On the various Omaha words for bison hunts, see Fletcher and La Flesche 1972:270–71.

For the types and naming of bison and buffalo, see Lott 2002; McHugh 1972; Reynolds, Gates, and Glaholt 2003.

In Numbers, Numberless

33 "Mr. Kipp told me," Audubon 1960, Vol.2:146.

35 "that from an eminence," Lewis 1966, Vol.2:420.

35 "The Buffalo are very numerous," Fidler 1991:76.

35 "At daybreak I was," Coues 1897, Vol.1:167.

35 "I will not attempt to," Pike 1966:161.

35 "it is *impossible to describe*," Audubon 1960, Vol.2:146.

36 "The immense quantity we saw," Dempsey 1977:189.

36 "I am conscious that with many," Brackenridge 1904:150.

36 "by the vapour which," Bradbury 1904:124.

36 "deep rolling voice," Southesk 1969:92.

36 On Audubon saying that chips were so abundant that a person could not step a few feet without coming across one, see Audubon 1960, Vol.2:105. "was soon covered with," James 1905, Vol.2:315.

36 "was soon covered with," James 1905, Vol.2:315.

36 "cow-yard," James 1905, Vol.2:315.

36 "the space they stand on," Glover 1962:267.

36 "They were in numbers," Dempsey 1977:189.

Tricks of the Trade

37 "Every spring as the river," Lewis 1966, Vol.1:175.

37 On Maximilian reporting eighteen-hundred dead bison damming the Missouri River, see Maximilian 1906, Vol.1:382.

37 "The slipperiness of the ice," Spry 1968:191.

38 "they followed them," Grinnell 1923, Vol.1:268.

For Maximilian reporting eighteen-hundred dead bison damming the Missouri River, see Maximilian 1906, Vol.1:382.

The Fats of Life

39 "us who had so long," Farnham 1906, Vol.1:203.

40 "we could not get any," Spry 1968:316.

40 "Our appetite was tremendous," Spry 1968:385.

40 "too poor to be worth," Lewis 1966, Vol.1:161.

40 "so extremely lean" James 1905, Vol.3:103.

40 "In the chase, the experienced," Gregg 1966, Vol.2:215.

40 "of course every one," McDougall 1898:224.

40 On Audubon observing that wolves also selected the fattest animals for attack, see Audubon 1960, Vol.2:124.

41 "I think that in cold countries," Dempsey 1956:12.

41 "but that the stomach," James 1905, Vol.2:297.

42 "At this time of the year," Wilson 1924:305.

For more references on evolution and classification of bison, numbers of bison, varieties of buffalo hunting by Plains Indians, and the role and importance of fat in game animals, visit www.aupress.ca.

CHAPTER 3: A YEAR IN THE LIFE

43 "ears were assailed by," Brackenridge 1904:149.

Calves

44 "The Calves in the Womb," Fidler 1991:73.

45 "the young calves, cut," Hearne 1971:253–54.

45 "are equal in flavour," Lewis 1966, Vol.1:192.

Mothers

45 "The principal beast," Maximilian 1906, Vol.2:345.

Fathers

49 "meat is not regarded," Glover 1962:310.

49 "openings are left," Coues 1897, Vol.2:518.

51 "Our folks have shot," Harris 1951:22.

Science and the Historic Record

54 "for having aimed at," Catlin 1851, Vol.1:27.

55 On Farnham riding around a village of Kansa Indians asking them if they were humans or beasts, see Farnham 1906, Vol.1:89–90.

55 "The lovers of Indian manners," Brackenridge 1904:114.

55 "The world would loose," Brackenridge 1904:128.

55 "savage, untutored, and heathen," Hind 1971, Vol.1:359.

56 "brave, steady," Glover 1962:258.

56 "is more detested," Glover 1962:259.

56 On Brackenridge complaining that Indians were foul smelling, see Brackenridge 1904: 114.

56 "Indians find the odour," James 1905, Vol.2:257.

56 "We are aware that," James 1905, Vol.2:256.

56 "people are all politicians," Ross 1972:252.

56 Many years have been passed," De Smet 1906:194.

57 "emerald furnaces," Southesk 1969:121.

57 "His appearance was now," Harris 1951:30.

57 "remarkably expert," Gregg 1966, Vol.2:283.

57 "with an accuracy," Gregg 1966, Vol.2:283.

57 "a bull, which I left" Palliser 1969:119.

57 "three buffalo," Coues 1897, Vol.1:170.

57 "too poor to be," Lewis 1966, Vol.1:161.

57 "had killed two poor Bulls," Glover 1962:186.

57 "a fine fat cow," Gregg 1966, Vol.2:148–49.

58 "so weak that if," Coues 1897, Vol.2:594.

58 "if possible, to pick out," Palliser 1969:226.

58 "a tolerably fat young bull," Coues 1897, Vol.1:178.

58 "got alongside of the cows," Palliser 1969:227–28.

58 "June the bulls," Morgan 1959:104.

58 "well-larded body," Farnham 1906, Vol.1:88.

58 "At this time of the year," Larpenteur 1898, Vol.1:21.

58 "We killed a bull," Coues 1897, Vol.1:310.

58 "bulls are beginning to get," Coues 1897, Vol.2:609.

58 "In the month of July," Glover 1962:305.

58 "Saw … six bulls," Audubon 1960, Vol.2:157.

58 "Saw Buffaloes," Audubon 1960, Vol.2:159.

58 "bison…was killed," James 1905, Vol.3:130–31.

58 "The Cows were fat," Glover 1962:54.

59 "I killed a Bull Buffalo," Henday 1973:26.

59 "I found them only," Coues 1897, Vol.2:490.

59 "Each of us soon killed," Coues 1897, Vol.2:492.

59 "I returned at sunset," Coues 1897, Vol.1:100.

59 "old out-straggling," Palliser 1969:107–08.

59 "Saw a few Bull Buffalo," Fidler 1991:14.

59 "Men running buffalo," Fidler 1991:27.

59 "My people killed," Coues 1897, Vol.1:161.

59 "flesh is not desirable," Kane 1996:267–68.

59 "four Bulls, no Cows," Glover 1962:167.

The Seasonal Round

63 "the buffalo in winter," Spry 1968:266.

The Season of Buffalo Jumping

65 "The Savages observe," Hennepin 1903, Vol.2:516.

67 "These [bulls] are generally," Gregg 1966, Vol.2:212.

67 "The cold was so severe," Dempsey 1977:49.

68 On seasonal changes in fat composition of Arctic reindeer, see
    Reimers, Ringberg, and Sørumgård 1982.

69 "are therefore killed," Harmon 1911:285.

69 "The Indians generally kill," Catlin 1851, Vol.1:254.

69 "I am informed by," Bradbury 1904:186.

69 "the Indians had certain spots," S.A. Barrett cited in Ewers
    1968:163–64.

    For more references on bison ecology, natural history, biology,
    calving patterns, female reproduction, fat cycles in pregnancy
    and lactation, the rut and fat cycles in male bison, bioenergetic

principles in large herbivores, and the bison seasonal round, visit www.aupress.ca.

CHAPTER 4: THE KILLING FIELDS

71 "The Great Father of Life," Schoolcraft 1851, Vol.5:50.

Finding Bison

73 "The Indians who reside," Harmon 1911:331.
   For George Frison's knowledge of bison hunting, see Frison 1987, 2004.

Drive Lanes

75 "From this entrance," Mathew Cocking cited in Ewers 1968:161.

81 "The most exciting phrase," Singh 2004:357.

Points in Time

For more on arrowheads found among the drive lanes at buffalo jumps in Idaho see Agenbroad 1976:6–9.

Ancient Knowledge

85 "It may truly be said," Hind 1971, Vol.2:104.

86 On Hind reporting 240 bison killed in a pound over several days, see Hind 1971, Vol.1:357.

86 On Father De Smet having witnessed six hundred bison brought in, see Lowie 1909:11.

86 "Pound being quite," Fidler 1991:58.

86 "Passed near an old," Dempsey 1977:78.

87 On the use of rocks at the Ramillies archaeological site, see Brumley 1976.

88 On the methods of corralling bison herds at Elk Island National Park, personal communication from Norm Cool, wildlife biologist, EINP.

88 "In the olden time," Grinnell 1923, Vol.1:264–65.

88 "on a slope," Spry 1968:197.

88 "might be only a fence," Grinnell 1962:229.

88 "so full does [the pound] become," Audubon 1960, Vol.2:146.

88 "When it [the pound] was full," Grinnell 1962:231.

89 "with the utmost silence," Hind 1971, Vol.1:358.

89 "wary old bull," Hind 1971, Vol.1:357.

89 "All around the corral," Weasel Tail as told to Ewers 1968:166.

Back to the Drive Lanes

91 "On each side of," Coues 1897, Vol.2:518–19.

96 "a tract is surrounded," Maximilian 1906, Vol.1:390.

96 On Mathew Cocking noting that the wings of the drive lane were made of sticks, with heaps of buffalo dung or old roots, see Ewers 1968:161.

96 "To this entrance," Spry 1968:197.

96 "From each side," Harmon 1911:286.

For historic and ethnographic descriptions of drive lanes, see Ewers 1968:161; Flannery 1953:56; Grinnell 1962:229–30; Harmon 1911:285–87; Hind 1971, Vol.1:357–58; Maximilian 1906, Vol.1:390; Spry 1968:197.

Deadmen

97 "was formed in a pretty dell," Hind 1971, Vol.1:357–58.

99 "Indians are stationed," Harmon 1911:286.

99 "Finally, when the buffalo," Grinnell 1962:229.

For the specific use of the term "Dead Men," see Hind 1971, Vol.1:357–58; Kane 1996:80.

In Small Things Forgotten

For the book *In Small Things Forgotten,* see Deetz 1977.

For more references on the nature and operation of drive lanes, the analysis of projectile points from the Plains, and historic and ethnographic accounts of buffalo pounds and jumps, visit www.aupress.ca

CHAPTER 5: ROUNDING UP

103 "When buffalo were needed," Mandelbaum 1979:54.

The Spirit Sings

105 "There is nothing relating," Bradbury 1904:177.

106 On archaeologists finding skulls placed in the fork of trees, see Frison 1991:254, 256.

106 "The life of the people," Fletcher and La Flesche 1972:271.

107 "every man … brings out of his lodge," Catlin 1851, Vol.1:127.

107 "Once the people could not find," Lowie 1922:355.

107 "carried with it," Mandelbaum 1979:177.

107 "the privilege of constructing," Mandelbaum 1979:177.

108   "Some shamans called," Lowie (*Religion of the Crow*) 1922:357.

109   "grave responsibility," Fletcher and La Flesche 1972:276.

109   "possess courage and ability," Fletcher and La Flesche 1972:276.

109   "He directed the march," Fletcher and La Flesche 1972:276.

109   "considered one of the most," Fletcher and La Flesche 1972:276.

109   "for on him all the people," Fletcher and La Flesche 1972:278.

109   "a man's hand," Fletcher and La Flesche 1972:281.

109   "those who look," Fletcher and La Flesche 1972:280.

109   "Come! that you may go," Fletcher and La Flesche 1972:280.

109   "It is reported," Fletcher and La Flesche 1972:280.

110   "dodging in and out," Fletcher and La Flesche 1972:282.

110   "a sacred one," Fletcher and La Flesche 1972:283.

110   "unrolled his pipe," Grinnell 1962:229.

110   "told his wives," Grinnell 1962:229.

111   "I saw a collection," Spry 1968:198.

111   "on which they hang," Spry 1968:198.

111   On archaeologists having excavated bison kill sites that show evidence for a central wooden pole with unusual artifacts around the pole base, see Stanford 1978.

111   "who had a wonderful," Southesk 1969:104.

111   "the pipe-bearer," James 1905, Vol.1:298.

112   "Before the carcasses," Mandelbaum 1979:55.

112   "the warriors are all assembled," Audubon 1960, Vol.2:145.

113   "so that they might," Mandelbaum 1979:58.

113   On the Omaha saving fat from around the heart of the buffalo for young children, see Fletcher and La Flesche 1972:332.

113   "Many of the Minnetarees," James 1905, Vol.2:63.

113   "In one of their villages," Maximilian 1906, Vol.2:375.

113   "there were formerly to," Grinnell 1923, Vol.1:268.

113   "We had been hunting," Glover 1962:259.

For more on magpies, see Grinnell 1923, Vol.1:256; stones sacred, see Densmore 1918:204–05; turtle hearts, see Fletcher and La Flesche 1972:332; fire flies, see Spry 1968:242; swallows and bluebirds pecking, see Dempsey 1973; rattles from snakes, see McDermott 1940:208; stuffed eagle in lodge, see Fidler 1991:65; eagle feathers as sacred, see Fletcher and La Flesche 1972:276; Lewis 1966, Vol.2:386; offerings in trees, see

Glover 1962:259; Maximilian 1906, Vol.2:375; bears sacred, see Schoolcraft 1966:184–85; won't eat bears, see Maximilian 1906, Vol.2:109; Wissler 1910:20; grizzly bear necklaces, see Glover 1962:249; James 1905, Vol.3:46; Kane 1996:266; use of weasel hides, see Ewers 1968:165.

The Nose of the Buffalo

114   "During our stay here," Bradbury 1904:149–50.
114   "provided he 'has the wind,'" Gregg 1966, Vol.2:217–18.
115   "it informed them of," James 1905, Vol.3:228.
115   "The wind happening to blow," James 1905, Vol.2:255–56.
115   "the wind was still," Coues 1897, Vol.2:577.
115   "it is most favorable," Coues 1897, Vol.2:519.
116   "Saw a good deal," Spry 1968:412.
116   "Great numbers of wolves," Brackenridge 1904:135.
116   "counted fifteen wolves," Bradbury 1904:150.
117   "they saw him several," James 1905, Vol.3:76.
117   "the herd of buffaloes," Catlin 1851, Vol.1:254.
117   "As is frequently the case," Kane 1996:82.
117   "perfectly aware that," Spry 1968:258.
117   On Fidler saying Indians intentionally let wolves feed on discarded carcasses, see Fidler 1991:64.

For the importance of wind in hunting buffalo, see Bradbury 1904:149–50; Gregg 1966, Vol.2:217–18; James 1905, Vol.2:255–56, Vol.3:228.

Fire this Time

117   "The grass of these plains," Glover 1962:181.
118   "When the fire passes," Harmon 1911:90.
118   "a sight the poor burnt," Dempsey 1977:260.
118   "set fire to the plains," James 1905, Vol.2:167.
118   "the fresh grass which," Lewis 1966, Vol.1:175.
118   "Along the Great Plains," Glover 1962:185–86.
119   "The most trivial signal," Spry 1968:254–55.
119   "setting fire to the grass," Schoolcraft 1966:279.
120   "driving whole herds from," Coues 1897, Vol.2:577.
121   "strikes a light with," Kane 1996:80.
121   "the herd must be," Coues 1897, Vol.2:519.

For bison killed in prairie fires, see Dempsey 1977:260; Harmon 1911:90.

Luring the Buffalo

121 "generally drive," Coues 1897, Vol.2:519.

122 "The antelope possesses," James 1905, Vol.2:227.

122 "A man who was very," Grinnell 1962:230.

123 "consisted in crawling," Kane 1996:268.

For antelope curiosity, see James 1905, Vol.2:227.

For bison curiosity, see Dodge 1959 (*The Plains of the Great West*):136.

For twirling and running to attract bison, see Grinnell 1962:230.

Buffalo Runners

124 "men consulted the leaders," Densmore 1918:439.

125 On Catlin reporting that the Sioux hid themselves "under buffalo skins," to trick their enemies, see Catlin 1851, Vol.1:130.

125 "following about in the vicinity," Catlin 1851, Vol.1:254.

128 "The mode of hunting," Lewis 1966, Vol.1:235.

128 "A gang of buffalo is frightened," Gregg 1966, Vol.2:217.

128 "bellowing like themselves," Henry 1969:300.

129 "At day-light, several," Henry 1969:300.

For more on Buffalo Runners, see Audubon 1960, Vol.2:145; Catlin 1851, Vol.1:254; Densmore 1918:439; Gregg 1966, Vol.2:217; Lewis 1966, Vol.1:234–35; Schoolcraft 1851, Vol.4:93.

Lost Calves

129 "all is ready," Audubon 1960, Vol.2:145.

130 "imitating the lowing," Dempsey 1989:115.

130 "This ruse is generally performed," Kane 1996:267.

131 "I had hoped to witness," Dempsey 1977:49.

131 "Their chief announced," Ewers 1958:83.

131 On Woolsey saying that a man might lure bison by imitating the sound of a cow bison for up to two days, see Dempsey 1989:115.

132 "carrying before them everything," Coues 1897, Vol.2:725.

132 "lives are sometimes lost," Coues 1897, Vol.2:725.

133 "Sometimes in this perilous," Lewis 1966, Vol.1:235.

133 "suddenly securing himself," Lewis 1966, Vol.1:235.

133 "would run forward," Flannery 1953:56.

134 "When the old men," Grinnell 1923, Vol.1:267.

For the use of the buffalo calf disguise, see Audubon 1960, Vol.2:145; Kane 1996:267.

Billy's Stories

136   On a comparison of early twentieth century Blackfoot stories in English and Blackfoot, see Uhlenbeck 1911.

137   "In winter, when the snow," Grinnell 1962:231–32.

The End of the Drive

137   "the buffalo appear," Hind 1971, Vol.1:358.

138   "A man stood," Ewers 1968:167.

139   "every man, woman, and child," Coues 1897, Vol.2:519.

139   "Young men are usually," Coues 1897, Vol.2:519.

139   "they are in a manner," Coues 1897, Vol.2:520.

For people along the drive lanes and methods of controlling the bison, see Ewers 1968:166–67; Grinnell 1923, Vol.1: 267; Hind 1971, Vol.1:358; Lowie 1922 (*Religion of the Crow*):357.

Of Illusions, Pickup Trucks, and Curves in the Road

143   "a long [downhill] slope," Harris 1951:34.

143   "We built a corral," Ewers 1968:166.

143   On bison increasing their speed running downhill, see McHugh 1958:9.

145   "The chute took," Mandelbaum 1979:54.

145   On curves in buffalo drives, see Mandelbaum 1979:54.

For more references on buffalo hunt ceremonies, ceremonial use of skulls, sacred parts of the carcass, wolves and bison, grizzly bears and bison, use of fire by Aboriginal people, bison aversion to smoke, visit www.aupress.ca.

CHAPTER 6: THE GREAT KILL

147   "poor affrighted," Catlin 1851, Vol.1:200.

148   "Still their advance," Gregg 1966, Vol.2:220.

148   "Late in the evening," Brackenridge 1904:150.

148   "were in such numbers," Spry 1968:258.

Leap of Faith

149   "A dreadful scene," Hind 1971, Vol.1:359.

151   "Be a bison," Lott 2002:158.

152   "it is then in vain," Lewis 1966, Vol.1:235.

153   "A sight most horrible," Hind 1971, Vol.1:356.

153   "the bawling and screaming," Spry 1968:197.

153   "The scene was more repulsive," Spry 1968:197.

153   "crammed more than," Spry 1968:197.

153   "A great number were," Spry 1968:197.

153   "run round and round," Spry 1968:197.

153   "with the sun," Spry 1968:197.

153   "I have frequently," Harmon 1911:286.

153   "Indians, even mere boys," Spry 1968:197.

153   "all busy plying bows," Spry 1968:197.

154   "After firing their arrows," Spry 1968:197.

Overkill?

155   "Nothing of the buffalo," Flannery 1953:58.

155   "The savages wage," McDermott 1940:196–97.

157   "ashamed," Harris 1951:34.

157   "regretted," Harris 1951:149.

157   "had no means," Harris 1951:149.

157   "temptation was," Harris 1951:152.

157   "ere long our consciences," Harris 1951:34–35.

157   "What a terrible destruction," Audubon 1960, Vol.2:107.

157   "one of the whole herd," Coues 1897, Vol.1:336.

157   "prevent them [the skulls] from apprising," Bradbury 1904:141.

157   "They could easily shoot," Dempsey 1989:116.

158   "The scene was a busy," Spry 1968:197.

158   "rushing off in a contrary," Dempsey 1977:49.

158   "It happens sometimes," Audubon 1960, Vol.2:146.

159   "But this method sometimes," Coues 1897, Vol.2:725.

For two provocative and important works on this subject, see Krech 1999 and Harkin and Lewis 2007.

Drop of Death

161   "Whilst the buffaloes were," Kane 1996:81.

162   "fired both barrels of my gun," Southesk 1969:80.

162   "vomits torrents of blood," McDermott 1940:192.

163   "are to the last directed," James 1905, Vol.3:145.

163   "trampled and gored to death," Audubon 1960, Vol.2:144.

163   "will run their horns into," Fidler 1991:74.

163   "narrowly escape," Fidler 1991:74.

For more on the numbers of buffalo killed at pounds and jumps, see Catlin 1851, Vol.1:199–201; Fidler 1991:58; Harmon 1911:70, 285–87; Henry 1969:301; Hind 1971, Vol.1: 357; Maximilian 1906, Vol.1:390.

For full eyewitness descriptions of killing bison at pounds, see Harmon 1911:285–87; Hind 1971, Vol.1:359; Spry 1968:197–98.

Bones on Fire

164 "The surrounding country," Harmon 1911:90.

165 "There was no wood," Maximilian 1906, Vol.2:196.

165 "On wet days," Mandelbaum 1979:93.

166 "when the Wind," Fidler 1991:58–59.

166 "It is needless to say," Hind 1971, Vol.1:357.

166 On the Assiniboine leaving openings in the pound for dogs, see Coues 1897, Vol.2:518.

166 On Catlin reporting one thousand dogs cleaning up the carcasses at a bison pound, see Catlin 1851, Vol.1:201.

166 On the effects of mass carcass decay, see Todd 1983.

166 "on account of the stench," Hind 1971, Vol.1:355.

For the debate about burned layers of bones at bison kill sites, see Frison 1970:6; 1991:231.

For Kehoe's arguments about burning at the Gull Lake site, see Kehoe 1973:39.

For the stench of buffalo kill sites, see Fidler 1991:86; Hind 1971, Vol.1:355, 357; Lewis 1966, Vol.1:235.

Let the Butchering Begin

168 "The process of cutting up," Harris 1951:36.

169 "Here I observed the filthy manners," Coues 1897, Vol.1:397.

169 "which we are accustomed," Lewis 1966, Vol.1:376.

169 "A hearty meal," Denig 1930:531.

169 "betakes himself to what is," Dodge 1959 (*Our Wild Indians*):276.

169 "and while still warm," Wilson 1924:252.

170 On hunters having arrows marked with personal designs, see Fletcher and La Flesche 1972:272.

170 "among the people," Grinnell 1962:230.

170 "the chiefs and the leading," Grinnell 1962:230.

170 On Lowie reporting that the buffalo runners among the Assiniboine received the fattest animals, see Lowie 1909:11.

170 On Henry (the elder) saying that chiefs were given the tongues, see Henry 1969:301.

170 "gives each tent an equal share," Coues 1897, Vol.2:520.

171 "no one will complain," Harmon 1911:287.

171 "any be displeased," Harmon 1911:287.

For Henry (the elder) saying that chiefs were given the tongues, see Henry 1969:301.

Bison Hide as Insulator

171 "The skin is in some places," Hearne 1971:251.

172 On Audubon telling of a Native hunter who approached a buffalo carcass to discover a grizzly bear inside, see Audubon 1960, Vol.2:65–66.

For the insulation of a bison hide, see Lott 2002:53–56.

For the neck portion of bison hide used as shields, see Grinnell 1962:227; Hearne 1971:251.

For more on the metabolism study at Elk Island Park, see Christopherson, Hudson, and Richmond 1978.

For more and finer hair on bison than cattle, see Lott 2002:55; Peters and Slen 1964.

For the use of infrared at Elk Island Park, see Lott 2002:55.

Back to the Assembly Line

175 "These animals spoil," Dodge 1959 (*Our Wild Indians*):253.

177 "Well do I remember," Palliser 1969:174–75.

177 "But what the tail of the beaver," Gregg 1966, Vol.2:212.

177 "is most extraordinary," Hearne 1971:253–54.

177 "In the operation of butchering," James 1905, Vol.1:300.

177 "It was no small matter," Hennepin 1903, Vol.2:520–21.

177 "The Natives generally cut," Harmon 1911:287.

For the fat content of bison tongue, see Emerson 1990.

For more references on numbers of bison killed in pounds, eyewitness descriptions of pounds, the butchering sequence of bison, visit www.aupress.ca.

CHAPTER 7: COOKING UP THE SPOILS

179 "The buffalo meat which the hunter," Gregg 1966, Vol.2:26.

179 "made for the purpose," Dodge 1959 (*Our Wild Indians*):287.

The Processing Site

180 "inordinate thirst," Schoolcraft 1851, Vol.4:106.

181 "the suffering is," Schoolcraft 1851, Vol.4:106.

181 "the means taken," Schoolcraft 1851, Vol.4:106.

181 "When there is no water," Harmon 1911:279.

181 "is always water," Spry 1968:187.

182 "converge from all directions," James 1905, Vol.3:143.

For the Vore site in Wyoming, see Reher and Frison 1980.

Day Fades to Night

184 "At the time of the," Dodge 1959 (*Our Wild Indians*):253.

184 "She must work," Dodge 1959 (*Our Wild Indians*):253.

184 "The life an Indian woman," McDougall 1898:12.

184 "throng of women and children," Catlin 1851, Vol.1:201.

Dried Goods

185 "Some meat was eaten," Turney-High 1941:37.

185 "Meat intended for winter use," Teit 1930:94.

185 "cut into broad," McDougall 1898:221–22.

187 "made a fire," McDougall 1898:222.

187 "The meat, with the exception," James 1905, Vol.1:301.

188 "Fat from shoulder and rump,' Mandelbaum 1979:58–59.

188 "The meat, in its dried state," James 1905, Vol.1:302.

188 "sixty or seventy pounds weight," Schoolcraft 1851, Vol.4:107.

Grease is the Word

188 "The large bones of the hind legs," Dodge 1959 (*Our Wild Indians*):273–74.

189 "a most delicious repast," James 1905, Vol.1:302.

189 "a treat whose value," James 1905, Vol.3:134.

189 "We cut the tough outer flesh," Wilson 1924:268.

189 "trapper's butter," Farnham 1906, Vol.1:202.

189 "till the mass became," Farnham 1906, Vol.1:202–03.

High Plains Cooking

191 "They make marrow fat," Harmon 1911:282.

Buffalo Chips

198 "Since leaving Pembina River," Spry 1968:110.

198 "so abundant that one meets," Audubon 1960, Vol.2:105.

198 "is amusing to witness," Gregg 1966, Vol.2:26.

198 On Harris wondering what friends back home would say if they could see him and Audubon carrying buffalo chips, see Harris 1951:167–68.

198   "produces an ardent," Schoolcraft 1851, Vol.4:109.

198   "makes a grand fire," Turnbull 1914:167.

198   "In dry weather it is," Gregg 1966, Vol.2:26.

198   "but when moistened, Gregg 1966, Vol.2:26.

199   "we had to use dried bison dung," McDermott 1940:188.

200   "endeavoured to kindle a fire," Maximilian 1906, Vol.2:196.

200   "even makes a hotter fire," Gregg 1966, Vol.2:26.

Hot Rocks

200   "An old method of preparing," Mandelbaum 1979:59.

Time for a Roast

206   "The Indian is a great epicure," Dodge 1959 (Our Wild
       Indians):273.

207   "Spits were put up everywhere," McDermott 1940:194.

210   "Cooked for dinner," James 1905, Vol.1:279–80.

210   On roasting pits dug inside the tipi, see Mandelbaum 1979:59.

Where Are the Skulls?

211   "Round an isolated tree," Maximilian 1906, Vol.1:318.

214   On Densmore describing how a medicine man from the Teton
       Sioux painted a buffalo skull and placed it on a bed of prairie
       sage, see Densmore 1918:444.

214   "It was believed," Densmore 1918:444.

214   "on the top of which is placed," Maximilian 1906, Vol.1:383.

214   "it was an honour," Bradbury 1904:141.

214   "hang a fresh buffalo's head," Farnham 1906, Vol.1:268.

214   "The buffalo skulls," Maximilian 1906, Vol.2:333–34.

215   "are obliged to drag," Maximilian 1906, Vol.2:332.

215   "with much pain," Maximilian 1906, Vol.2:333.

215   "a semicircular row of sixteen bison skulls," James 1905,
       Vol.2:253.

215   "Our interpreter informed us," James 1905, Vol.2:253.

       For how skulls were used in ceremonies, see Bradbury
       1904:141; Densmore 1918:444; Farnham 1906, Vol.1:268–69;
       Grinnell 1923, Vol.1:268; James 1905, Vol.2:253; Lowie 1922
       (*Religion of the Crow*):355, 357; Mandelbaum 1979:54; Maximil-
       ian 1906, Vol.1:318, 383; Vol.2:333–34, 375.

Packing Up, Among the Bears

216   "We had not left the fort," Kane 1996:266.

217 "when he saw a bear," Palliser 1969:281.

217 "and leaving the carcass," James 1905, Vol.3:50.

218 "soldiers saw him," Audubon 1960, Vol.2:66.

218 "without doubt, the most daring," James 1905, Vol.3:47.

218 "frequently pursues," James 1905, Vol.3:47.

218 "nearly dragged one of the hunters," Dempsey 1989:115.

219 On Thompson recounting a grizzly bear attack on natives, see Glover 1962:248–49.

219 "the death cry," Glover 1962:248.

219 "one of his thighs," Glover 1962:248.

219 "sprung on the first," Glover 1962:249.

219 "They found him devouring," Glover 1962:248.

219 "The first poor fellow," Glover 1962:249.

219 "one of the most esteemed," Kane 1996:266.

219 "highly esteemed, and dignify," James 1905, Vol.3:46.

219 On the recovery of a set of grizzly bear foreclaws from an Alberta archaeological site, see Brink 1988.

219 "until nothing but," Glover 1962:249.

219 "devouring a dead buffaloe," Lewis 1966, Vol.2:394.

For historic encounters with the Plains grizzly bear, see Glover 1962:248–49; James 1905, Vol.3:46–47; Kane 1996:266; Lewis 1966, Vol.2:394; Palliser 1969:281–82; Spry 1968: 412, 414–15.

For more references on historic and archaeological accounts of bison butchering, foods consumed at the kill, foods preserved by drying and smoking, desire for and use of bone marrow and grease, Aboriginal cooking methods, cooking experiments at Head-Smashed-In, use and abundance of buffalo chips, stone boiling and roasting, use of brains in tanning and bison skulls rare at other sites, visit www.aupress.ca.

CHAPTER 8: GOING HOME

221 On Father Hennepin remarking on the strength of Native women, see Hennepin 1903, Vol.1:147.

For Napi stories in Blackfoot culture, see De Smet 1906:243–44; Ewers 1958; Grinnell 1962; McClintock 1968:337–48.

Buffalo Hides

224 "Whilst in the green state," James 1905, Vol.1:312.

224 "They had Shields," Glover 1962:173.

225 "In buffalo robes," Southesk 1969:307.

226 "The hide is extended," James 1905, Vol.1:312.

227 "for the convenience of manipulation," James 1905, Vol.1:312.

227 "They then take it out," Harmon 1911:288.

227 On Culbertson noting that meat and fat scraped from the buffalo hide were cooked, mixed with dried berries, and eaten, see Culbertson 1952:84.

227 "esteemed a most rare dish," Culbertson 1952:84.

227 "The hide of the buffalo-bull," Grinnell 1923, Vol.1:255–56.

227 "had been 18 days," Dempsey 1977:94.

227 On Bradbury's team having to eat their moccasin soles, see Bradbury 1904:232.

Pemmican

229 "As the Indians use no salt," Harmon 1911:282.

229 "as they incline to migrate," Gregg 1966, Vol.2:214.

229 "immense herds of bisons," James 1905, Vol.2:239.

229 "upon all the plain," James 1905, Vol.2:239.

230 "In making this pemmican," Turney-High 1941:38.

230 "when carefully melted," Glover 1962:312.

231 "A much finer grade," Grinnell 1962:207.

231 "a trough made of," Grinnell 1962:206.

232 "about thirty inches," Glover 1962:312.

233 "shovelled into one," Grinnell 1962:206.

233 "When the bag was full," Grinnell 1962:206.

233 "If kept in a dry place," Harmon 1911:23.

233 "the staple food," Glover 1962:313.

233 On Audubon saying that men on the barges subsist almost entirely on buffalo meat and pemmican, see Audubon 1960, Vol.1:499.

233 On Stefansson's experiments with eating an all meat diet, see Lieb 1926.

234 On Catlin's first kill of the largest bull, see Catlin 1851, Vol.1:27.

Snow Falling on Cottonwoods

235 "The beauty of an Indian camp," Fletcher and La Flesche

1972:279.

For more references on methods of tanning and seasonal use of bison hides, pemmican (making, taste, ingredients, longevity), tannic acids as preservatives, visit www.aupress.ca.

CHAPTER 9: THE END OF THE BUFFALO HUNT

237 "It is truly a melancholy," Catlin 1851, Vol.1:256.

237 "The air was foul with," Dodge 1959 (*Our Wild Indians*):295.

238 "saw two bull buffalo," Morgan 1959:159.

238 "on getting on board," Harris 1951:95.

238 On an example of the senseless slaughter of bison, see Harris 1951:30–31.

238 "would jump aside," Harris 1951:30.

238 "He proved to be very poor," Harris 1951:31.

The Skin of the Animal

239 "The danger from Indians," Dodge 1959 (*Our Wild Indians*):293.

240 On Dodge's estimates of bison hides and pounds of meat and bones hauled from the west by train for the years 1872–74, see Dodge 1959 (*The Plains of the Great West*):140.

240 "at least five millions," Dodge 1959 (*Our Wild Indians*):295.

240 "They are usually," James 1905, Vol.1:174.

242 "It is at this time," Morgan 1959:104.

242 On accounts of buffalo derailing trains, see Dodge 1959 (*The Plains of the Great West*):121–22.

243 On the effects of disease on Native people of the Plains, see Binnema 2001:119–28; Isenberg 2000:53–62, 113–20.

244 "In winter, there are," McDermott 1940:197.

244 "It is impossible to make," McDermott 1940:197.

244 "man in his savage," Hind 1971, Vol.1:359.

244 "I am almost ashamed," Harris 1951:34.

244 "We now regretted," Harris 1951:149.

244 "It would be highly desirable," James 1905, Vol.2:256–57.

245 "They left nothing behind," Grinnell 1923, Vol.1:266.

245 "They keep the Hoofs," Hennepin 1903, Vol.1:150.

The Last of the Buffalo Jumps

247 "The *arms* of the wild Indians," Gregg 1966, Vol.2:283.

247 On Pike putting nineteen balls into a bison, see Pike 1966:155.

247 "Big Ribs, a Northern Cheyenne," Grinnell 1923, Vol.1:263–64.

248 "White Cloud says," Morgan 1959:99.

248 "An arrow kills more efficiently," McDermott 1940:192.

248 "If the arrow has not," McDermott 1940:192.

248 "the Indian is apt to kill," Gregg 1966, Vol.2:216.

249 "They heard the Report," Hennepin 1903, Vol.2:520.

249 "Sometimes the young men," Harmon 1911:285.

Rivers of Bones

251 "far as the eye," Maximilian 1906, Vol.2:50.

251 "The land was covered," McDermott 1940:188.

251 "Buffalo Bones, & dung laying," Turnbull 1914:167.

251 "bones and skulls, scattered," Maximilian 1906, Vol.2:246.

252 "constantly finding the skulls," Southesk 1969:58.

252 "The plains are all strewn," Southesk 1969:254–55.

252 "and before many years," Audubon 1960, Vol.2:131.

252 "I fear we shall soon be deprived," Schoolcraft 1851, Vol.5:50.

253 "real food," Flannery 1953:58.

253 "To those who had been," Flannery 1953:58.

253 "There is no earthly consideration," Ross 1972:260–61.

253 "The buffalo melted away," Dodge 1959 (*Our Wild Indians*):294.

Final Abandonment of Head-Smashed-In

254 On Fidler's early written records of native life in the Canadian west, see Fidler 1991.

254 On Fidler's accounts of driving bison to a cliff, see Fidler 1991:36.

254 On Lewis and Clark seeing the carcasses from previous jumps, see Lewis 1966, Vol.1:234–35.

254 On James describing how jumps worked based on Native informants, see James 1905, Vol.2:281–82.

255 "Where we encamped yesterday," Fidler 1991:36.

255 "the men brought another," Fidler 1991:36.

255 "Horses are sometimes used," Coues 1897, Vol.2:520.

255 "After this preparation," Harmon 1911:286.

For an Aboriginal narrative of what must have been one of the last buffalo jumps, somewhere near Head-Smashed-In, see Ewers 1949; 1968:166–67.

For more references on the near extermination of bison, changes in Plains culture due to horses, accounts of the prairies littered with bones, visit www.aupress.ca.

CHAPTER 10: THE PAST BECOMES THE PRESENT

277 On the work done by Joe Crowshoe and Roger McDonnell, see McDonnell 1984.

For articles on the development of Head-Smashed-In Buffalo Jump, see Brink 1992, 1996; Cannon and Cannon 1996; Johns 1988; Johns and Le Blond 1989; Sponholz 1992.

For more on the involvement of the Blackfoot people in the development of the interpretive centre, see Brink 1992; Slater 2006.

For the architecture of the Head-Smashed-In Interpretive Centre, see Johns 1988; Johns and LeBlond 1989.

For more references on archaeological studies of Head-Smashed-In and other buffalo jumps, general Plains archaeology and buffalo hunting, and Plains Indians, visit www.aupress.ca.

References Cited

Agenbroad, L. "Buffalo Jump Complexes in Owyhee County, Idaho." *Tebiwa* 1 (1976). D.C.: University Press of America.

Audubon, Maria R. *Audubon and His Journals.* 2 vols. New York: Dover Publications, 1960.

Bement, Leland. "Bonfire Shelter: A Jumping off Point for Comments for Byerly et al." *American Antiquity* 72 (2007): 366–72.

Binnema, Theodore. *Common and Contested Ground: A Human and Environmental History of the Northwestern Plains.* Norman: University of Oklahoma Press, 2001.

Brackenridge, H.M. *Journal of a Voyage up the River Missouri Performed in 1811.* Early Western Travels: 1748–1846, edited by R. G. Thwaites, vol. 6 (part 1, pp. 21–166). Cleveland: Arthur H. Clark, 1904.

Bradbury, John. *Travels in the Interior of America in the Years 1809, 1810, and 1811.* Early Western Travels: 1748–1846, edited by R. G. Thwaites, vol. 5. Cleveland: Arthur H. Clark, 1904.

Brink, Jack W. "Buffalo Jump." *Horizon Canada* 89 (1986): 2120–25.

-----. "The Highwood River Site: A Pelican Lake Phase Burial from the Alberta Plains." *Canadian Journal of Archaeology* 12 (1988): 109–35.

-----. "Blackfoot and Buffalo Jumps: Native People and the Head-Smashed-In Project." In *Buffalo,* edited by John Foster, Dick Harrison, and I.S. MacLaren, 19–43. Edmonton: University of Alberta Press, 1992.

-----. "An Example of *In Situ* Preservation of Archaeological Resources, A UNESCO World Heritage Site, Head-Smashed-In Buffalo Jump." In *Archaeological Remains In Situ Preservation.* Proceedings of the Second ICAHM International Conference, 5–12. Montreal: ICOMOS International Committee on Archaeological Heritage Management, 1996.

Brumley, John H. *Ramillies: A Later Prehistoric Bison Kill and Campsite in Southeastern Alberta, Canada.* Archaeological Survey of Canada, Mercury Series, 55. Ottawa: National Museum of Man, 1976.

Byerly, Ryan M., Judith R. Cooper, David J. Meltzer, Matthew E. Hill, and Jason M. LaBelle. "On Bonfire Shelter (Texas) as a Paleoindian Bison Jump: An Assessment Using GIS and Zooarchaeology." *American Antiquity* 70 (2005): 595–629.

-----. "A Further Assessment of Paleoindian Site-Use at Bonfire Shelter." *American Antiquity* 72 (2007): 373–81.

Cannon, D., and A. Cannon. "Archaeology's Public: A Perspective from Two Canadian Museums." *Canadian Journal of Archaeology* 20 (1996): 29–38.

Catlin, G. *Illustrations of the Manners, Customs, and Condition of the North American Indians: In a Series of Letters and Notes.* 2 vols. London: G. Bohn, 1851.

Christopherson, R.J., R.J. Hudson, and R.J. Richmond. "Comparative Winter Bioenergetics of American Bison, Yak, Scottish Highland and Hereford Calves." *Acta Theriologica* 23, no. 2 (1978): 49–54.

Coues, E., ed. *New Light on the Early History of the Greater Northwest. The Manuscript Journals of Alexander Henry, Fur Trader, and David Thompson, Official Geographer and Explorer of the North West Company.* 3 vols. New York: Francis P. Harper, 1897.

Culbertson, Thaddeus A. *Journal of an Expedition to the Mauvaises Terres and the Upper Missouri in 1850.* Edited by John F. McDermott. Bureau of American Ethnology, 147. Washington: Smithsonian Institution, 1952.

Darragh, Ian. "The Killing Cliffs." *Canadian Geographic* 107 (Oct./ Nov. 1987): 55–61.

Dawson, G.M. *Report on the Region of the Vicinity of the Bow and Belly River, Northwest Territory. Geological and Natural History Survey of Canada, Report of Progress 1882-1883-1884:1c-169c.* Ottawa: Queen's Printer, 1885.

Deetz, James. *In Small Things Forgotten: The Archaeology of American Life.* Garden City, N.Y.: Anchor Press, 1977.

Dempsey, Hugh A. "Donald Graham's Narrative of 1872–73." *Alberta Historical Review* 4, no. 1 (1956): 10–19.

-----. "A History of Writing-On-Stone." Unpublished manuscript on file, Royal Alberta Museum, 1973.

-----, ed. *The Rundle Journals 1840–1848.* Calgary: Historical Society of Alberta and Glenbow-Alberta Institute, 1977.

-----, ed. *Heaven is near the Rocky Mountains: The Journals and Letters of Thomas Woolsey, 1855–1869.* Calgary: Glenbow-Alberta Institute, 1989.

Denig, E.T. *Indian Tribes of the Upper Missouri,* edited by J.N. B.Hewitt, 375–628. Bureau of American Ethnology, Annual Report, 46. Washington, 1930.

Densmore, F. *Teton Sioux Music.* Bureau of American Ethnology, 61. Washington: Smithsonian Institution, 1918.

De Smet, Father P.J. *Oregon Missions and Travels Over the Rocky Mountains, in 1845–46.* Early Western Travels: 1748–1846, edited by R. G. Thwaites, vol. 29, 103–424. Cleveland: Arthur H. Clark, 1906.

Dibble, D.S., and D. Lorrain. *Bonfire Shelter: A Stratified Bison Kill Site in the Amistad Reservoir Area, Val Verde County, Texas.* Miscellaneous Papers, 1. Austin: Texas Memorial Museum, 1968.

Dodge, Colonel Richard Irving. *Our Wild Indians: Thirty-Three Years' Personal Experience Among the Red Men of the Great West.* 1883; New York: Archer House, 1959.

-----. *The Plains of the Great West and Their Inhabitants: Being a Description of the Plains, Game, Indians, &c. of the Great North American Desert.* New York: Archer House, 1959.

Emerson, Alice E. "Archaeological Implications of Variability in the Economic Anatomy of *Bison bison*." Unpublished PhD dissertation, Washington State University, 1990.

Ewers, J.C. "The Last Bison Drives of the Blackfoot Indians." *Journal of the Washington Academy of Sciences* 39 (1949): 355–60.

-----. *The Horse in Blackfoot Indian Culture.* Bureau of American Ethnology, 159. Washington: Smithsonian Institution, 1955.

-----. *The Blackfeet: Raiders on the Northwestern Plains.* Norman: University of Oklahoma Press, 1958.

-----. *Indian Life on the Upper Missouri.* Norman: University of Oklahoma Press, 1968.

Fagan, Brian. "Bison Hunters of the Northern Plains." *Archaeology Magazine.* May/June 1994: 37–41.

Farnham, Thomas J. *Travels in the Great Western Prairies, the Anahuac and Rocky Mountains, and in the Oregon Territory, vols. 28 and 29. Early Western Travels: 1748–1846,* edited by R.G. Thwaites. Cleveland: Arthur H. Clark, 1906.

Fidler, Peter. *Journal of a Journey over Land from Buckingham House to the Rocky Mountains in 1792 & 3,* edited by Bruce Haig. Lethbridge: Historical Research Centre, 1991.

Flannery, R. *The Gros Ventres of Montana: Part 1 Social Life.* Washington: The Catholic University of America Press, 1953.

Fletcher, A.C., and F. La Flesche. *The Omaha Tribe.* 1911; Lincoln: University of Nebraska Press, 1972.

Frison, George C. *The Glenrock Buffalo Jump,* 48CO304. Plains Anthropologist Memoir 7, 1970.

-----. "Prehistoric, Plains-Mountain, Large Mammal, Communal Hunting Strategies." In *The Evolution of Human Hunting,* edited by M.H. Nitecki and D.V. Nitecki, 177–223. New York: Plenum Press, 1987.

-----. *Prehistoric Hunters of the High Plains.* 2nd ed. San Diego: Academic Press, 1991.

-----. *Survival by Hunting: Prehistoric Human Predators and Animal Prey.* Berkeley: University of California Press, 2004.

Glover, Richard, ed. *David Thompson's Narrative 1784–1812.* Toronto: The Champlain Society, 1962.

Gregg, Josiah. *Commerce of the Prairies.* 2 vols. Reprinted, March of America Facsimile Series 71. Ann Arbor: University Microfilms, 1966.

Grinnell, G.B. *The Cheyenne Indians: Their History and Ways of Life.* 2 vols. New Haven: Yale University Press, 1923.

McDonnell, R.F. "Pis'kun: Some Ethnohistorical Considerations of the Blackfoot Communal Buffalo Hunt." Unpublished report on file, the Royal Alberta Museum, Edmonton, 1984.

McDougall, John. *Pathfinding on Plain and Prairie: Stirring Scenes of Life in the Canadian North-West*. Toronto: William Briggs, 1898.

McHugh, T. "Social Behavior of the American Buffalo (*B. b. bison*)." *Zoologica* 43, no.1 (1958): 1–40.

-----. *The Time of the Buffalo*. New York: Alfred A. Knopf, 1972.

Morgan, Lewis H. *The Indian Journals, 1859–62*, edited by Leslie A. White. Ann Arbor: University of Michigan Press, 1959.

Palliser, John. *Solitary Rambles and Adventures of a Hunter in the Prairies*. Rutland, Vermont: Charles E. Tuttle, 1969.

Peters, H.F., and S.B. Slen. "Hair Coat Characteristics of Bison, Domestic X Bison Hybrids, Cattalo, and Certain Domestic Breeds of Beef Cattle." *Canadian Journal of Animal Science* 44 (1964): 48–57.

Pike, Major Z.M. *An Account of Expeditions to the Sources of the Mississippi, and Through the Western Parts of Louisiana, to the Sources of the Arkansaw, Kans, La Platte, and Pierre Juan, Rivers*. March of America Facsimile Series. 1810; Ann Arbor: University Microfilms, 1966.

Pringle, Heather. "Boneyard Enigma." *Equinox*. March/April 1988: 87–103.

-----. "Killing Fields: Head-Smashed-In Buffalo Jump, Alberta." In *In Search of Ancient North America*, 149–67. New York: John Wiley and Sons, 1996.

Reeves, B.O.K. "Six Millenniums of Buffalo Kills." *Scientific American* 249, no. 4 (1983): 120–35.

Reher, C.A., and G.C. Frison. *The Vore Site, 48CK302, A Stratified Buffalo Jump in the Wyoming Black Hills*. Plains Anthropologist Memoir 16, 1980.

Reid, Gordon. *Head-Smashed-In Buffalo Jump*. Calgary: Fifth House, 2002.

Reimers, E., T. Ringberg, and R. Sørumgård. "Body Composition of Svalbard Reindeer." *Canadian Journal of Zoology* 60 (1982): 1812–21.

Reynolds, H.W., C.C. Gates, and R.D. Glaholt. "Bison (*Bison bison*)." In *Wild Mammals of North America: Biology, Management, and Conservation,* edited by G.A. Feldhamer, B.C. Thompson, and J.A. Chapman, 1009–60. 2nd ed. Baltimore: John Hopkins University Press, 2003.

Ross, Alexander. *The Red River Settlement: Its Rise, Progress and Present State.* 1856; Edmonton: M.G. Hurtig, 1972.

Schoolcraft, Henry Rowe. *Historical and Statistical Information Respecting the History, Condition and Prospects of the Indian Tribes of the United States.* 6 vols. Philadelphia: Lippincott, Grambo, 1851.

-----. *Travels Through the Northwestern Regions of the United States.* 1821; Ann Arbor: University Microfilms, 1966.

Singh, Simon. *Big Bang: The Origin of the Universe.* New York: Fourth Estate, 2004.

Slater, Bryony. "Blackfoot Consultation and Head-Smashed-In Buffalo Jump Interpretive Centre." MA thesis. University of Newcastle, 2006.

Southesk, Earl of. *Saskatchewan and the Rocky Mountains: A Diary and Narrative of Travel, Sport, and Adventure, during a Journey through the Hudson's Bay Company's Territories, in 1859 and 1860.* Rutland, Vermont: Charles E. Tuttle, 1969.

Sponholz, E. "Head-Smashed-In Buffalo Jump: A Centre for Cultural Preservation and Understanding." In *Buffalo,* edited by J. Foster, D. Harrison, and I.S. MacLaren, 45–59. Edmonton: University of Alberta Press, 1992.

Spry, Irene M., ed. *The Papers of the Palliser Expedition 1857–1860.* Toronto: The Champlain Society, 1968.

Stanford, Dennis J. "The Jones-Miller Site: An Example of Hell Gap Bison Procurement Strategy." In *Bison Procurement and Utilization: A Symposium,* edited by L.B. Davis and M. Wilson, 90–97. Plains Anthropologist Memoir 14, 1978.

Teit, J.A. *The Salishan Tribes of the Western Plateau,* edited by Franz Boas, 23–396. Washington: Forty-Fifth Annual Report of the Bureau of American Ethnology, 1927–28, 1930.

Thomas, D.H. "Head-Smashed-In Buffalo Jump." In *Exploring Native North America*, 52–61. Oxford: Oxford University Press, 2000.

Todd, L.C. "Taphonomy: Fleshing out the Dry Bones of Plains Prehistory." *Wyoming Archaeologist* 26, nos. 3–4 (1983): 36–46.

Turnbull, T. *Travels from the United States Across the Plains to California.* Proceedings of the State Historical Society of Wisconsin, 151–225. State Historical Society, Madison (Separate Note No. 158), 1914.

Turney-High, H.H. *Ethnography of the Kutenai.* American Anthropological Association, Memoir 56, 1941.

Uhlenbeck. C.C. *Original Blackfoot Texts.* Amsterdam: Johannes Müller, 1911.

Wilson, Gilbert. *The Horse and the Dog in Hidatsa Culture.* New York: Anthropological Papers of the American Museum of Natural History, vol.15, 125–311, 1924.

Wissler, C. *Material Culture of the Blackfoot Indians.* New York: Anthropological Papers of the American Museum of Natural History, vol. 5, part 1, 1910.

Index

United Nations
Educational, Scientific and
Cultural Organization

Head-Smashed-In
Buffalo Jump
Inscribed in 1981

This publication is licensed under a Creative Commons License, see www.creativecommons.org. The text may be reproduced for non-commercial purposes, provided that the original author is credited.

Please contact Athabasca University Press at aupress@athabascau.ca for permission beyond the usage outlined in the Creative Commons license.